BONES

BONES

A FORENSIC DETECTIVE'S CASEBOOK

DR. DOUGLAS UBELAKER & HENRY SCAMMELL

M. Evans and Company, Inc.
New York

M. Evans and Company, Inc.
216 East 49th Street
New York, New York 10017

Library of Congress Cataloging-in-Publication Data

Ubelaker, Douglas H.
    Bones : a forensic detective's casebook / Douglas Ubelaker &
Henry Scammell.
        p.   cm.
    Originally published : New York : Harper Collins, 1992.
    Includes index.
    ISBN 0-87131-904-7
    1. Forensic anthropology. I. Scammell, Henry. II. Title.
GN69.8 .U2 2000
614'.1—dc21   99-049352

Designed by Jessica Shatan

Printed in Canada

9 8 7 6 5 4 3

To life.

CONTENTS

ACKNOWLEDGMENTS

The authors wish to acknowledge the assistance and perspective they have received from the following investigators, prosecutors, medical examiners, anthropologists, attorneys, agencies, institutions, and other sources in the collecting and telling of the stories in this book. We also wish to acknowledge our debt to numerous additional sources who, because of the status of related cases, cannot be identified.

FEDERAL BUREAU OF INVESTIGATION
Washington, DC
  Joseph Dizinno
  Robert Fram
  Gene O'Donnell
  William Tobin

GEORGE WASHINGTON UNIVERSITY
Washington, DC
  James Starrs

NATIONAL MUSEUM OF NATURAL HISTORY
Smithsonian Institution
Washington, DC
  Erica Bubniak
  Douglas Owsley
  Robert Mann
  T. Dale Stewart
  John Verano

OFFICE OF THE ARMED FORCES MEDICAL EXAMINER
Armed Forces Institute of Pathology
Washington, DC
  William C. Rodriguez

OFFICE OF THE CHIEF MEDICAL EXAMINER
Washington, DC

DEPARTMENT OF PUBLIC SAFETY, STATE OF ALASKA
Fairbanks, Alaska

DIVISION OF STATE POLICE, STATE OF DELAWARE
Dover, Delaware

OFFICE OF THE STATE ATTORNEY
Pensacola, Florida
    Joseph A. Schiller

FLORIDA STATE MUSEUM
UNIVERSITY OF FLORIDA
Gainesville, Florida
    William R. Maples

HILLSBOROUGH COUNTY SHERIFF'S OFFICE
Tampa, Florida

GEORGIA BUREAU OF INVESTIGATION
Atlanta, Georgia
    Gary L. Nicholson

UNITED STATES ATTORNEY'S OFFICE, DISTRICT OF HAWAII
Honolulu, Hawaii

CLARK COUNTY SHERIFF'S OFFICE
Dubois, Idaho

KANSAS STATE UNIVERSITY
Manhattan, Kansas
    Michael Finnegan

JEFFERSON PARISH SHERIFF'S OFFICE
Harvey, Louisiana
    Lt. Gene Ferrin
    Capt. Walter Gorman
    Chief Richard Rodrigue
    Lt. Susan Rushing

THOMAS E. WEISS
New Orleans, Louisiana

OFFICE OF THE CHIEF MEDICAL EXAMINER
Baltimore, Maryland

MARYLAND STATE POLICE
Berlin, Maryland
    Philip R. Fort

CAMBRIDGE POLICE DEPARTMENT
Cambridge, Maryland

FALL RIVER POLICE DEPARTMENT
Fall River, Massachusetts
    Tom Joaquim
    Alan Silvia

MASSACHUSETTS STATE POLICE
Middleboro, Massachusetts
    Paul Fitzgerald
    Kenneth F. Martin

BUTLER COUNTY CORONER'S OFFICE
Poplar Bluff, Missouri

DOUGLAS COUNTY ATTORNEY'S OFFICE
Omaha, Nebraska
    Sam Cooper

CORNELL UNIVERSITY
Ithaca, New York
    Kenneth A. R. Kennedy

THIRTY-FOURTH PRECINCT
Police Department of the City of New York
New York, New York

OFFICE OF THE CORONER
Akron, Ohio

DEPARTMENT OF PUBLIC SAFETY
East Liverpool, Ohio

MACEDONIA POLICE DEPARTMENT
Macedonia, Ohio

OFFICE OF THE SHERIFF, PUTNAM COUNTY
Ottawa, Ohio

MULTNOMAH COUNTY SHERIFF'S DEPARTMENT
Portland, Oregon
Lt. Rod Englert

OFFICE OF THE CORONER, DAUPHIN COUNTY
Harrisburg, Pennsylvania

PUERTO RICO DEPARTMENT OF JUSTICE
San Juan, Puerto Rico
Minerva Ramos

UNIVERSITY OF SOUTH CAROLINA
Columbia, South Carolina
Ted A. Rathbun

OFFICE OF THE UNITED STATES ATTORNEY
Rapid City, South Dakota
Robert A. Mandel

UNIVERSITY OF TENNESSEE
Knoxville, Tennessee
William M. Bass

UNIVERSITY OF TENNESSEE REGIONAL FORENSIC CENTER
Memphis, Tennessee
Hugh E. Berryman

OFFICE OF THE CHIEF MEDICAL EXAMINER
Burlington, Vermont
Paul L. Morrow

DEPARTMENT OF PUBLIC SAFETY, DIVISION OF STATE POLICE
Waterbury, Vermont
Nicholas A. Ruggiero

CRIMINAL INVESTIGATIONS DIVISION, CITY OF MANASSAS
Manassas, Virginia

STATE OF VIRGINIA MEDICAL EXAMINERS' AND PROSECUTORS' OFFICES
Richmond and Goochland, Virginia
    Leah Bush
    Edward Carpenter
    Carolyn M. Coyne
    Marcella Fierro

DEPARTMENT OF PLANNING AND NATURAL RESOURCES
Government of the Virgin Islands of the United States
Charlotte Amalie, St. Thomas, VI
    Elizabeth Righter

SNOHOMISH COUNTY PROSECUTOR'S OFFICE
Everett, Washington
    Helene Blume

KING COUNTY MEDICAL EXAMINER'S OFFICE
Seattle, Washington
    William B. Haglund

OFFICE OF THE ATTORNEY GENERAL
Seattle, Washington
    Gregory Canova

SPOKANE COUNTY SHERIFF'S OFFICE
Spokane, Washington
    Clyde R. Ries

MADISON POLICE DEPARTMENT
Madison, Wisconsin
    Det. James I. Grann III

TETON COUNTY SHERIFF'S DEPARTMENT
Jackson, Wyoming

THE ROYAL HONG KONG POLICE
Hong Kong
    Dr. Yip Chi-Pang

BONES

1

HELPING HANDS

On the morning of May 24, 1980, a pretty, soft-eyed twenty-one-year-old woman set out from her Arlington, Virginia, apartment, headed for her job as a chemist at the Quantico Marine Base a few miles to the south of the city. Like most of the people in this book, she never got where she was going. Two days later, her green 1974 Pinto was found on a deserted road near Frederick, Maryland, in the opposite direction to Quantico, engulfed in flames.

The Maryland police could determine right away that the fire had been set, but that in itself meant little. Lots of cars are burned by vandals after stealing them for joyrides, and lots are burned by their owners for insurance. By comparison, it is only rarely that a fire is set to destroy the evidence of some other crime. The Maryland police obtained the owner's name from the Virginia registry of motor vehicles, and the registry in turn notified the police department in Arlington.

By then the girl had been missing for more than forty-eight hours, but until the two police departments compared facts and matched her disappearance in one state with the discovery of her burning car in another, neither jurisdiction had any particular reason to treat their part of the case as anything other than a routine matter. Now, with obvious cause for greater alarm, detectives carefully searched the wreckage of the car and interviewed her two roommates and several of the neighbors for some clue as to what might have happened to her. She was originally from Puerto Rico. She had worked at the Marine base for the past seven months and hoped eventually to enter Georgetown University Medical School. She played the guitar and flute.

But there was nothing at all in either the Pinto or her apartment that could provide any clue to where she had gone. Yes, it was possible something terrible had happened, even that she was dead. But in the absence of any useful leads, her file remained stuck in the never-never-land of Missing Persons. Its status didn't change for the next two and a half years.

In July 1982, human skeletal remains were found scattered across a 30-foot circle in a blackberry patch near Oilville in Goochland County, a rural section of central Virginia. It was the height of summer and the finders were a group of berry pickers. Harvesters of natural crops have always played an important role in the science of anthropology, and in modern crime detection they are among the forensic scientist's best allies. Despite such scientific advances as ground-penetrating radar and magnetic resonance imaging systems that can define decayed bodies when they are almost invisible to the unaided eye, no machine has yet been made that surpasses hunters and gatherers—along with man's ancient friend the dog—for the discovery of lost bodies.

There were numerous signs of animal activity in the area, and the lower portion of the skeleton in the berry patch was missing. Fortunately the upper part, including the skull, was relatively complete, and near the bones police recovered the remains of blue jeans and a red jersey. They even determined the likely cause of death: a brown shoelace still in place around the victim's neck. But this time the jurisdictions were too widely separated and the time of discovery too long after the disappearance for police at either end to connect the skeleton to the missing chemist. Besides, Goochland was far south of Arlington or Quantico Marine Base—well away from Frederick, Maryland, where the car had been found two years before.

The Goochland County case was labeled a homicide, and the bones and other evidence were carefully gathered up by investigators from the sheriff's department and turned over to Virginia's deputy chief medical examiner. From there they were sent to the laboratories of the

Department of Anthropology, National Museum of Natural History, at the Smithsonian Institution in Washington, D.C.

The case was addressed to a curator named Dr. J. Lawrence Angel, and was delivered to his office in a cardboard carton. The slight, balding, scholarly Angel, then in his early sixties, was one of my earliest colleagues and friends in the Department of Anthropology.

Although the Smithsonian's relationship with the FBI had started decades before, at about the time Angel had been born, he was still only the third scientist in line of succession as the Bureau's primary consultant in forensic anthropology—and the first to "go public" with his art. Partial to bow ties, he smoked cigars, still spoke with a trace of his original Devonshire accent, and in his spare time read mystery novels, including those of Agatha Christie and P. D. James. He didn't mind at all that he was sometimes called Sherlock Bones by an admiring press.

In common with his predecessors—and with his successor—Larry Angel was primarily a scientist and only incidentally a forensic sleuth. He loved his work, whether it was the analysis of skeletons from Homer's Greece or the 2,000-year-ago city of Herculaneum, or the occasional, perhaps weekly, assignment like this one from the police or FBI. After all, the crime work didn't usually take that long, and it was always interesting.

A few days after the agents made their delivery, Dr. Angel carefully removed the remains from the carton and systematically laid them out on a tabletop in his office, approximating the relationship they had occupied in life. The job was made slightly easier by the fact that some of the bones, such as the neck portion of the spinal column, were still articulated. But for the most part, perhaps even before wild animals had found the body and strewn it about the berry patch, the connective tissues had lost their integrity and the bones had become disconnected.

The reassembly process began with the skull, to which the short column of cervical vertebrae was still attached. Below that he laid in the manubrium of the sternum, then fanned out the eight left ribs and the eight right ribs on either side of center, noting teeth marks, probably from a dog or fox, on both ends of the central thoracics.* He laid in the right scapula, both clavicles, and the long humeri and ulnae from the arms. There was only one radius, the other long bone of the fore-

---

*For details of technical terms, see the Glossary on pp. 297–299.

arm; it was from the left side, and Dr. Angel noted that its head had been bitten off postmortem.

He came to the hands. He carefully dealt out the left hand's metacarpals and the basal phalanges of the fingers. The left little finger in particular attracted his attention, and he made a mental note to examine it more thoroughly later. From the right hand, the box contained only metacarpals 2 and 3; both displayed crushed distal shafts and, like the left radius, had lost their heads to animals.

By the time he was finished, there were some bones left over, but none of them fit in the missing bottom half of the body. Dr. Angel sought the opinion of a Smithsonian expert on animal skeletons, and the extra pieces were tentatively identified as coming from a sheep or deer. But there was no pelvis, no lower extremities, no vertebral column below the cervicals.

In general, the skeleton lacked any odor or grease, and most of the cartilage had disappeared. The bones had been stained irregularly a drab brown to reddish color by vegetation or soil. The left posterior part of the skull was slightly sun-bleached, which suggested it had lain face down for most of the period since the body had become skeletonized. Angel did a simple chemical analysis of the reddish silt extracted from the shoulder girdle and jaw bones; it showed a neutral pH of 3.5, consistent with his estimate of a time since death of between 1.5 and 3 years.

The anthropologist contemplated the puzzle on the table. The favored means for determining sex in forensic cases is from an examination of the pelvic bone, but in this case that was part of the missing lower half of the body. However, the skull contained other indicators, and from the smoothness of the brow ridge Angel had recognized at the outset that this one was unmistakably female.

For age, he examined the sutures in the skull—the fracture lines between the plates which allow for growth through childhood and adolescence before uniting at maturity. Consistent with those lines, he noted that the closures in the epiphyses of the shoulder and the basilar synchondrosis of the sphenoid and occipital bones were both fairly recent. Finally, there were the teeth. He assessed the development of the roots of the third molar. She had been between eighteen and twenty-four years old.

Despite a long palate and pronounced prognathism—a possible indicator of ancestry in which the jaw extends beyond the upper part of the face—the victim was probably white.

She had been only 4'10" to 5'1½" tall. Her bony frame was slight

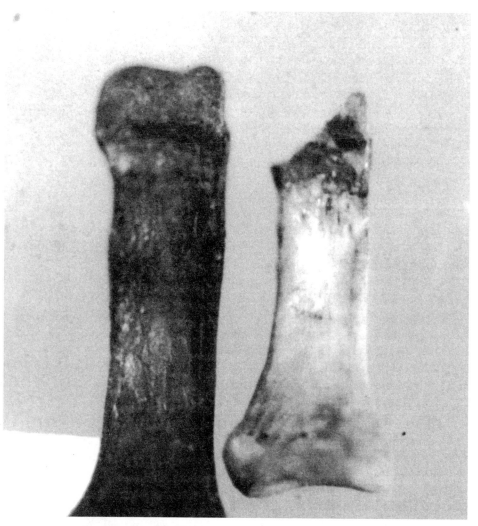

Normal phalanx and altered phalanx recovered with Goochland skeleton.

but rather broad-shouldered and very wiry. The attachment crests for deltoid, pectorals, biceps, supinator, and arm muscles were large and sharp, including those for anterior deltoids. Dr. Angel knew the latter muscles are stressed by both nursing mothers and factory workers, and he entered that information in her file.

The skull was unexpectedly large. She had a strong chin, and a rather narrow face with a thin, slightly beaky, asymmetrical nose. There were no obvious scars of healed injuries.

Angel went back to the left hand to examine a striking peculiarity of the basal phalanx on the left little finger. A very small section—he estimated three and a half to five millimeters—of the distal joint had been amputated by a diagonal cut. It could have been caused by anything, before death or after, but it was the kind of detail that can be of enormous significance to the forensic anthropologist. The fracture had some of the characteristics of a parry wound, received when the victim defended herself against the thrust or slashing of her killer's knife. He studied the severed end carefully, then returned to his examination of the rest of the bones on the table.

He looked for a long time and with great care, but there were no corresponding cuts on the facial bones, and he could find no knife marks on any of the other bones recovered from the berry patch. Angel knew it was possible, even without collateral indications, that the severing of her fingertip could be related to the victim's murder. In his report, he wrote that it might be a defense wound, but it could equally well be the result of an accident, perhaps with a meat-packing machine, shortly before death.

Although the lower half of the body was missing, the victim's jeans had been recovered near the scattered bones. The medical examiner had suggested that they had been removed from the body shortly before or after death, indicating probable rape. He also noted the presence of a ligature, still twisted around what was left of her cervical vertebrae. After rereading the police report to be sure it made no reference to a tree from which she could have hanged herself, Angel set down the shoelace as another indication of probable murder.

A few weeks later, encouraged by the amount of detail in Angel's report which the anthropologist had been able to infer from the shape of the cranium, authorities in Virginia requested a facial reproduction. Based on precise measurements of the skull and using his natural gifts as the son of a sculptor, Angel and an artist in Richmond collaborated in reproducing the head of the victim as she had looked in life.

A picture of the result was run in the *News Leader* in Richmond, the nearest large city to the discovery site. It was a pretty face. The eyes were soft and almond-shaped, and the expression was serene but slightly quizzical, as though she too were bemused by the mystery of her identity and the circumstances of her death. The following January, six months after the discovery in the berry patch and partly with the help of the reconstruction, the remains from Goochland were connected at last with the missing girl from Arlington.

Once that link was made, final proof was a matter of simple routine, with confirming checks against her dental records from Puerto Rico. There were no arrests and no strong suspects, but the need for resolution about the fate of the victim is usually a more compelling emotion than any impulse for justice or revenge, and with the identification of the remains the family and friends of the victim were finally able to put to rest their hopes and fears and give proper expression to their grief. The crate containing the murdered girl's bones was sent back to Virginia, then to Puerto Rico for burial, and her case became just one more folder in the file of unsolved crimes.

The years passed. Larry Angel reduced his forensic casework, and my own began to grow steadily. In 1977, he took a much-deserved sabbatical. At that time he was not only helping out authorities in Virginia but also was handling all referrals from the FBI and a number of other agencies. I agreed to take on the work from the FBI during his sabbatical. When he returned, the arrangement became permanent, although he continued to work on those cases sent to him directly from the District of Columbia, Virginia, and other jurisdictions. By the time Larry died in 1986, any vague recollection I may have had from hearing him tell about the woman in the berry patch had been overlaid by the hundreds of other FBI assignments that had passed through the Smithsonian—and through my own offices—in the interim. But if I had long since stopped thinking about Larry's old case, the police in Virginia had not.

In May 1991, I was contacted by the Commonwealth's Attorney in Goochland County. He told me an arrest had been made in an ancient case which he was now prosecuting. The evidence had originally been examined by Dr. J. Lawrence Angel, and a potentially critical element in the case was the observation Dr. Angel had made of a cut bone at the tip of the victim's left little finger.

The prosecutor said the family remembered Dr. Angel had requested that key parts of the evidence—they weren't sure, but thought it was something to do with the throat—be kept apart from the rest of the remains for possible future use in court. Could I check around the Smithsonian for whatever evidence Dr. Angel had saved? The case was coming to trial shortly, and it was fairly urgent. I dropped what I was doing, called our collections manager, Dr. David Hunt, and we both set about searching for the missing parts.

When Larry Angel had died, in keeping with the tradition at the Smithsonian all his unpublished notes, slides, and records were sent down to the National Anthropological Archives. Because I had worked with Larry for several years, I knew that a trip to the archives would be a lot like doing an archaeological dig into a part of my own past, and I viewed the prospect with a mixture of curiosity and trepidation. Part of the trepidation was because the volume of Larry's work had been formidable, and I also knew he had his own peculiar indexing system.

The files were located on the first floor of the museum, and I dutifully descended to begin my search. After some considerable effort I figured out the system he had used for tracking his forensic cases, searched through those that had originated in Virginia, and succeeded at last in finding his folder on the eleven-year-old murder.

Some of the details came back to me as I glanced through it on my way to a table in the reading room of the archives. There was a picture of the facial reproduction, and another photograph, added when her identity had been established, from the victim's family album. I was impressed once again by how closely the forensic sculpture from the skull in the berry patch had anticipated the appearance of the girl from life. I sat down and pored through the folder from beginning to end. The file included measurements as well as some routine photographs done in the format Larry always followed in recording a forensic skeleton. But there were no pictures of the severed fingertip, and no bones. Dr. Hunt had searched the collection records as well, but with no better results.

Although the search through the archives didn't produce the results the prosecutor was hoping for, my next avenue of inquiry was to try tracing the evidence back through the original chain of referral. I contacted the Virginia Medical Examiner's Office, which had sent this case to Angel in the first place, and they were able to locate a rather blurry photograph of the bone in question. It didn't prove to be much of a victory. When a copy finally reached my office, I had to tell the prosecutor that it would not be possible for me to base any reasonable testimony on such a picture in court. Without being able to examine the actual bone under a microscope, I could not say anything more than that it had been cut. In any event, without the bone itself, the best I could have given him would have been an informal opinion. The rules of evidence in court require a witness to speak from his or her own observations, not from the reports of others.

The prosecutor was persistent. He said the victim's family thought they remembered that Larry Angel had examined the finger and had been given permission to keep it. I knew that the same medical examiner, Dr. Marcella Fierro, was in charge of the case as ten years earlier, and it was my own experience that she runs a very tight ship. Whenever I find any signs of trauma on the bones she sends my way, she usually asks me to return them so she can do the tests herself, make her own observations, and carefully control the flow of evidence. Good habits don't usually change, and I felt certain she would not have let any of the bones remain with the FBI or the Smithsonian. That assumption was bolstered by a record that Fierro had conducted such a test on the missing hand, which meant she had it after Larry Angel discovered the cut. It convinced me that all the remains had been turned back to Virginia and in turn passed along to the family for the funeral, and that the hand was buried along with the rest of the skeleton in Puerto Rico. In any event, I knew I wasn't about to spend the rest of my life searching the archives and collection, so I told the prosecutor what I thought had happened and said we had gone as far as we were able.

Apparently I was persuasive. A few days later, the prosecutor called again. "Dr. Ubelaker, how would you like to go to Puerto Rico to supervise the exhumation?"

Puerto Rico is a long way to travel for that kind of project, but it happened that the request coincided with another call I had received a short time earlier about an important new archaeological find in the Virgin Islands. Archaeology and forensic anthropology are closely related, and the application of those sciences to the understanding of our ancient past has always had the first claim on my interests and professional commitment, ahead of modern murder and forensic detection.

The call from the Virgin Islands was an attempt to recruit me as a volunteer; as is common in such emergencies, the project had almost no funding, and I expected my participation would be largely at my own expense, including part of the travel. I was anxious to help out and would have been happy to contribute a few days of my time, but getting there would be costly. Finding financial support for research and travel is a constant struggle for most scientists, and I was certainly no exception. I had already nearly exhausted existing resources on trips to professional meetings and maintaining my laboratory, so this new request to go to Puerto Rico raised some interesting possibilities.

As is usually the case in such finds, the discovery in the Virgin Islands occurred by accident. A tract of land on St. Thomas was being cleared for a K-Mart near Charlotte Amalie, and someone noticed that the bulldozers were turning up ancient pottery. The territorial archaeologist quickly arrived at the scene and recognized a large, rich, and unusually complex pre-Columbian site, which included a number of ancient burials. She realized that local expertise was not available to excavate them properly, and requested that I fly down to give her some guidance on setting goals and procedures. "If I go to Puerto Rico," I asked the Virginia prosecutor quickly, "can you arrange for me to swing by St. Thomas?"

I thought I heard a groan on the other end of the line. The prosecutor was already juggling a very complex case of his own, and I was sure he wasn't staying up nights trying to think up ways to advance the sciences. Despite his own pressures, however, he agreed to look into it. Clearly he recognized that I was willing to invest some of my time, and it would have been difficult for him to decline this archaeology excursion. A few days later, as the result of a happy accommodation between the two poles of a forensic anthropologist's career demands, I found myself on St. Thomas.

It soon became apparent how good a job the organizers of the dig had done in rallying the community around their project. There wasn't a lot of money, but restaurants had pledged free meals for the scientists who came to help, the local hotels contributed accommodations, and volunteer workers—thoughtful, competent people who were willing to take directions—had converged from all over the island. From my experience in other archaeological digs in various places in the world, I had come half expecting to learn my bed was a hammock in a corn crib. Instead, I was surprised and delighted to find myself billeted in one of the best hotels on the island, complete with a wet bar and a Jacuzzi right in the room.

I didn't get to spend much time in the tub. The real delight of the trip was the opportunity it provided to get out from my desk, leave the paperwork behind, roll up my sleeves in a beautiful location and, despite the blazing hot sun, return to doing the work that had attracted me to the field in the first place. For the next three days, I donated my labor and observations to the excavation, charting, recording, and study of the funerary remains of a people whose arrival from

South America predated the voyages of Columbus by more than half a millennium.

The find was located in a relatively flat, elevated area of the island. The complex site had been a fairly large community, and there was evidence of houses and other structures, with individual burials interspersed among them. It provided my first example of an unusual burial practice I had never seen before, although I knew of a few instances documented in other parts of the Caribbean. The funeral bundles of two infants were found, one above the other, and although the limbs were very tightly flexed, the knees were splayed out like frogs' legs and the feet joined together, with the toes pointing inward, as though they had been preserved intact in the very act of swimming into the afterworld.

Most of my time was spent on the recovery of those two interments. When I was finished, I gave my notes and photographs to the woman in charge, returned to my luxury hotel, where I showered away the 1,000-year-old dust of a population that had long since vanished from the earth, changed my clothes, and headed back to the airport feeling thoroughly refreshed by the three-day break.

The coordinator assigned by the Puerto Rico Department of Justice to help me through the legal side of the exhumation was a bright young attorney named Minerva Ramos, chief of the department's Extradition Division. Two of her staff met me as I walked through the gate and escorted me to her downtown office. Ms. Ramos shook my hand and said the disinterment was scheduled at Los Cipreces Cemetery for just after sunrise the next morning. Her regular job was in no way connected with the purpose of my trip, but it was immediately apparent she was wonderfully organized and energetic, spoke perfect English, and clearly knew how to get things done. I was not at all surprised when she told me she was frequently recruited to offbeat challenges like this one. Everything had been arranged down to the last detail.

The reason for the early hour was to accommodate the cemetery management, who wanted the exhumation to be finished and the plot resealed before people began arriving with flowers to pay visits to loved ones. Grave digging is a common enough activity in that environment, but exhumation is another matter, and it was reasonable to anticipate some people might find the sight disturbing.

Our arrival at Los Cipreces was greeted by a large yellow Ford backhoe and a dump truck. We made a brief stop at the office for the necessary exchange of paperwork and to meet the delegates from the cemetery, the Medical Examiner's Office, and the funeral home, then we formed a short cortège behind the two larger vehicles, driving slowly to the gravesite under the pall of their diesel plumes.

We got out of our own cars and trucks while the heavy equipment rolled off the roadway and across a short strip of grass. The truck dropped its tailgate. The backhoe coughed a couple of times as its bucket genuflected to the headstone, then pushed powerfully forward and lifted off an eight-foot strip of sod as though it were a tablecloth. It took a longer time to shovel out the three feet of soil that overlay the vault, but eventually the heavy concrete slab that covered it was revealed, straps were attached to the proper rings and bolts, and the vault lid was raised from the hole and placed next to the heaps of dirt and wrinkled lawn on the back of the truck.

Most people who have ever peeked beneath the coffin at a graveside service for a glimpse of our common future know that in modern cemeteries the hereafter is usually lined with cement. The simple hole in the ground went out with Boot Hill, replaced by a vault of cinderblock or slab, designed for double or triple occupancy and built to last until the Resurrection. We knew that there had been two burials in this particular vault, and that our task would be somewhat simpler because the coffin we were exhuming was on top. What I didn't know until the concrete cap was removed was that the water table in this particular location was only a few inches below the surface. Buoyed up by pressure from below, the top casket bobbed gently in the dark pool.

This was not a welcome discovery. Water can be very destructive, especially when mixed with chemicals. I knew there had been nothing to embalm in this instance, but chemicals are also sometimes used in the analysis of bone cases, and there was a similar risk from natural acid leaching out of the soil. With a neutral pH, water doesn't make a lot of difference, but combined with materials that are either highly acidic or highly alkaline, the result can be extremely corrosive, and I was immediately concerned for the condition of the evidence. The good news was that the casket was floating; but the buoyancy could have come from the wood or from the coffin beneath, so that was no proof that the seal had held.

Two cemetery workers rolled up their sleeves and reached down into the pool to attach leather straps, the backhoe coughed again, and the coffin was raised into the air. To my great disappointment, water was pouring out of it from every seam. I knew there was another box containing the bones inside, so the casket was lowered to the ground, the straps were loosened, and we set about taking off the lid.

By then, despite the early start, our efforts had begun to attract an audience. The first visitors of the day were arriving at the cemetery, and I noticed several people watching us from a respectful distance, some with flowers destined for nearby graves still in their hands, as the leaky coffin was hoisted up from its watery resting place. It was clear from the expressions on their faces that this was not the kind of thing they expected to see, and when the lid came off, a couple of them dropped their flowers and moved quickly away. At the same time, those with different impulses or stronger curiosity came closer, craning for a look at whatever horrible thing was within.

Besides the water and the yards of bloated, decaying fabric from the coffin liner, all they saw of course was the smaller box in which the bones of the victim had been shipped from Virginia a decade earlier. Made of plain brown wood and closed with nothing more than a few nails, I knew that it, too, was bound to be filled with water. We had already stayed too long in what was becoming a very busy cemetery, so we made arrangements for the grave to be closed and the casket stored until our return, loaded the smaller box into the medical examiner's wagon, and headed for the gate.

On the way across San Juan, the water that had filled the box from the casket began to drain out. From Ms. Ramos's automobile I could see that it was running across the floor of the medical examiner's wagon, and a steady stream of brownish fluid was splashing out from under the back door. I could also see that we weren't the only ones to notice, although from the expressions on the faces of people in passing vehicles and along the roadside, we were probably alone in knowing that the fluid was nothing more than muddy water. The sides of the wagon were clearly marked with the seal of the medical examiner, and it was understandable that anyone who saw the stream beneath the door might imagine the worst. It was a relief for everyone when we finally reached our destination.

Before I agreed to come to Puerto Rico, I had raised the question of what kind of facility would be available for my examination of the evidence. The prosecutor made the appropriate queries and called back to assure me that arrangements had been made with the Instituto de Ciencias Forenses de Puerto Rico. I had never heard of it, but the name immediately inspired reassuring images of spotless laboratories with gleaming modern equipment, devoted to state-of-the-art research on toxicology and forensic remains. We shortly discovered that the Forensic Science Institute was the San Juan morgue, and if any traces remained of the impulse to trust my expectations, they vanished when the promised facilities turned out to be one of the autopsy tables.

All of the tables were in use when we arrived, and we were advised there would be a short delay. While we were waiting, Ms. Ramos and I walked around the morgue looking for the medical personnel who were scheduled to help me examine the bones. When we finally located them, they were at work on the autopsy of a baby, and they indicated we could wait there with them while they finished. One of the examiners may have read the expression on my face, or perhaps he offered his comment because he assumed professional interest on my part. "Newborn," he said, nodding down at the tiny body under his knife. "Mother rolled over on her in bed."

"What a tragedy." From the long habit of my science, I pictured the scene in my mind, then added, "And how terrible for the mother, living with what she did."

The doctor concentrated on his work, shaking his head. "That's what we all thought with the first one. Now we're not so sure. This is the second child she's lost that way."

Ms. Ramos looked away, and I followed her eyes around the busy room. There were three autopsies in various stages of completion—one of them a black man who had obviously died of gunshot wounds—and I counted rolling tables with six more shrouded bodies awaiting their turns. The atmosphere was close, pungent with the odor of recent death. When I looked back at the young attorney, I could see she was getting paler and I asked if she would prefer for both of us to wait outside. She nodded gratefully. As we sat on the front steps of the facility, gulping fresh air, I thought I heard her whisper to herself, "How did I ever get into this one?"

A few minutes later, obviously better, she excused herself and went back inside. She made several telephone calls, searching for last-minute alternative sites where we could study the remains, but to no avail. It was with considerable chagrin that she returned to the steps and admitted failure; we would have to continue waiting our turn.

In due course a table became available, and after it was washed down, one of the examiners helpfully lifted the crate to the table and pried up the lid. Inside, several layers of plastic were lashed around yet another box, this one shaped like a miniature coffin, wrapped inside and out with white linen and tied with a pink bow. As I untied the ribbon, I couldn't help thinking we were within sight of the end of a long quest—long not only because of the geography I had covered in the trip, but because this search for a tiny piece of the truth about the past had itself begun a generation earlier, near the end of Larry Angel's long career, and was now about to complete its circle.

I opened the box. As I had expected, the remains were wet and very dirty from all the muddy water that had been standing so long within the casket, so I decided to wash each one before examining them, and to do an inventory at the same time. The bones were loose in the box, and as I started to lift them out, I saw something else lying at the bottom of the small casket.

It was a torn plastic bag, and even before I had lifted it all the way out of the box I recognized the small cylindrical metacarpals and basal phalanges of fingers. Across the front of the bag in indelible marker was written "LEFT HAND." Below it was a smaller bag, tightly sealed, labeled "GOOCHLAND" and with a description of its contents in the same writing. I moved my own fingers across the lettering on the pouch.

I had seen that same penmanship just a few days earlier, while reviewing the forensic file one last time before this trip. But that same handwriting was also part of my earliest recollections as a young graduate student, newly arrived at the Smithsonian some twenty years before, when I had first met Larry Angel. Seeing his meticulous hand again here in this unlikeliest of places, so unexpectedly out of context and yet so perfectly in context, was almost as vivid an experience as suddenly hearing his voice or being buoyed up once again by the flash of his wide smile.

Carefully, I unsealed the smallest package. Inside, as promised, still intact despite its two years in the berry patch and remarkably dry after nearly a decade in the underground pool, was the cut phalanx.

I held up the pouch to the others around the table. "An old colleague," I said, pointing to the words. "Dr. Lawrence Angel. One of my first teachers."

And, I thought to myself, still teaching.

2

IMPOLITE SOCIETY

J. Lawrence Angel was born on March 21, 1915, in London, England, the son of a Devonshire sculptor and an American classicist mother, and he died on November 3, 1986, at George Washington University Hospital at the age of seventy-one. What happened in between, and to a large extent in tandem, were a great scientific career and the coming of age of the new profession of forensic anthropology.

Larry's education began in England. When he was thirteen his parents moved to America, so he left Ovingdean School in Sussex for the Choate School in Connecticut. Seven years later he received an A.B. from Harvard, magna cum laude and Phi Beta Kappa, and three months after that he entered graduate school there to study anthropology under Earnest Hooton.

Hooton was something of an academic folk hero. He had become curator of the Peabody Museum at Harvard just before the Great War at the age of twenty-seven, and in 1931, the year Larry started college, Hooton's celebrity received another big boost from the popular success of his book *Up from the Ape*. Although he was American-born and more than twice the age of his enthusiastic young graduate student, they had much in common. A Rhodes Scholar, Hooton had studied at Oxford from 1910 to 1913 and was partial to things English. Moreover, his immense popularity as a lecturer was due in part to his wit and love of humor, qualities he could not have helped but perceive were equally prominent in Larry Angel.

(In one famous story making the rounds at the time, the professor was approached before class by a Radcliffe student warning him that other women in his newly integrated anthropology seminar were going to rise up in a body and walk out the next time he exceeded propriety in his often graphic anatomical descriptions. Hooton listened politely, thanked the emissary, and proceeded to deliver the most conservative, cautious, circumspect lecture of his career—on a tribe of aborigines on a South Pacific island so remote that it was connected to the rest of the world only by a mail boat that stopped twice a year. Five minutes before the bell, almost as an afterthought, Hooton cited a remarkable effect of their isolation on the evolution of the male members, as it were, of this island culture: like Darwin's finches, this race of men had developed a spectacular adaptation, distinguished by—well— by the world's largest sex organs. Almost apologetically, the professor held up his hands to illustrate, and the distance between his opposing palms was truly awesome. As promised, the women in the class arose as one and headed angrily for the exit. "Please, ladies, please," Hooton called after them. "I can appreciate your enthusiasm, but this haste is unnecessary; the next mail boat doesn't leave until August.")

Like many other anthropologists of his time, Larry started out in the classics. His field work took him to New Mexico, Arizona, and Georgia, but also to Greece and Turkey. He developed an intense commitment to two areas of study: the interpretation of the human skeleton, and the geographic area of Greece and the Near East. He told me that both aspects of that commitment owed to parental influence: he had been fascinated by the skeleton that hung in his father's studio, and his mother had given him much of his early exposure to Hellenic literature and art.

After a couple of years as a teaching assistant at Harvard and a year at Berkeley, Larry received his doctorate from Harvard in 1942. By then, skeletal anatomy and classical anthropology had become the focus of his professional career, and he taught anatomy, conducted research, made frequent trips to Greece, and worked as a research associate in the museum at the University of Pennsylvania for a decade and a half after World War II.

As far as I know, Larry Angel never saw a forensic bone case until he was forty-seven years old. But by the time he arrived at the Smithsonian in 1962, three major factors were moving into alignment to produce a revolution in the ways anthropology was used for detecting and solving crimes. One factor was a postwar rise in the public's appreciation of the role of science in general. This included a new perception that detective work could take place as effectively in the laboratory as on the streets. The second was the recognition within the law enforcement community that skeletons often contained clues to crime which were completely inaccessible through conventional methods of forensic examination, but which became vividly obvious through classic techniques of anthropology.

The third was a gradual acceptance within the profession of anthropology that the anthropologist might play a broader role in society, and that service to the law was both honorable and necessary. This was by no means self-evident among those who worked in the "pure" sciences. Anthropologists began to recognize that even in forensic cases, important knowledge could flow in both directions. Police work might just be a source for invaluable data about present populations that was unavailable from ancient sources.

Larry didn't need much encouragement. He quickly recognized that solving a police case could be just as exciting and rewarding as unraveling the mysteries of a tomb in ancient Greece or Egypt, and often considerably easier. By the time he died, J. Lawrence Angel was recognized throughout the world, not just in the academic sector but by the general public, as one of a handful of experts who led forensic anthropology out of the closet and into full legitimacy.

Anthropologists love to divide almost everything into time periods, and it should surprise no one that three such eras have been identified in the evolution of forensic anthropology.

The period prior to 1939, which stretches from about the midnineteenth century until the start of World War II, is now viewed as the Dark Ages of the science as an instrument of law. Anatomists and physical anthropologists were consulted now and then on forensic remains, and sometimes they testified in court, but with very little visible impact on the academic development of their profession. Some of those early forensic cases attracted enormous fame for expert witnesses who would far rather have escaped the attention.

The Parkman murder in 1849 entailed testimony by a professor at Harvard Medical School who examined a victim who had been murdered, mutilated, partially burned, and dumped into one of the school

Aleš Hrdlička

T.D. Stewart

J. Lawrence Angel

latrines by a thoughtless colleague; that would be a tough one even by today's standards. In another case fifty years later, a physical anthropologist named George A. Dorsey found himself drawn into a spectacular courtroom battle with an anatomist over the source of certain small bones discovered amidst the sludge in the bottom of a sausage maker's vat in Chicago. Dorsey's view prevailed in court, with the jury accepting his thesis that the exhibits had previously occupied important positions in the anatomy of the sausage maker's late wife. But in the larger arena of peer opinion, Dorsey suffered such ridicule and scorn—both from the medical profession and from his own colleagues—for having stooped to such an unseemly forum and for having the temerity to stand up to an M.D. that he never offered his professional expertise in any other courtroom.

It was a classic sort of battle between pure and applied science, and in those days it was drawn along clear class lines. But it continued to dog forensic research in years to come. Larry Angel's early mentor, Professor Hooton, acknowledged he had examined some dozen police cases in thirty years, and although he published an important overview in 1943 on the medical-legal aspects of physical anthropology, he never wrote a professional paper on a single one of those cases.

Even the scientist described most frequently as the founder of American physical anthropology, the Smithsonian's own Aleš Hrdlička, was reticent about that side of his work. The first physical anthropologist on the staff of the National Museum of Natural History, Hrdlička came to the Smithsonian in 1903 to head up the newly founded Division of Physical Anthropology. Seven years later he was promoted to full curator, and in 1918 became founding editor of the *American Journal of Physical Anthropology*. It was under his direction that the museum's world-famous reference collection of human remains grew to near its present level of some 33,000 individual skeletons. And it was also during his tenure, when the museum got new neighbors across the street in the mid-1930s, that the science of anthropology first became available on a reliable, systematic basis, in service to the Federal Bureau of Investigation. It was Hrdlička, a consummate scientist, who formalized the Smithsonian's relationship with the FBI. Yet for all the times that he was consulted for forensic examinations in the years before his death in 1943, he spoke of them rarely in private, mentioned them hardly at all in public, and wrote never a word.

The 1939 publication of W. M. Krogman's "Guide to the Identification of Human Skeletal Material" in the FBI's *Law Enforcement Bulletin* is now thought by many to be the historical event that finally brought forensic anthropology out of the closet. It vividly demonstrated the potential contributions of physical anthropology to a nationwide forensic community. Perhaps even more importantly, it was the first bold statement by a respected anthropologist to his colleagues that forensic applications could be a legitimate and useful aspect of their science. The date of its publication marks the beginning of what is now defined as the second era of forensic anthropology, from 1939 to 1972.

Like many important landmarks, Krogman's "Guide" looms larger in the rear-view mirror than it appeared in passing. For many more years, forensic work continued to be regarded professionally as outside the mainstream of physical anthropology. But it was largely because of publication of the "Guide" that law enforcement agencies throughout the country began calling on anthropologists for their expertise. In 1942, Hrdlicka's only student, Dale Stewart, began to consult regularly with the FBI. Other prominent figures in the fields of academe— notably H. L. Shapiro, F. E. Randall, and Charles E. Snow—were consulted extensively throughout the balance of the war. Dale Stewart, Ellis R. Kerley, and Charles P. Warren assisted the military services with identifications during the Korean hostilities.

Krogman published subsequent papers on the forensic side of his work in 1943 and again in 1962. Others followed, including a major publication by Stewart in 1970.

The third and present era began with the founding, in 1972, of a Physical Anthropology section within the American Academy of Forensic Sciences. The new organization gave a legitimacy and rallying point for all the previously unconnected anthropologists who were scattered about in the field. Instead of going off on their own and having no other constituency than the police departments which they served, they now were presented with a dynamic forum for the exchange of knowledge and the advancement of their work as a science.

The section's fourteen charter members formally staked out the boundaries of their field. The orphan had been owned, and in 1978, a program was introduced to certify diplomates in forensic anthropology in much the same way physicians are certified in their field by a board of specialization. Certification was based on academic credentials and rigorous examination. Eight initial diplomates were certified that March, and a group of fourteen more, including J. Lawrence Angel, Ph.D., passed through in November. The number of certified diplomates has grown steadily since, although not as fast as section membership. Forensic applications of physical anthropology were headed for respectability at last.

The diplomate program was a further step toward the establishment of forensic anthropology as a solid subdiscipline. Anyone can call himself an anthropologist, and prior to a method of accreditation, most police departments and lawyers who needed to draw upon this type of forensic skill and experience for the first time were confronted with a lot of confusing choices and potential risks. Assuming they found someone who had been legitimately trained as an anthropologist, their "expert witness" could easily have spent his (or her) entire career as a specialist in non-human primates without looking at a single human bone.

Those two events—the founding of the section and the certification program—also marked the beginning of a new age of enlightenment in publishing. Of the 1,008 articles appearing in the *Journal of Forensic Sciences* during the 20 years from 1956 through 1975, only 14 were related to physical anthropology; in the 12 years following, there were 70. The number and percentages both continue to grow, and the frequency of forensic bone studies in other publications has soared as well.

A precipitating factor in Larry Angel's involvement with the forensic side of his profession came when he found himself the recipient of Dale Stewart's mantle as the Smithsonian's bone consultant for the FBI. Because of Larry's anatomical background, and perhaps also because of his natural intellectual propensity for puzzle solving, he took to the new role, in Stewart's words, "like a duck to water." He examined six forensic cases in 1962; by the time of his death, his 24-year Smithsonian career total stood at 565.

Like others who came before him, Larry Angel's many contributions to forensic anthropology are only hinted at in his bibliography. For all the twenty-two years he performed forensic analysis at the Smithsonian, Larry's papers on the subject consisted of two short, co-authored articles in the FBI *Law Enforcement Bulletin*. A lot of the other things he wrote had great relevance to forensics—on TMJ formation, obesity, the reaction area of the femoral neck, general vs. dental health, patterns of fractures, secular change in the skeleton, and skeletal features related to sex, age, and individuation—but they never directly addressed forensic applications.

The balance started to change by the end of his life, but not by much. In the end, out of more than one hundred publications in his bibliography, only seventeen focus on themes related to forensic anthropology, and a mere seven address that subject head-on.

I can think of one area particularly in which I wish Larry had written for publication. In his reports to the FBI, he delighted in combining detailed anatomical observation with speculation about the individual's geographical origin, lifestyle, or occupation. There are some good examples in these passages from cases in his last year of life:

> The tibia feels more dense and is flattened from side to side (platymeric) as if from muscle pull. But the tibial flattening slopes at 4 degrees, less than average in the U.S., and the opposite of a skier's or mountaineer's adaptation.

*   *   *

> Signs of occupation include strong rotator cuff, deltoid insertion, pectoralis crest and vertebral border of scapula, suggesting active use of upper extremities; in the distal femur a strong crest among the (missing) abductor tubercle. The pubic pectin is sharp. These all suggest a "cowboy" or at least someone active on horseback. I don't know if shepherds in Montana use horses or not; I note the belt buckle.

*   *   *

> Stress marks on anterior part of rotator cuff and at costo-clavicular ligament insertion (especially on right) suggest work in a factory or possibly with horses, but not as a jockey.

*   *   *

> Occupational suggestions include extremely marked attachments for pectoralis major muscles (on clavicles and humeri especially), strong muscles around the elbows and also scapulae, and unexpected exostoses at origin (above hip socket) and insertion (on top of patellae) of the rectus femoris muscles. Hands are muscular and quite big. The man seems to have jumped from a height to produce injuries to hip and foot....Was he a shipyard worker or a factory bench worker (who got involved with crime or drugs)?

The data sheets in the archives, summarizing Larry Angel's immense forensic caseload as well as his lifetime of contributions to classical anthropology, show the real balance in his research. And despite the often lofty condescension of colleagues who considered themselves purer scientists for having escaped the notice of the public, so did the abundant evidence of Larry Angel's celebrity. He was profiled in media ranging from *Smithsonian* magazine and *Science Digest* to *The Washington Post* and *People* magazine. All that attention by the press obviously had a lot to do with the increased general awareness by the public of the importance of forensic anthropology in police investigations. Viewed beside his other life as a classicist, it seems to split his image in two. Neither image is real.

Over the years, the forensic casework drew him in, both in terms of his productivity and the way he presented himself to the world, and by the time he died it had totally dominated his persona with the public. But to his professional peers and heirs, who were more inclined to judge him by his publication record, the forensic side amounts to little more than a footnote. Neither record provides any insight into what may have been Larry's greatest contribution, which was as a teacher.

He was a natural, and everyone who ever came in contact with him on a professional level, no matter how casually, went away richer for the experience. He regularly lectured on forensic topics, taught physical anthropology at George Washington University each spring, and each fall taught a course in forensic anthropology, primarily for forensic pathologists. As far as I know, the forensic course never was advertised, but each year the waiting list was greater than the capacity of the room. Two years before he died, Larry estimated that more than half the medical examiners in the entire country had taken his course—a remarkable impact for someone whose primary commitment was to research in an institution not normally associated with teaching. I have kept the course alive, and it still draws turn-away crowds.

Larry Angel's contributions to forensics changed the field. But whatever his fame did for his science, it didn't change Larry. He loved to sing. He sang around the office, quietly and unobtrusively, and those of us who got to know him usually could tell from the melody what type of work he was doing, particularly when he was collecting data from a skeleton. And he was always smiling, whether in the middle of an abstruse intellectual exchange or when occupied with his normal workaday activities—such as positioning the most odoriferous forensic case on the window ledge in his laboratory and leaving the window just sufficiently ajar to attract the curiosity of passers-by. (Larry and I agreed that we could probably come up with a pretty accurate formula for computing time since death, based on elapsed time between the arrival of the body and the first complaint about the odor by a non-forensic colleague.) He was a hard act to follow.

I'm a different generation and I came to the Smithsonian far earlier in my life than Larry did, so when I inherited the same role I saw it in a different way—and it has changed even more in just the short time since Larry Angel left us. Larry started out in the classics, in ancient Greece and elsewhere, and he remained true to those interests for the rest of his life. When he got to the Smithsonian and Dale Stewart passed him a plate which included forensic work, I'm sure Larry accepted it at first as just one of those things that came with the territory—and like many of his colleagues then he probably viewed it mainly as a way of obtaining useful data on contemporary populations. There are now people who get their degrees specializing in forensic anthropology, which was unheard of when Larry Angel was in school and still not possible as recently as when I got my own doctorate. These are people who may casually study pre-Columbian America or ancient Greece, but the bulk of their training is in police work.

When I first joined the Smithsonian I did an occasional forensic assignment, and I was amused at how much time Larry Angel spent on these cases and at how it was undeniably shaping his public persona. The old attitude was still very much alive in those days among academicians—especially those who hadn't ever been called on to do any forensic examinations themselves—that police work was a branch of show business, and that to become involved at all carried the risk of being drawn off into the irrelevant and the bizarre. Those days are gone. A substantial science has now evolved, along with all the academic trappings of a legitimate subdiscipline, and such pioneers as Hrdlička, Krogman, Stewart, and Angel have been succeeded by a new generation of giants with names like Kerley, Bass, Maples, and Snow.

Down in the archives of the museum, there is a 1977 review letter from Larry Angel's principal contact at the FBI. It says that although "his primary interest is not in forensic work, Dr. Angel's endeavors in this field have enabled him to report findings that were initially missed by pathologists, coroners, and local physical anthropologists."

Someday my own files will come to rest in the same archives, near or beside Larry Angel's. I'd be pretty proud if they contained the same kind of letter. It's not a bad way to be remembered.

3

ABEL AND AFTER

he Silence of the Lambs is based on the premise that you have to be outside the framework in which most of us are trapped to be able to understand how another kind of mind operates. To use that story's example, it is very difficult to understand where a sociopath is coming from if you don't understand how his mind works and if you don't have a sociopath's databank. In the analysis and understanding of crime, physical anthropology offers techniques and perspective which often transcend the conventional framework, supplying an order that allows us to see and understand things others might miss or from which they would draw no meaning.

For example, in examining the skeletal remains of a suspected murder victim, a county coroner who is relatively unfamiliar with skeletal anatomy thinks he has found cut marks on the bones. He reports them to the police investigators as coming from a knife. A forensic anthropologist who has seen lots of these cases before is able to interpret the marks differently, and recognizes them as the tooth marks of a scavenging carnivore. The distinctions are extremely fine, but tell that to a presumably innocent man the police are about to charge with murder. The experience to distinguish carnivore marks from trauma at the time of death stems from observations on hundreds or thousands of bones, not only from forensic contexts but from archaeological excavations as well.

Experienced forensic anthropologists have examined thousands of bones from all time periods and from all over the world, and are beneficiaries of tens of thousands of examinations made by others in the field. They know what happens to a skeleton after the passage of a month, a decade, a century, two thousand years. They know what happens when a skeleton is left on the prairie after an Indian massacre and buried years later by a passer-by. They can distinguish between evidence of murder and the results of a dog passing by and helping himself to lunch. Those experiences supply the context in which suspected or known murder cases can be interpreted far more precisely than before.

Conversely, forensic work supplies a lot of knowledge that sharpens one's wits for interpreting the past. If I'm excavating a site in Ecuador and find ten thoracic vertebrae that are still articulated, still in anatomic order, I start to ask myself, how many weeks after death did that individual lie around—what stage of decomposition was the body in—before someone came along and put him in the ground? The answer comes from forensic cases where we routinely see similar situations and which comprise a good database for making accurate estimates.

Until fairly recently, physical anthropology was viewed as almost exclusively the science of mankind's past. It is now generally accepted that the methods we've developed in our attempts to interpret the lives of vanished populations can help us understand the modern world. Conversely, scientific study of contemporary groups of people have led to analytical techniques used by physical anthropologists to gain access to the ancient world. Analysis of patterns of modern violence can illuminate what happened several centuries ago to the occupants of some of the world's deepest shaft tombs in Ecuador, just as the knowledge we have gathered from fossils in the Sinai, from before the time of Moses, can contribute clues to the identity of a murder victim whose skeleton is found scattered about a blackberry patch in Goochland, Virginia.

Many of the benefits on both sides of this new equation are related to the rise of anthropology as a forensic science. In this relatively recent union between anthropology and the law, the flow of knowledge and its associated benefits runs in both directions.

That concept takes a little getting used to. The increase and diffusion of knowledge for its own sake is the charter of the Smithsonian Institution. In its classical application, physical anthropology carries no value judgments, involves no ethical decisions on the scientist's part other than an obvious obligation to the truth, and has little or no consequence beyond the generation of knowledge. From the outside, it's sometimes tempting to regard science in general as cut and dried, and an area like archaeology as nearly irrelevant, with no connection between the past and the present.

From the inside, the connection has been there from the start. There is a direct link between our ability to discover and examine the social, economic, political, and environmental systems of past societies and the ability to understand these same factors at work in the world today.

When I initially came to the Smithsonian full-time in 1971, my interest in forensics was only marginal. Before going into the Army, I was trained in forensic anthropology at graduate school with Bill Bass, Ellis Kerley, and the late Tom McKern. But all of them had moved on by the time I returned to Kansas for my doctorate, so I finished up the degree with other people on my committee, including the Smithsonian's Dale Stewart, who served as chairman. My real focus was on the ancient past, and when I completed my degree and went to work, my first projects for the Smithsonian took me to Latin America, and such South American sites as Ayalán in coastal Ecuador.

Part of the impetus for that work came from my good luck in meeting a man named Earl Lubensky, the U.S. consul general to Guayaquil. An avid archaeologist who later earned a Ph.D. in this field, Earl had extensive contacts in Ecuador throughout the business and cultural communities, and one of them was the owner of a large farm on the southern coast. Almost all large farms in that part of the world contain archaeological remains, but Ayalán proved to be particularly fertile. Earl had initiated extensive excavations there. When we met, he encouraged me to become involved because it was also an extensive cemetery site.

In 1973 I went down with him and we unearthed a number of large burial jars, each containing up to twenty-five skeletons. They were relatively recent, dating to the Late Integration Period, which was sometime between A.D. 900 and 1300, and I wrote a monograph on our work. But that introduction led to my meeting numerous other archaeologists in the area, and over the next several years I worked at a variety of different sites covering a wide span of time. The breadth of

Burial urn from the Ayalán site.

Working at the Ayalán site. At bottom, excavators sift soil for fragments.

this research enabled me to develop a profile of the whole sweep of history in that part of the world, and we are now able to plot what happened to those peoples through time and space as we can in very few other areas. By working with large samples, we were able to determine the frequencies of various diseases and other conditions, not only to document them but to see how they changed with time.

That work has enabled us to tell all kinds of stories about the ways in which cultures evolve and what kind of impact they have on the peoples who create them. With the rise of agriculture, as we saw them beginning to live in larger, denser communities, we also were able to chronicle their increased problems with anemia, parasitism and other disease, the adverse impact of a more sedentary life, and the decline in life expectancy. One of the most fascinating stories to develop from this work was the rise of porotic hyperostosis, an anemic condition thought to reflect iron deficiency. Through our analysis of the distribution of the sites and the time periods involved, we were able to make a strong argument that the disease was caused by a hookworm similar to a modern-day parasite still found in coastal Ecuador.

Very few of the skeletal remains found by anthropologists speak of violent deaths, although this may be more true in some parts of the world than in others. When they do speak of such violence, they usually illuminate important cultural practices related to religious beliefs, criminal punishment, or warfare, often with great eloquence.

Sometimes when the skeletal evidence of violence is found, it is supported by written or pictographic records of the related events: battles, torture, beheadings, eviscerations, mutilations, and the setting out of dead bodies to feed carrion-eating birds. An outstanding recent find of this sort is the excavation, in the mid-1980s, of mutilated human remains from a thirteenth-century slaughter pit at Pacatnamu on the north coast of what is now Peru.

As reported by my colleague John Verano, the bodies were recovered from a deep trench just outside the entrance to the ancient city's principal ceremonial site. There were fourteen of them—all male and all young—probably the victims of three separate rituals of sacrifice and mutilation. Each group was commingled at its level in the pit, but the levels were separated by layers of sand, trash, and building rubble, indicating the passage of months or possibly years between the rituals in which they were killed. The deepest layer of such refuse extended to the top of the pit, and consisted of melted adobe, collapsed wall materials, and wind-blown sands which had accumulated in the centuries since the city itself had died.

The last group to be thrown into the pit were four victims found six feet below ground level. Some small fragments of plain fabric, perhaps a loincloth, were found under one of the bodies, and the rope remnants of what appeared to be hobbles were still tied around the ankle bones of two of them. Each skeleton showed signs of mutilation at the time of death, including puncture wounds in the ribs and other bones from repeated stabbings in the chest and abdomen, some of which went all the way through to the spine.

Several fragments of sharpened animal bones were found mixed in with the remains of the victims, apparently broken off from the stabbing instruments that had been used to kill them. One of those sharpened fragments was found to fit precisely into a stab mark in a vertebra of the body from which it was recovered. The minimum number of provable stab wounds in each body ranged from five to nineteen, and their angles indicated multiple attackers. The angles also suggested the victims were on their backs rather than standing at the time of the thrusts, probably tied to a horizontal post, perhaps even an altar, which provides another possible explanation for the ankle ropes.

One other element of the sacrificial rite, evident in the remains of all four victims, was the removal of the left radii. The radius is the smaller of the two long bones in the forearm, the one nearer to the thumb. In the course of cutting out that bone from one of the victims, a large part of the hand was apparently cut loose without being separated entirely; a cluster of several finger bones was found at a point halfway to the elbow, most likely folded back on a flap of tissue when the radius was twisted free.

Group Two, about six inches deeper in the pit, consisted of eight more bodies. All of the injuries to this group were different from the first; there were no signs of the puncture wounds that told of stabbing, and none of the forearms was lacking a radius, but the trauma that they did exhibit were more numerous and diverse. They suffered from broken necks and limbs, slashed throats, cracked skulls. Three had lost their left legs, one was beheaded, and two more were apparently torn to pieces. Near the foot of one of them were the remains of a black vulture, killed perhaps when it had come down into the slaughter pit to scavenge on the carrion.

Six inches further down were the remains of the first two victims. One had been decapitated, and in both bodies the arms and legs had been wrenched so violently that the heads of the long bones were pulled from their sockets in the shoulders and hips. Like three of the bodies in the middle group, their chests had been cut open with the

Skeletal remains recovered at the site at Pacatnamu, Peru.

stroke of a blade, which slashed or bisected the breastbone and severed the left costal cartilage of numerous ribs. Fractures in the back where those same ribs joined the spine suggested the violent spreading apart of the incision for access to the internal organs, perhaps including the beating heart.

Based on his observation of bleaching and surface cracking in a mandibular (lower jaw) bone from the upper level, and in ribs from the middle level, Verano deduced that both groups of skeletons had remained on the surface for a period of weeks or months before being covered by fill. Some period of surface exposure was confirmed by soil studies at all three levels, which produced abundant evidence of scavenging insects and their larvae.

Although the three groups were separated by time, space, and the nature of their injuries, they shared a number of common attributes. They all carbon-dated to the early part of the Late Intermediate Period, between A.D. 1160 and 1380. They were all within an age range between fifteen and thirty-five, all male, all apparently robust. And many of them—far more than would be the case if they represented a random sampling of the general population—showed signs of healed injuries to the bones. Two had recovered from broken ribs, two showed hip deterioration which may have been injury-related, and one had recovered from a depressed fracture of the skull. To Verano, these old trauma were signs of their lives as soldiers, and perhaps as war captives to the people who had later killed them.

If this catalogue of anthropological inferences from the skeletal remains in Peru reads like Larry Angel's report on his examination of the murder victim from Virginia, it is because the detective work is nearly identical. Verano approached the ancient killings with the same intention, and armed with the same insights and the same technology, as a forensic anthropologist brings to his or her investigation of a modern crime. The two avenues of inquiry are both served by the same discipline, and each supports the other.

That discipline served the great anthropologist Louis S. B. Leakey thirty-five years ago when he examined debris recovered from Olduvai Gorge, the now dry bottom of an ancient lake some 300 feet below the surrounding Serengeti Plain in Tanzania. Analysis of artifacts and bone fragments suggested the possibility that our collateral ancestors had used tools for skinning and cutting up game nearly 2 million years ago. Dale Stewart's 1969 review of Leakey's work also offers the possibility that these same materials include an early hint of hominid cannibalism.

Dale also called attention to possible early evidence of human warfare: healed injuries to the shoulder of a Neanderthal skeleton in Germany, dating four hundred centuries before Christ, which so altered the shape of the bones that the owner would not have been able to feed himself with his left hand.

At about the same time as the aftermath of the hypothetical battle that left the disabled Neanderthal veteran nursing his injuries on the Alpine slopes of Central Europe, another sojourner faced a violent confrontation some 1,500 miles away, at the eastern edge of the Sahara in the area now called Sudan. He didn't do nearly as well, but his death provided his eventual heirs with a legacy of astonishing wealth.

This second Paleolithic man was probably a trader or some kind of merchant. He was well into his twenties or older, solidly muscled but not particularly heavy or tall. He was right-handed, and there was a good possibility he excelled with the javelin. He had been in fights before; there was an old, healed parry fracture in the bone of his right forearm, circumstantial evidence that he had beaten his adversary in at least one prior battle even with a broken arm.

But none of his past triumphs helped much when he was attacked · by at least two assailants while crossing the fertile floodplains of the Nile. He was pierced twice or more by stone-tipped weapons, perhaps arrows, or spears, or possibly knives. The tips of two of the weapons penetrated the bone and broke off; one bladelet of chalcedony and another of chert were found in the body between the lowest ribs and the spine, and it was probable they had injured the distal ends of his right ulna (the bone of the forearm) and left humerus (upper arm bone) in their passages. He dropped to the ground, pitching face forward into the damp soil, and was preserved where he had fallen for the next forty thousand years.

That's a lot of drama to extract from a pile of ancient, shattered bones, and it would be hard to imagine two scientists better equipped for the task than Dale Stewart and Larry Angel, both of whom were members of the team commissioned to examine the remains and describe them for the scientific literature. If there are cosmic reasons for the way things occur in life, maybe that explains why this early victim of murder lay so long in the rich and ancient soil of the Wadi Kubbaniya before being discovered in 1982. As Walt Whitman once said, to have great drama, it is also necessary to have a great audience.

Larry and Dale collaborated on another exhumation a few years earlier which required no digging and very little travel, and that time I was with them. Our celebrated subject was enshrined just across the street from our offices in the "Castle" of the institution that bears his name. James Smithson's perilous proximity to the National Museum of Natural History probably made him a likely subject for disinterment and anthropological examination anyway, but such a fate was virtually guaranteed by his personal history.

An Englishman who was born illegitimately eleven years before America became a nation, and who died in Italy in 1829 at the age of sixty-four, Smithson had never set foot in America. But he was educated at Oxford, became a fellow of the Royal Society at the nearly unprecedented age of twenty-one, established a brilliant reputation as a research chemist, and was sympathetic to the promise and purpose of the newly emerging country he never saw. When he died, his inheritance was bequeathed to the "United States of America, to found at Washington...an establishment for the increase & diffusion of knowledge among men."

Smithson's body was dug up the first time when it was removed in 1903 from the British Cemetery in Genoa. His skull was displayed to the press by the American consul in Italy, and his skeleton was extensively examined by Alexander Graham Bell in America, and photographed by Mrs. Bell, before its enshrinement with full state honors the following year in the bosom of the institution he created. In 1973 Smithson's crypt was reopened and his bones were examined again.

As in any forensic case, Larry and Dale insulated themselves as fully as possible from learning anything in advance about their subject which might color their analysis of his remains. As Smithsonian employees, however, there was no way they could unlearn what they already knew, and Smithson's first disinterment and subsequent transatlantic crossing in the winter of 1903 were a well-established part of the institution's lore. The evidence of postmortem trauma—broken ribs and a part of the spine—were therefore attributed to that passage. They estimated his age at death as between fifty and sixty-five, and his height as slightly under the average for modern Americans or for English aristocracy of his own era. He was also slight in build, but with a long trunk, a large chest, and strong hands and arms. He had lost seventeen teeth during life, five more were abscessed at the time of his death, and the remainder on the left side of his mouth showed wear from a pipe. His teeth also showed patterns of arrested growth from early childhood, perhaps related to weaning.

There were no signs of growth arrest in his bones, although he apparently suffered from a poor diet, even to the point of some anemia, and also may have had a minor shoulder injury as a young child.

The Maryland ossuary. At right, the author lies across a board in order to remove soil without disturbing the remains.

The darker patch of earth at left marks a burial pit. Below is the pit after excavation.

The correct anatomical arrangement of the articulated skeleton in this section of the ossuary contrasts with the confusion of disarticulated remains.

Occupational indicators pointed to a vigorous, hardworking life and also to a fair amount of time spent bending over a desk. And in the kind of detail that Larry Angel, in particular, was so fond of, the report concluded with the observation that characteristics of the right little finger suggest Smithson may have played the violin, piano, or harpsichord.

At the start of my career with the Smithsonian, Dale Stewart and I excavated an ancient ossuary in southern Maryland. An ossuary is a community grave in which a large number of bodies and skeletons, usually accruing over a period of several years, are all collected at a single site and buried at the same time. This particular ossuary had been discovered by a landowner when a fence line was being erected in 1971. Dr. Stewart had previously worked at this site, so when the post-hole auger came up with bone instead of dirt, the landowner called the Smithsonian. Ossuaries not only offer a rare glimpse of burial customs of peoples living in the area before Captain John Smith and the formation of Jamestown, but also an opportunity to learn about their health, life expectancy, and other demographic factors. Our excavation recovered the skeletal remains of over 150 individuals. The dig provides a good example of how knowledge gained by forensic work can be used to solve archaeological problems.

Using microscopic analysis of bones and X-rays of teeth, I was able to reconstruct the ages at death of everybody in that sample, then group them all together to make a life table, the same kind of life table that insurance companies use today to determine premium rates based on likely life span.

The table told me that when members of that society were born, they could expect to live an average of nineteen or twenty years, but if they survived the first five years of life, they could expect to live another twenty-three years. This was based on evidence of high infant mortality, a lot of infectious and respiratory disease, plus other indicators at the site that their hygiene was far from ideal. Their first challenge was to survive the highest risk period, from ages one to five; but even though the mortality rates dropped after that, old age as we know it today was extremely rare.

One of the basic uses of a life table is to calculate the crude mortality rate, which is how many people die per thousand per year in a given population. In southern Maryland just prior to the establishment of the European beachhead at Jamestown, the crude mortality rate was approximately 5 percent. That information can be very useful. Starting with a count of the number of dead people in the ossuary, extrapolating the mortality rate based on the distribution of ages, and then using other means to determine the length of time the ossuary was in use, it became possible to estimate with fair reliability the total number of people in the population during that period. This all depended, however, on our accurately determining how long the ossuary was in use.

While we were involved in this excavation in Maryland, it occurred to me that the clue to the length of use rested in our observations on the degree of articulation of the bones. It was an idea that grew out of many years of observations on modern forensic cases.

From our work in forensic science, we knew that the process of decomposition follows a predictable course, that the muscles and ligaments gradually decompose to the point that when a skeleton is picked up or otherwise disturbed at any time beyond a certain period after death, it will fall apart. At earlier stages, certain desiccated ligaments hold together some of the vertebrae or other parts, and the integrity of the body diminishes as time since death increases.

Obviously, a body that was buried within a week of death would be nearly intact at the time of interment; this isn't enough time for a skeleton to fall apart before it goes into the ground. If death occurs three months before the burial, enough decomposition sets in so that an excavator would be likely to find a skeleton in segments, but not completely fallen apart. If death had occurred two years before the burial, there would not be any soft tissue left at all, and the bones would be isolated.

Based on that logic, when we excavated the ossuary we carefully recorded which bodies were in their correct anatomical relationship and which were not. I reasoned that the longer the time interval in which this ossuary had remained open, the greater the number of bodies that would be disarticulated. If they had an ossuary burial ceremony once a month, then it would be reasonable to expect that nearly every body would be a complete, integrated skeleton. If the ceremonies were once every twenty years, then the opposite would be the case. Assuming a constant rate of death, we were able to calculate the length of time represented by this particular ossuary as four years. And from that, we knew the size of the community it served was approximately one thousand people.

This raised an interesting archaeological puzzle: where did all those people live? A series of test pits from around the area of the ossuary suggested that the site could not have supported more than two hundred people.

Logic and experience suggested that the people in the ossuary did not all come from that site, but that various villages came together to bury their dead communally. That was similar to the known practices of the Hurons during the period in the region of the Great Lakes, and the Jesuits who documented Huron mortuary customs indicated that the villages rotated the site every ten years—about half as frequently as in Maryland.

Interestingly enough, there was some evidence in Maryland even during historic times, i.e., in the period since the arrival of the Europeans, that this same social structure and ritual were still around. In 1612, Captain John Smith of Jamestown fame made a map of all the villages in that area, and he concluded there were about twenty-eight villages forming a loose political structure. Only five had a chief's house, which implied that each chief presided over an average of five or six other villages in the complex. To our delight, we found that our estimate of the population served by the ossuary was roughly equal to John Smith's own estimates of the aboriginal population in each area under a single chief.

What Smith actually estimated was the number of fighting men which each of these villages could muster, and they averaged around fifty per village. From the life table study, I was able to demonstrate that for every male between the ages of twenty and forty, there were three to five other people, so the population per village was about two hundred, and five villages would bring the total up to around one thousand.

Smith had the considerable advantage of being there at the time he was making his count. Three and a half centuries later, we couldn't have done any of the calculations to arrive at his result without the knowledge acquired from our forensic work.

We examine bones for the insights they contain to the culture in which their owners lived, and through skeletal evidence of such practices as head deformation or the mutilation and reshaping of teeth, we can understand some of the patterns that reflect their social evolution. We make observations on how tall they were, and through the comparison of samples try to work out the relationships between one population and another. By these means we trace their migration histories. Often we work in tandem with archaeologists, and when they find that a tribe makes pottery more closely resembling one group than another, we try to determine if these parallels match up biologically as well. Were A and B related genetically, or were they different but simply trading pottery?

Another discipline with which physical anthropologists work in close parallel is that of medicine. We have an enormous range of ways to measure the health of populations, not just to measure the history of disease. We do that as well by finding instances of tuberculosis and treponemal disease such as syphilis in the New World, for example, or by tracing the history of parasitism. But our goal for these discoveries, through the excavation and anthropological study of samples, is to determine the impact and frequency of some of these conditions on the host populations. It doesn't do a lot of good to find one questionable example of tuberculosis or syphilis. The important questions are: how many people had it, how severe was it, and how did it relate to everything else they had and did? Frequency of these diseases provides a key to the overall quality of life—not just the impact of disease on population numbers, but the kinds of stress the people were under, the effects on their lives of what they ate, the environment they were living in, and a myriad of other factors.

In Ecuador we tried to do that by looking at material from a number of different sites and different time periods. Fortunately the body of data is now large enough that we have been able to trace the prehistoric populations far back in time, all the way to the Santa Elena sample—findings which predated agriculture and the invention of ceramics. These were semi-nomadic hunters and gatherers who lived between 8,250 and 6,600 years ago. We compared the condition of the population then with later descendants, who were first learning to develop ceramics, beginning to experiment with agriculture, and living in permanent settlements. Those comparisons, in turn, can be related to the periods in which Ecuadorans had developed highly sophisticated civilizations—and were doing some terrible things to each other.

An anthropologist can not only trace the cultural changes that were going on during those periods but indicate the biological impact of the way they lived and of the diseases associated with their times and ways of life. Before the benefit of such scientific insight, speculation on human life in the ancient past generally divided between extreme optimists who saw the descendants of Adam and Eve as still tenants of Eden, and extreme pessimists like Thomas Hobbes, who three centuries ago offered the following description of man living in nature, without the blessings of civilization: "No arts, no letters, no society, and, which is worst of all, continual fear and danger of violent death, and the life of man solitary, poor, nasty, brutish, and short."

There may be some truth in each assumption, depending on time and circumstance; but overall, physical anthropology has been able to develop a far more accurate ancestral portrait. We know, for example, that the evolution of most cultures followed a pattern from the nomadic life of the hunter-gatherer to the more settled existence of farmers and pastoralists, and from there to trade and commerce. We also know that the course of any kind of evolution inevitably entails a constant trade-off between good news and bad news.

The good news for nomads who decided to settle down was in the improved living conditions of permanent settlements and better control over their food supply. The bad news was reduced exercise, less varied diet, and new problems of public health from increased population densities.

The question of why people settle down is still being debated. Some believe it happens when population densities reach a certain critical level that no longer permits mobility, so they invent agriculture in place of the hunter-gatherer economy that had supported them up to that point. Others argue that cause and effect take place in just the opposite order, that the invention of agriculture stimulated those population densities once people became anchored to the land they farmed. The jury is still out, but my guess is that the rise of cities will prove to be the result of a combination of the two influences working in tandem.

My roots extend to an agricultural community of low population density in northeast Kansas. Although we lived in the town of Everest (population about 400), I grew up working on area farms, hauling hay, cultivating grain crops, and working with cattle. I enjoyed the country life, but it became clear to me early on that my career trajectory likely did not include farming.

In my senior year of high school, I was accepted at the University of Kansas. An uncle was a physician in South Haven, Kansas, several aunts were nurses, and my first goal for college was to get into pre-med; it was assumed by everyone that I was headed in the same direction as my uncle. That assumption was fatally derailed, however, when I decided to meet my freshman science requirement with an introductory course in anthropology.

My teacher was a young professor named William Bass. It was a large lecture class, and because Bass was known throughout the university as a wonderful teacher, I was just one of hundreds who took the course. However, my interest in his subject was hardly a case of love at first sight. Even after several months, I could take anthropology or leave it alone. Then one day that all changed as the result of a mistake made by a computer in grading an hour exam.

When I visited his office to see him about the error, Bass happened to mention that he had just received a grant to do some archaeological field work in the Dakotas that summer. He told me the site had been occupied by American Indians prior to the arrival of Lewis and Clark in the early 1800s, and was one of the places painted by George Catlin in his many trips down the Missouri and its tributaries. A dam was being built for flood control, and soon the whole site would be submerged; his goal was to salvage as much as possible before the rising waters destroyed it forever. As I was about to leave his office, Bass offered me a job as a field hand at the excavation. The project had an undeniable element of romance to it, enhanced by urgency. I weighed it against the prospect of yet another backbreaking summer of hauling hay, and accepted on the spot.

By the end of that summer, my career path had been bent irretrievably away from medicine and into anthropology. I'd looked forward to a good time, and the excavating had been even more fun than I'd expected. But the real impact of the experience was in my new appreciation of knowledge for its own sake. The site held so many secrets worth knowing, so many stories that deserved telling, and so much information that illuminated our own culture as well as the ones we were studying—all brought back to life through the careful application of science and technology in ways I'd never before imagined. I was thoroughly hooked. On returning to school, I plunged into more advanced offerings in anthropology, and I also took my first course in skeletal anatomy.

I recall a term paper I wrote for that course, on the femur, that became something of a landmark in my own journey of discovery. It was on everything one could learn about a person from studying nothing more than the thigh bone. From that one body part it was possible to determine that the owner was human, how tall he had been, and to estimate his sex, age at death, ethnic origin, body weight, patterns of locomotion, clues to certain diseases, even possible indications of how he had earned his living—and, sometimes, how he had died.

Writing the paper introduced me to the literature of the field and, in the course of gaining my first exposure to a variety of techniques which have since occupied a good portion of my life, I also came to appreciate how young this science really was. The techniques I learned about were absolutely fascinating, and part of my new enthusiasm came from the realization of how much room there still was for their improvement.

After writing that paper, I was working for a local farmer and friend named Rex Bruning of rural Everest, cutting sunflowers out of his soybean field. The sunflower may have been the state emblem, but it was generally regarded by farmers as an unwelcome intruder in the cash crops of Kansas. I had developed a knack for eliminating the pesky plant with a corn knife, and I was so good at it I could perform this task while practically jogging through the rows. One day I was cutting sunflowers with Rex's wife, Pauline, and she was questioning me about the university life. What on earth could anyone hope to learn, she wondered, from a bunch of old bones?

I could tell by how her nose wrinkled when she said "old bones" that anthropology was not high on her list of reputable professions, at least not compared to raising soybeans, so I told her all about the femur. I'm not sure I ever convinced her about the merits of anthropology, but it was probably clear to her from my enthusiasm that my days of cutting sunflowers were numbered.

Many years later, I found myself on a train crossing through field after immense field of sunflowers in Hungary, on my way to a scientific meeting near the Russian border. When I expressed amazement at their abundance, a colleague told me they were a cash crop, raised for their oil. I looked back at the passing landscape, but in my attempt to see the familiar flower in a new light, I found myself in the grip of a strong impulse from my youth. I wanted to get off the train and run through the fields as I had years before in Kansas, cutting down the tall plants with deft flicks of my corn knife as I passed, leaving column after column behind me in neat rows.

I managed to resist the impulse, but when it had passed it was quickly replaced with another image. I envisioned a small army of Hungarian teenagers, employed as I had been to run through the fields of sunflowers, only instead of cutting at the tall stems they were reaching down between them and rooting out the soybeans growing in their shadows.

The same year I wrote on the wonders of the femur, I also took an independent reading and research course, and for it I did a study on Indian pendants. The pendants were made in part from the blue glass seed beads which the fur traders offered for barter in the early 1800s. The beads were not only used in their original form, but were ground down to form a paste that the Indians redesigned into new shapes, and these forms were then heated to the point where the paste fused. A century and a half later it was easy enough to find good examples of the new art form created by this process, but the really exciting part of the project was the discovery of several of the firing pans used to fuse the new objects. In one case, the firing had been done in an old rifle butt plate, with remnants of the blue glass paste still stuck to the metal.

After studying the ethno-historical literature for early descriptions of this process, I borrowed a kiln in the art department and initiated some experiments to see if I could replicate the technique well enough to copy some of the early ornaments. In the process we learned a lot about the specifics of how the Indians had done it, and we also gained useful insights into which of the early accounts of this process were correct. Doing it myself taught me something else about scientific experimentation. It's a useful way to solve problems, and you don't have to settle for what the books tell you, especially when they contradict each other. With a little ingenuity, you can prove or disprove almost anything through testing. So it was as a sophomore that I published my first scientific paper: "Arikara Glassworking Techniques," in the archaeological journal *American Antiquity.*

Despite all this reinforcement, the bend in the road of my career was not as obvious to me at the time as it now seems in retrospect. I announced my major in anthropology, which was a perfectly acceptable way to preserve my pre-med intentions, took all the requisite courses in chemistry and physics, and continued to believe I was still headed toward becoming a medical doctor. Fortunately, large dams take a long time to build and often even longer to fill, so my summers were spent in research and running archaeological digs in the same area of the Dakotas where the hook had first been set.

In 1968, the year I graduated from college, *Time* magazine's cover for commencement week showed a student receiving his degree in one hand and an M-16 rifle in the other. In America's fervor to send all its sons to Vietnam, graduate deferments had been abolished and the Selective Service System had become one of the country's truly democratic institutions. I was never inclined toward the military by nature, and like a lot of other graduates that year I was against that particular war in principal. More than that, I had been caught up in a love of knowledge, and I saw all my enthusiasm and momentum on a collision course with the nation's purpose. It was a frightening time.

Although I was finished with college, I was still running a dig that summer in the Dakotas, by then on a grant from the National Geographic Society, so I wrote my draft board in Kansas to postpone my military physical until that fall. They responded to that request by transferring my file to South Dakota. A couple of days later a truck arrived at the dig with a large woman from my new draft board, telling me to stop work immediately, to fall in line with the other boys from that area, and to get my physical. I did as I was told.

For the following several months I appealed my status, which was 1-A, and managed to complete a year of graduate school in anthropology, still at the University of Kansas. But the appeals process was eventually exhausted and I was drafted into the Army. Like hundreds of thousands of other kids in the same position, I accepted the inevitable and tried to make the best of a bad thing. Because of my size and the muscles I'd developed from hauling hay all those years during my teens, or possibly because they were impressed by my intellectual credentials, the Army chose to assign me to the Military Police. I was trained in Georgia, then sent up to Washington, D.C., to ply my new trade. I couldn't have picked a better place or a worse job.

Then I got an unbelievably lucky break: I landed a new assignment as a microbiology technician in the military hospital laboratory. In this best of both worlds, I lived out the balance of my military career. Yet another lucky break, in the scheduling of my work week at the hospital, allowed me to forge an informal but highly productive affiliation with the National Museum of Natural History at the Smithsonian Institution.

I had first visited the museum back in 1968, as a college senior, while researching archaeological collections from the Dakotas. I had made a new discovery: small grooves in the teeth which were evidence the Indians had used toothpicks, probably in an attempt to temporarily relieve toothaches. The practice was apparently unknown to the academic community, and I was anxious to determine whether there were any teeth with these grooves in the collections of the Smithsonian. The visit did more than advance my research project, for it was then that I met some of the legends in the field who up to then were only names in textbooks. One of those legends was T. Dale Stewart.

Dale had joined the museum in 1924, while still an undergraduate at George Washington University. He worked in the relatively new Department of Anthropology in what amounted to an apprenticeship to the curator, and on receiving his B.A. he went on to Johns Hopkins University, with Aleš Hrdlička's approval, to study medicine. When he received his M.D. in 1931, he became assistant curator of physical anthropology; thirty years later he succeeded Hrdlička as head curator, and a year after that became the museum's director. His career began shortly after the emergence of physical anthropology as a distinct scientific discipline, and it embraced most of the milestones of his profession.

Dale was expert in the morphological dating of ancient remains. At one point he challenged the master by reexamining the Melbourne (Florida) skull, contradicting Hrdlička's opinion that it was related to recent Indians of the region, and reopening the possibility that it dated back to the era of the extinct animal remains with which it had been found. He introduced a couple of his own candidates for membership in the select club of North American anthropological antiquities— Tepexpan man from Mexico and Midland man from Texas—and in 1957 he became one of the few Americans to be honored with an invitation to help recover, restore, and research several important Neanderthal skulls in Iraq. He had written over two hundred scientific publications, including *The People of America* and *Personal Identification in Mass Disasters*, and held numerous international awards for his contributions to physical anthropology. His accomplishments were legion.

The coincidence of my beginning a professional career in anthropology on the eve of Dale Stewart's retirement apparently held some of the potential chemistry for which the Smithsonian is famous. The decision was made to replace the grand old man of anthropology with the fledgling from Kansas. I was hired with the understanding I would finish my degree in the following year, and then return to Washington.

4

THE OTHER ARMY
OF THE POTOMAC

In the summer of 1983, on an Indian reservation in the Dakotas, a guest at a late-night drinking party announced that it was time for him to go home. Gary Cheyenne, one of the other partygoers, said that he and his brother were leaving as well, and he offered a ride in his pickup truck, which the first man gratefully accepted. Instead of following their initial plan, however, the three drove a little way down the road, then pulled off to the side to have another few drinks from a bottle one of them had brought from the party. A short time later, the driver slid out from behind the wheel, retrieved the car jack from under the seat, and swung it against his passenger's head with enough force to crush his skull.

Cheyenne and his brother then attempted to bury the victim in a nearby dry creek bed. The earth was too hard to dig by hand, so they left the body, journeyed a short distance to the house of a relative, and then returned to the arroyo with the necessary equipment: a length of clothesline, the pole it was tied to, some gloves, and a shovel. They lashed the body to the pole in the traditional manner for the transportation of kill—head at one end and feet at the other—then put on the gloves, and with the pole on their shoulders carried the litter and its contents out into the Badlands. Eventually they became exhausted and set their burden down. One of them began digging, but before the grave was finished, the handle broke off the shovel. By this time their energy and enthusiasm were pretty well exhausted, so they rolled the body into the shallow hole, covered it over as well as they were able, and headed back to the truck.

Ten months later a cattleman was checking his stock on horseback when he noticed a number of vultures in the sky and followed them to where they were dropping to the ground. Cattle sometimes break a leg or get into other kinds of trouble, and the presence of carrion birds was a sure sign, even from a great distance, that something was dying or dead. The last thing the horseman expected to find was a human body, and it took a moment to recognize what he was looking at. Vultures don't dig, but the corpse had been pulled partially out of the ground by larger animals, and some of the bones were strewn around a wide area in the vicinity of the grave. His horse shied, and the rider had to pull hard on his reins to stop him from running.

When the police secured the scene they found no papers or other evidence of identity, but they were pretty sure whose body it was; the remnants of clothing agreed with a missing person report filed shortly after the fatal party. They gathered up the bones, expecting they would be able to confirm their assumption about the identity by matching dental X-rays with the shape of fillings in the teeth. It wasn't going to be that easy. The reservation had good dental facilities, but the dentist's office management was not up to the same high standard, and no one had the slightest idea what had become of his records.

In the course of searching for them, the police came across some other radiographs they thought might do almost as well: chest X-rays taken a couple of years earlier at a local medical center. They had heard that it was sometimes possible to identify remains from comparisons of the bones, so they sent the chest films along with the skeleton to the FBI. That technique of identification was not nearly as well accepted or widely practiced as comparisons of the teeth, but it represented a possible fallback if all else failed, and I was glad for some insurance. I set aside the large manila envelope and started instead with an examination of the skull.

It was obvious the victim had suffered a massive blunt-force trau-

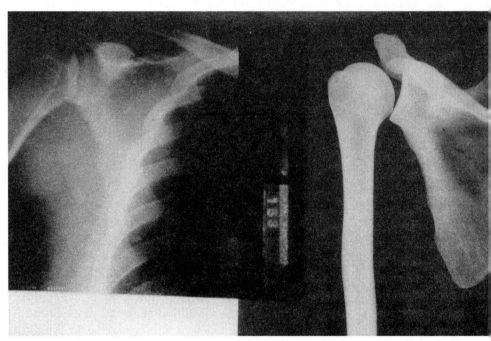

A radiograph taken of the victim's shoulder in life (left) shows an unusual configuration on the lateral border of the shoulder blade that exactly matches bones recovered in the Badlands.

ma to the side of the head. By that time the police had arrested the two brothers; one of them had admitted that a car jack had been the murder weapon, although the question was still open as to which one of them had struck the mortal blow. The bending of the bone was forensic proof that the crushing trauma was perimortem, which is the short way of saying it had occurred at about the time of death, and it appeared to be the cause. I sorted through the rest of the bones for other signs of trauma and found none. But what I did find—a healed fracture, and an anomaly in the development of the shoulder blades— greatly increased the potential value of the medical X-rays; I reached for the envelope.

When I held one of the films to the light in the ceiling over the examining table, those features in the radiograph matched exactly with the bones in the disarticulated body. The radiograph taken during life revealed anatomical details of the shoulder area, including the upper part of the humerus, the scapula, and collarbone; careful comparisons with those same bones recovered from the shallow grave in the Badlands revealed many small anatomical landmarks in common, and no discrepancies. In particular, the lateral border of the shoulder blade displayed an unusual configuration that matched exactly between the X-rays and the recovered bones. This was one case in which I knew my testimony would make a difference, and when the police sorted out which of the brothers had swung the car jack, I was not surprised that they asked me to fly to the Dakotas to appear at the trial.

I would not have been surprised either if the defense decided to challenge my positive identification on the witness stand. I was prepared for it. I had compared the shape of the skeletal scapula with hundreds of American Indian scapulae from skeletons in the Smithsonian collection. All of those skeletons were distinct. Even though the scapula from the Badlands matched exactly with the X-rays taken of the alleged victim in life, it matched none of those from the collection. However, the challenge never came.

On the witness stand, I positively identified the victim, and I affirmed the medical examiner's testimony that the crushing blow to the skull was consistent with the scenario about the murder weapon. I'm not sure what kind of reaction to my testimony I expected to see from the defendant, but I clearly recall how impressed I was, as I glanced at him across the courtroom while delivering that testimony, that there was no reaction at all.

The defendant was only in his twenties, and he gave the impression of being the only one in the courtroom who was unaware that

The "other army of the Potomac." Collections of the National Museum of Natural History at the Smithsonian include more than 30,000 skeletal remains.

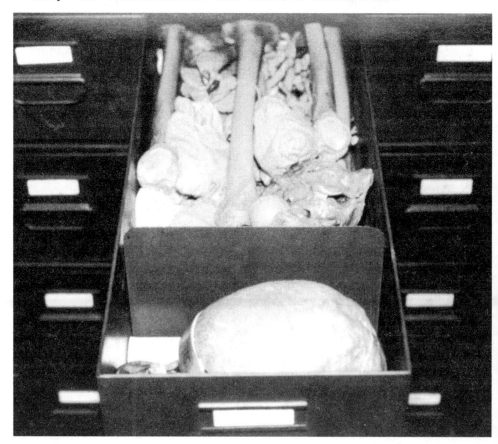

the rest of his life was at stake. He remained totally expressionless throughout; from all I could tell by his face, anything I had to say about the identity of the victim or the cause of death could as easily have been in another language or about people he had never met. A class of students from a local girls' high school was in the courtroom, apparently for an afternoon's civics lesson, and the contrast between the uniformed, intensely interested, obviously privileged schoolgirls and the dark, emotionless, impregnable demeanor of the defendant only deepened my sense of his isolation. Knowing it would be over soon after my testimony, I decided to see the trial through to its end. The schoolgirls didn't stay for the verdict, which was guilty of murder in the second degree, but they didn't miss much: his expression never changed.

Perhaps in his own mind, Gary Cheyenne's life had already been defined by two events, and whatever was decided by the court about his guilt or his future was no longer relevant. For this was not his first murder. He had killed before, at the age of seventeen, but had been tried as an adult and served seven years in federal prison. In that killing as in this one, he had smashed the victim in the head and buried him in the Badlands.

In forensic anthropology as in any other science subject to the tests of law, knowing that a thing is unique, such as the shape of the murder victim's scapula, is of little value unless that uniqueness can be proven and quantified in court. The scientific basis for proof is not to be found in some agreed-upon measurement locked in a vault at the National Bureau of Standards, or an immutable law of nature such as the decay rate of a radioisotope. Instead, it consists of precise reference data, scientifically compiled from tens of thousands of sources in over a century of careful recovery, examination, and measurement of human skeletal remains. Without such reference data, it would be difficult for any anthropologist to make even the most basic inference about age, sex, race, time since death, cause of death, and in some cases even whether the remains were human.

Outside my office, in large green drawers which rise in stacks nearly 16 feet from floor to ceiling on both sides of the long corridor, and stretch in a labyrinth of such corridors throughout a large portion of the immense third floor of the National Museum of Natural History, is the world's largest such collection of human bones. It is the anthropological equivalent to the National Bureau of Standards or the laws of nature, containing the skeletal remains of more than 33,000 individuals of all ages, races, shapes, and sizes, compiled in over a century of extraordinary scientific effort and representing millennia of human development, particularly in North and South America. A reporter once described this unequaled scientific treasure as "The Other Army of the Potomac." Its members range from volunteers, some of whom lived in our own lifetimes, to conscripts from humankind's earliest prehistory.

Probably the last thought in the minds of the anthropologists who amassed this army was that it would ever play a major role in fighting crime. It was assembled as a standing resource for the solution of other kinds of mysteries: where we came from, how we lived, where we are headed. But once a body has lost its soft tissue and gone to bones, a single drawer in this collection of human skeletal remains contains far more data for analyzing, interpreting, and identifying the victims of crime or misadventure than all the millions of fingerprints ever recorded. The collection provided the data I needed to positively identify the body from the Dakota Badlands, and in one degree or another it or a similar resource has helped with every forensic study in this book.

In January 1978, when a hunter discovered a human skeleton partially protruding from the frozen ground near a grove of trees in a rural area of Ohio, there was little useful information in the small amount of soft tissue left on the body. The county coroner asked for help from anthropologists at the local university. Based on data derived from reference collections, they identified the remains as having belonged to an adult black female whose living height was about 5'5".

Analysis by local dental specialists found no fillings but several cavities, noting that some teeth were missing from before death and some since. The dentists removed two other teeth and cut them horizontally to determine age (again based on research data derived from reference collections), which was estimated at between thirty-seven and forty-seven years. The dental examiners also noted a hole in the cranium they thought could be representative of trauma from around the time of death.

Next, an X-ray dispersion analysis system attached to a scanning electron microscope identified radiopaque particles embedded in the bone of the left temple, and indicated they were primarily composed of lead. A local radiologist confirmed the presence of the fragments, and that the perforation was consistent with a gunshot wound.

In subsequent years, circumstantial evidence accumulated that the skeleton might represent a missing local woman, and in the absence of personal dental or medical records for her identification, the cranium, mandible, and a facial photograph of the suspected victim were forwarded to the FBI for analysis. In January 1991, thirteen years after the initial discovery, they arrived at the Smithsonian.

I confirmed that the bones originated from a young adult black female. Evidence for trauma was largely confined to the left side of the head: two circular perforations, 7 mm and 9 mm across, near the rear of the left temple, and a third hole, more irregular in shape and measuring about 8 mm by 11 mm, behind where the left ear had been. The two circular holes were beveled internally, which is a characteristic of entrance sites, and were relatively free of radiating fractures. The irregular hole was not beveled, and fractures radiated from the site throughout the rest of the skull; one of the fracture lines curved all the way around to the left eye orbit, and part of that bone had subsequently broken off and was missing. Another radiographic analysis confirmed the presence of the radiodense particles, and that they were concentrated in the vicinity of the two entrance sites, although one such particle was also detected in the right side of the cranial vault.

The photograph that had been sent along with the bones was compared to the articulated cranium and mandible (using a computer-enhanced system described in Chapter 14), and it revealed an exact match. Obviously if such matches occur frequently when comparisons between photographs and skulls are made at random, then the match in this case would have no significance. Even if it happened only one time in a hundred, a perfect match still wouldn't be of much use in forensic terms. To determine the degree of likelihood that the match meant the photo and skull were from the same person, we turned once again to the collections.

Of over thirty thousand human remains in the collection, only fifty-two were identified as even approximately agreeing with the characteristics of the recovered skeleton with respect to race, sex, and range of age. All fifty-two were from the Terry Collection, a sample of late nineteenth- and early twentieth-century individuals of known identity on permanent loan to the Smithsonian from the state of Missouri.

For both the Ohio forensic case and each of those fifty-two Terry Collection individuals, we recorded the height of the upper face (nasion to prosthion) and lower face (prosthion to gnathion), then calculated their ratio. The result for the skull from Ohio was .69. The ratios for the other fifty-two ranged from .48 to .84, but eighteen of them were within a single point of the ratio for the murder victim, which meant that one third of the Terry Collection skulls compared closely with the one from Ohio.

We then measured those eighteen and the forensic skull in the other direction, by the width at the cheekbones (anthropologists know this as the bizygomatic breadth, zygion to zygion), and drew a second set of ratios with the upper facial lengths measured earlier. The result for the Ohio skull was the lowest of all at .49, while the ratios for the other skulls varied from .52 to .62. That meant that *none* of the Smithsonian skulls exactly matched the murder victim, but of the thirty thousand skulls in the collection, we had narrowed our search down to the closest four.

These four closely matching crania were then compared to the Ohio facial photograph by means of computerized superimposition. Because of other differences in the proportions of the face, the contours of the cranial vaults, the shape of the jaw, and additional disparities, none of them exactly matched the photograph.

By proving that not a single one of more than thirty thousand skulls in the Smithsonian's collection could be made to fit, and that only the skull from Ohio had matched perfectly, we had assembled convincing evidence that the skeleton from the field and the woman in the photograph were almost certainly the same person.

Even in cases where the results are not that definitive, they can still have value in establishing probability and, in some instances, indicating the direction in which further research is likely to provide conclusive proof.

I made one positive identification in a Massachusetts court based on nothing more than an X-ray of a fragment of the murder victim's mutilated skull and a medical X-ray of her sinuses, taken while she was alive. It is unlikely that such testimony would ever have been permitted in a murder trial unless I had been able to quantify my observations and conclusions with reference data from the Smithsonian collection and the scientific literature.

In purely spiritual terms, it might be argued that there is an inherent risk in such a powerful tool as the Smithsonian collection. Life and death are more than numbers, averages, and the laws of probability, and too great a reliance on statistics can separate an anthropologist or any other forensic scientist from the moral consequence of his or her findings and opinions. I have two answers to such a suggestion.

First, there can never be a negative moral consequence to the truth, and in order to protect the truth every science demands complete objectivity of its practitioners. Statistics promote objectivity. The power of the data in the collections is the best possible guarantee that justice will be served by the truth, and not just by guesswork and good intentions. Exactly the opposite of separating the scientist from moral consequence, objectivity binds him to it.

My second answer is that objectivity is one thing, and aloofness is another. I don't know of a single medical examiner or forensic anthropologist who suffers a broken heart every time a carton of evidence arrives or who weeps, like the policeman in *Twin Peaks*, at the scene of every violent crime. But by the same token I don't know of many who consider themselves completely immune to such a risk. Scientific objectivity doesn't blind us to our personal values or normal human feelings, and it certainly doesn't make us emotionally bulletproof. Sometimes a professional situation can become an intensely personal one when least expected.

That's exactly what happened in 1991 with a case from Nebraska. A partial skeleton had been recovered near the Missouri River, and police suspected it belonged to a man who had disappeared from that area ten years before while in his early twenties. A lot of evidence was submitted with the query, and was parceled out to its proper places within the FBI. The parts coming to me were the bones, some chest X-rays taken during life, and photographs of the recovery site. I was told there was some urgency in the case, even though it could have been a decade old, and so I went to work on the skeleton promptly. In fact, I recall being impressed at the attention the case was being given when officials from the referring agency showed up at the Smithsonian to observe the procedure and get the results as soon as possible.

Small roots were present in the vertebrae, and I found weathering cracks on the one scapula that was recovered. There were no signs of bleaching from exposure to the sun, but the anterior surface of the right femur was green, which indicated long-term exposure to copper. I noted from the report that a number of coins, none newer than 1981, had been found in the victim's pants pocket, so I assumed from the stain that some of them had been pennies.

I inferred the victim was a male, based on comparisons of the pelvis and other bones with measurement data from the collections.

I estimated his height at about 5'10½", based on measurement of the long bones, using formulae derived from the collections. Everything I used to estimate his age at death similarly came from collection statistics. The victim could have been as young as nineteen or twenty, or as old as twenty-seven; most likely he was in his early twenties.

In an attempt to confirm the identity, I compared the shapes of the vertebrae of the recovered skeleton with those visible in the chest X-ray taken during life. The comparison revealed a close match of several anatomical details that we rarely see in skeletons. The skeleton appeared to be that of the missing young man.

Realizing that the identification might one day be challenged in court, I once again turned to our collections for confirmation. I retrieved several other vertebral spines of skeletons from the green drawers in the hall outside my office, rearticulated them in the same manner as the bones in the medical radiograph, then took them over to the FBI and X-rayed them for comparison. The spines from our collections were all distinct from those that had matched in the earlier comparison. We also surveyed the collection to find any vertebrae which demonstrated the same unusual features displayed by the bones and X-rays from Nebraska. We found none.

Taken together, those data allowed me to confirm the identity of the victim as that of the missing young man—and if necessary to support that confirmation in court. Because of the urgency, I telephoned my results across the street to the FBI.

Several months passed. Then, on the last afternoon before the Memorial Day weekend, I received a telephone call from the victim's mother. What could I tell her, she asked, about whether the bones I examined had belonged to her missing son.

The call caught me completely unprepared, and I asked her in return what the police had already told her about my report. She said they had told her nothing. I realized there could have been a number of reasons for the delay: perhaps there was still a loose end; maybe they were waiting for a report on some of the other evidence to come back from the FBI; they could have been waiting for some other source. Or perhaps there had been a slip-up in the system and whoever was responsible had simply forgotten to relay my findings to the family.

Whatever the reason, I realized instantly it would not justify keeping the truth from her for even a moment longer, and I told her that in my opinion the bones were those of her son. After ten years, ending the uncertainty can bring relief as well as sorrow; she accepted the information with great strength, and expressed her gratitude for what I had done.

It wouldn't hurt if everybody who does this type of work got a call like that from time to time, as I'm sure a lot of us do. It's a good reminder that every forensic case involves the living as well as the dead, that there are more victims of murder or misadventure than those whose remains pass through our hands.

We are responsible to them all.

5

PARTNERS IN CRIME

iolent crime is a growth industry. The last full year on which I have a report from the FBI is 1990, and it shows 1,820,130 violent crimes, a 12-month increase of more than 10 percent and up more than a third for the decade. By the same token, murders and non-negligent manslaughters in 1990 showed good growth with 23,440 killings, a one-year gain of 9 percent.

There are a lot of people who see opportunity here. For a start, consider the hardware involved. Firearms usage was at an all-time high as manufacturers around the world worked overtime to supply the 9,923 handguns, 743 rifles, 1,237 shotguns, and 944 unspecified guns used in these killings, not to mention the millions more manufactured to defend the survivors.

Cutting and/or stabbing instruments in 1990 accounted for another 3,503 deaths, up from the year before but admittedly lower than the 3,957 victims claimed by knives, saws, hat pins, ice picks, and sharp sticks in banner year 1986.

In an economy where creativity is king, it's no surprise that blunt-instrument usage was down to 1,075 murders, the lowest for the sector since 1987. However, another low-tech favorite, murder by fire, went just the other way, reaching record levels in the last reporting period with 287 victims.

What has happened, some may ask, to the other old standards? Are such relatively prosaic murder weapons as the fist, the shod foot, even the simple unadorned hand that does nothing more than shove its victim from a high window or a subway platform, now considered hopelessly primitive and out of date? Not at all: hands, fists, feet, and shoving, collectively referred to as "personal weapons," held their own in the FBI report with 1,112 recognized results—and very likely a lot more that were not recognized as victims of murder.

Poison, often the instrument of choice in the classics of crime fiction, actually accounted for fewer deaths in 1990 than any other category of weapon reported by the FBI—a total of only eleven victims. That low figure may encourage the belief that poison works better than any other type of weapon because so few of its recipients are identified as murder victims—but that's a thesis more properly addressed by a medical examiner than by a forensic anthropologist.

Exactly that thesis was addressed quite recently, in 1991, although not by the FBI, when America's twelfth President, Zachary Taylor, was exhumed and autopsied on the suspicion he had been murdered by his successor, Millard Fillmore.

This was probably a bit of a disappointment to academics, especially the former humanities professor from Florida who is largely credited with whipping up interest in the theory, that no evidence of murder could be found on the body. If Fillmore had indeed killed Taylor, it would have been the only significant landmark in either of their otherwise thoroughly undistinguished administrations. The absence of any poisonous residue in Taylor's bones or hair leaves us with less exciting alternatives. The cause of death given in the contemporary press: Old Rough and Ready killed himself with a surfeit of cherries and chilled buttermilk after only sixteen months in office. The likelier cause was some sort of gastrointestinal infection.

Taking the broadest view of the explosive growth in criminal enterprise, the FBI Uniform Crime Report analyzes its potential for career development.

On the enforcement side, the Bureau reports that 2.2 full-time police officers are employed for every 1,000 Americans countrywide. If civilian employees are counted as well, that number rises to 3.1 per 1,000. All told, some 12,400 city, county, and state police agencies together employ 523,000 officers and 191,000 civilians, comprising a law enforcement work force of almost three quarters of a million people.

Unhappily, the numbers for the competition are equally robust. Although the overall crime rate was up by only 1.4 percent in the last reporting period, America's prison population over the previous decade grew by a whopping 134 percent. Even in relatively slow 1990, the need for new accommodations continued to explode at the rate of 1,100 additional prison bed spaces per week. Right now, three quarters of a million Americans—a number equal to the *combined* populations of Savannah, Georgia, Schenectady, New York, Salem, Oregon, Odessa, Texas, Little Rock, Arkansas, and Fall River, Massachusetts—now reside in America's state and federal prisons.

Some planners see an answer to that need in the increasing popularity of the death penalty, but so far their hope is in vain. America is one of only four industrialized nations (with human rights champions Russia, South Africa, and China) still taking the lives of their citizens, and the process here is nowhere efficient enough to significantly increase space. Time between initial proceedings and execution often runs ten years or more. Some appellate courts, like those in California, spend half their time on capital cases.

Executions don't save money. On the contrary, taxpayers in Texas pay an average of $7 million per legal killing, and in Florida the cost is over $3 million. In Massachusetts, where the death penalty has not yet been restored, the cost of life imprisonment without parole averages a comparatively trifling $900,000.

Another number is worth citing for those not persuaded by economics. Such monitoring organizations as Amnesty International, the NAACP, and the ACLU say that approximately 10 percent of those executed in the United States in this century were subsequently proven innocent of the crime for which they died.

Even so, today there are 2,210 condemned prisoners awaiting death in America. More than half are in the South. Only five are in federal prisons.

The federal government may not be big in executing criminals, but it certainly is a major factor in catching them. The FBI offers such cooperative services as fingerprint identification, scientific analysis, police training, and the immense retrieval and computing power of the National Crime Information Center to other authorized law enforcement agencies throughout the country. The Bureau's own crime-fighting priorities are focused most closely on terrorism, drugs (in shared jurisdiction with the DEA), espionage, organized crime, white-collar crime, and violent crime. The great majority of FBI referrals to my office are in that last category.

Although the FBI Laboratory is organized by specialty, much of the evidence sent to it requires more than one type of examination. A bloody banknote recovered as robbery loot, for example, could contain latent fingerprints and traces of marking dyes from an explosive packet, as well as fibers from the trunk of the getaway car. It is the responsibility of the FBI's Evidence Control Center to assign priorities and distribute the evidence to the appropriate examining units in the proper sequence. The choices depend on a lot of factors, some of them subjective. In normal circumstances, the Hair and Fiber Unit might be first on the list because their queries would do least to alter the appearance or character of the material being analyzed. Conversely, Identification would probably be the last stop because the chemicals used to disclose latent fingerprints can destroy some of the evidence contained in bloodstains, and they can also complicate or preclude the analysis of dyes which might be required to prove the source of the money. If the material taken in evidence contains human skeletal remains, then somewhere in the process it is automatically assigned to Hair and Fiber. It's from this department that evidence finds its way across the street to the Smithsonian.

In general, the FBI sorts physical evidence into two categories. The first is the kind that can be positively identified by specific source and/or identified with a particular place or person, such as fingerprints, handwriting, bullets, tool marks, shoe prints, and glass or wood whose broken parts can be pieced together and matched. The second category is the sort of evidence for which there is more than one source and which therefore can be positively identified only by class. For the most part, this second group includes such things as soil samples, hairs and fibers, blood and other body fluids, and fragments of paint, wood, glass, and plastic. However, even a fingerprint, a tire tread, or a spent bullet becomes class rather than specific evidence if nothing of known origin is found to match it.

Due course first involves the Q-ing and K-ing of all the items to be studied. Q stands for question item, and K for known. If the origin of an item has been positively established, such as a blood sample removed from a victim, then the scientist logging in the evidence gives it a K. If the blood sample was recovered from a knife found beside railroad tracks with no obvious means of identification, then the blood becomes a Q.

Each known and questioned item receives a number. The blood

sample from the victim might be K-1, and the sample from the knife might become Q-1. A shoe found a few yards from the victim may or may not be related to the victim, and would be given a Q number as well. If the shoe had still been on the foot, then, like the initial blood sample, it would be a K.

The police often strongly suspect the identity of the skeletal remains which the FBI Hair and Fiber Unit refers to me for study, but even the strongest suspicion is not the same as proof, and the Evidence Control Center never confuses assumptions with facts. Most bone cases arrive in my office marked with a Q.

One result of the Q and K system is to reduce the possibility that judgments by others, however compelling, are allowed to erode the scientific process or take the place of fact. Forensic scientists in particular can't risk finding camels in clouds. Every step in the FBI's handling of crime data is carefully designed to assure the integrity of evidence, the appropriate disinterest of the examiners, and the scientific reliability of results.

Sometimes the evidence of a crime is a product of the same technology used to analyze it. The FBI Engineering Section can do amazing things with tape recordings, for example, proving whether they are authentic and free of tampering, interpreting such non-voice sounds as gunshots or radio noise, and identifying the numbers dialed on a telephone. Experts can greatly increase audibility by elimination of most background sounds, and in cases where they have a second voice sample, they can sometimes identify a suspect by matching voice patterns. Spectrographic print matching is still a new science and at this point the results are provided only in support of criminal investigations, not courtroom testimony.

The Engineering Section also has astonishing expertise in other forms of electronic analysis. Its members can identify the various "boxes" used to beat the telephone company out of their payment for toll calls and pay phones. They locate and identify telephone taps and other bugging devices, including those that can steal any conversation in the room even when the phone is not in use or when no phone is present. They can tell which electronic system was used to trick a burglar alarm, override time clocks, detonate bombs, open locks, or crack safes, and the Engineering Division knows how to recognize those gadgets as well.

Probably the best-known activity of the FBI, dramatized in thousands of gangster films and television dramas for two thirds of a century, is related to fingerprints. The Identification Division was established in 1924, consolidating the fingerprint records of the federal penitentiary in Leavenworth, Kansas, with those from the National Bureau of Criminal Identification, and the division has maintained world leadership in the size and utility of its collection ever since. Today, the prints of one of every four Americans, including those of every living citizen ever booked on criminal charges, all unidentified bodies where printing was still possible, and every known victim of amnesia, are listed in this file. It is accessed some 34,000 times every day by law enforcement agencies throughout the United States and around the world.

The file also contains some four hundred sets of prints that are taken from the feet and classified by patterns in the area behind the big toes—just in case.

In criminal cases, most print identification is the result of the police arresting a suspect, or the wrong person applying for a job requiring a security check. But in some ways the most exciting aspect of this science is in the area of latent prints, where participation in a criminal act is inferred, and frequently a suspect is identified, from the often invisible pattern left behind on a document, a piece of furniture, a murder weapon, or even on the victim's skin. Latent prints can often be made visible by chemicals, photographed, then lifted from the recording surface by the application of peeled transparent tape.

The latent specialists also frequently are called upon to identify a dead body that has been discovered too late to get a clear set of fingerprints; after a certain point in decomposition, no amount of skill at inking or rolling produces a classifiable result. That isn't necessarily the end of the line; if police can name likely individuals whose print records are then run for comparison, even partial or fragmentary inked prints can sometimes be matched. And if they can't, the referring authority is sometimes then encouraged, with the approval of appropriate local forensic medical authorities, to sever the victim's hands and send them in a 70 percent solution of alcohol in an unbreakable, airtight container to the FBI Laboratory for direct analysis.

As Lady Macbeth was aware, a durable—and sometimes first—indication that a violent crime has been committed is the discovery of blood. It is common for police or passers-by to report blood on highways, carpets, porches, walls, and on the seats, floor, or in the trunks of automobiles, even when no body is immediately present. It is also common for suspects to explain away that blood as belonging to a dead animal—most often a dog, deer, or duck—even when those respective bodies are missing as well. The FBI's Serology Unit can tell when they're lying.

The uses of forensic serology go far beyond locating crime scenes, discovering violence, or bursting alibis. It can identify a murder weapon. It can help exculpate suspects who claim truthfully that the blood on hands or clothing is their own. It can determine whether blood is human and, when not, name the family of animal.

All forensic serology attempts to classify human blood into one of the four ABO groupings, and beyond that the FBI Serology Unit uses the art of electrophoresis—analyzing fluids and gels under the influence of electrodes—to identify blood by such characteristics as red cell enzyme and serum protein. But conventional blood examination protocols have limits. They don't reveal conclusive data on the age of the bloodstain, they tell little about racial affiliation, and they can't be used to prove the identify of the source.

Most such limitations are reduced, not just in the analysis of blood but of other body fluids and tissues, when the examination is focused on deoxyribonucleic acid, or DNA. Evidence from blood and bloodstains, from wet or dried saliva, from semen and vaginal fluids and tissue samples, when matched with other samples extracted from known sources, can prove or disprove identity with varying degrees of scientific certainty. When no such comparison fluid or tissue sample is available, even a bucket of blood from a supposed murder site would be almost useless. But when such matching is possible, visually and by computer, the DNA in a single drop of dried blood could be enough to place the victim or perpetrator at the scene of a violent crime.

Microscopic examination of hairs and fibers recovered from a crime site can sometimes be used for the same purpose, but not always with the same evidentiary weight. If a rape or murder victim was wearing an angora sweater, and the assailant had on a pair of corduroy trousers, then the positive identification of angora hairs on the pants and/or corduroy lint on the sweater suggests the probability, perhaps even the likelihood, that they came in contact. The same applies to the identification of suspected instruments of assault, where hairs from the victim may adhere to a hammer or board from the crime scene.

The FBI can determine a lot from a single strand of hair, such as whether it is human, the owner's race (and sometimes sex, depending on the presence and condition of the root), how it was removed, and if it has been bleached, dyed, or otherwise altered. An analyst can even specify whether it came from the scalp, chest, brows, lashes, underarm, pubic area, feet, hands, nostrils, or elsewhere on the body. If the hair is non-human and species identification is important to the investigation, analysis can determine whether it originates from a rat, dog, cat, cow, or some other animal. However, because it exhibits only class characteristics, even though hair is often introduced as strong circumstantial evidence, by itself it cannot be used to positively identify its owner.

Fibers are subject to similar limitations. Examined in the same laboratory, they are identified as being animal, vegetable, mineral, or man-made. Fiber evidence, although usually circumstantial, has been used successfully in court to identify the origin of ropes used in murders, to match lint on the victim with clothes worn by the killer, and to establish the probability that botanical samples from a questioned locale originated at the same place as a sample from a known source. The FBI's hair and fiber specialists also identify wood species and match wood fractures and cuts. Their more arcane activities include the analysis of fabric impressions, the sourcing of clothes through manufacturers' label searches, even the identification of feathers.

Bureau chemists test human serum and tissue samples for each of the four basic classes of toxin. They can determine the quantity and weight of an abused drug or a pharmaceutical involved in a crime, indicate its active pharmaceutical ingredients, and test for drug traces on clothing, luggage, currency, and inside automobiles, boats, and airplanes.

When it is suspected that a fire has been set for insurance fraud, revenge, as a result of pyromania, or to cover a crime such as a theft or murder, FBI chemists use gas chromatography to determine what combustibles were used to start it. They identify them from the arson debris and sometimes perform chemical comparisons from samples taken from the car, clothes, or skin of suspects.

This same analytical resource detects the use of chemicals in malicious destruction, identifies caustics or debilitating substances in assault cases, even specifies lubricants used in sex crimes. The FBI can identify dyes that may adhere to stolen money, flash papers, and water-soluble papers which can burn or dissolve instantly in the event of discovery in espionage and gambling cases, stolen chemicals, smokeless powder, and every kind of tampered product from hair tonic to foot powder.

There's a story from America's whaling days about an old captain who could reckon the location of his ship to within a mile in any part of the world, just from the smell of the mud on the sounding lead. One night, when his ship was becalmed off an unknown coast in a fog bank, he told the bos'n to take such a sample from the ocean floor and bring it to his cabin, so the captain could take a sniff and tell the pilot what bearing to set. The bos'n was convinced the old man was a fraud, so instead of casting the lead over the side, he dipped the end into a flowerpot in the forecastle and returned to the cabin. The captain sniffed at it, suddenly paled, and sat bolt upright in his bunk. "Hats off, Hearties," he said. "Cape Cod has sunk, and we're directly over Widow Snow's garden."

Not even the FBI can say for sure whether a soil sample came from Widow Snow's garden. But it can say for sure if it did not, and it can usually offer a fair degree of scientific certainty as to whether it did. If the sample in question were taken from the driveway of a robbed Cape Cod bank, for example, and scrapings from a suspect's shoes exhibited the characteristics of Georgia clay, FBI mineralogists might suggest the local police look elsewhere for their perpetrator. Conversely, if the scrapings matched, some characteristics can be so unusual and specific as to eliminate any reasonable doubt that they came from a single source.

Depending on the nature of the crime, soil samples from tire treads can also sometimes be matched with the same degree of scientific certainty—and of course the treads themselves can leave prints at the scene of a crime, particularly in the loose soil near a burial site. Consider the following scenario.

Cadillac Frank murders rival mobster Big Al and buries the body at a toxic waste dump. The next day, one or another of Big Al's extremities is seen sticking up out of the shallow grave. Later that day, Cadillac Frank hears on his radio that police have recovered the body, and realizing he will be a suspect, he acts quickly. Criminals know about tread prints and soil samples because they watch the same late shows as the rest of us, so he changes his tires and hoses down the car. When detectives examine the vehicle an hour later, it's gleaming with fresh wax, the hubcaps are spotless, and naturally there is no match between the tread marks found at the burial site and the four new tires.

Fortunately, the police in this case have read the FBI's *Handbook of Forensic Science*, and Cadillac Frank has not. The detectives carefully remove the mud which is laminated to the lower inside surface of the fenders, mark and seal the samples, and along with similar soil samples taken from near the tread prints at the burial site, they send them off to the FBI.

The mineralogy of the site soil is characteristic of the latest lamination of mud from under the fenders. And paint, glass, and other man-made materials contained in the mud are similar to the seemingly extraneous materials in the soil at the dump. Cadillac Frank goes to jail. Big Al gets a real funeral. For the FBI, it's all in a day's work.

In glass fracture patterns, some of which require the painstaking reassembly of a melange of shards, scientists find clues to the direction of impact, sequence of occurrence, and the approximate angle of impact of a bullet. These determinations can sometimes resolve questions of who fired first if there is more than one person shooting, and where they were standing—or sitting, in the case of someone in a car. Glass is also useful in associating a suspect with a crime scene. If the suspect flees and is later arrested, microscopic particles recovered from clothing and even from hair can be compared optically for consistencies with broken glass from the site.

Probably next to fingerprints and criminal records, the FBI is best known for the evidence which Bureau scientists can extract from firearms, shell casings, and spent bullets. Like fingerprints, if the right kind of information is available, then the FBI's conclusion is accepted by the courts as positive. One such positive conclusion is that a bullet or shell case was or was not fired from a particular weapon.

Ammunition gets marked in a lot of different ways: scratching against anomalies in the breach or chamber; grooves in the barrel; the action and shape of the firing pin; the rifling in the barrel which gives a slug its spin; marks made by a flash suppressor or silencer as the slug passes out the end of the barrel or by the extraction and ejection of the spent case. Spent shot can also be compared with other ammunition still in the weapon or in the suspect's possession, and the analysis of lead composition in slugs and pellets can identify the manufacturer and provide strong circumstantial links between suspects and crimes.

Spent wadding, which leaves a shotgun right behind the pellets or slugs, can also help determine the gauge and sometimes the manufacturer of the shell. Even microscopic amounts of gunshot residue can often be detected on clothing or other surfaces surrounding the point of entry, and when the shot was fired at close range there is frequent evidence of smudging and singeing.

Lady Macbeth would have been perhaps a bit more cheerful about having used a knife if she knew that discharging a firearm can leave residues of the spent primer on the hands of a murderer; although they usually become visible only through chemical enhancement and microscopic analysis, those residues can be as damning as blood. As a rule, primers are a mixture of antimony, barium, and lead. Despite some persistent mythology, primer residues don't ordinarily become deeply embedded in the skin; on the contrary, they wear off or wash off fairly easily, and as a rule the FBI will not examine swabs from samplings conducted more than six hours after a shooting.

In one form or another, fingers, feet, body fluids, chemicals, and firearms all leave a characteristic signature. But in bone cases, many of those signatures have deteriorated or disappeared by the time the evidence arrives for examination by a forensic anthropologist. The skin has desiccated and fallen away, body fluids have dried and vanished, chemicals have done their work and leached into the soil, and firearms, if any were used, have found their way back to the gun cabinet or to the bottom of a lake or river. Long after death, however, the path of a bullet or the strokes of a knife may still be clearly printed in the bones. And in some cases, so are the marks of a tool or other instrument that was used to murder.

Taken alone, the impressions of tool marks in bones would not seem to have much, if any, forensic value. It's common in murder, and virtually the rule in cases where the remains are nothing more than a skull or a few scattered bones, that such tools are nowhere to be found. But the fact is, many impressions in bones can be identified by their patterns alone to provide strong circumstantial evidence of murder. A hammer leaves a variety of signature imprints—from the peen, from the claw, and from the side—which can identify the class of instrument even when the tool itself is missing. Surprising to some, because of their repetitive motion, saws, files, and grinding wheels generally do not—although recent research by Dr. Steve Symes of the Department of Pathology at the University of Tennessee in Memphis indicates that sometimes even saws can leave telltale marks when they are used on bone.

Tool-mark identification is a particular specialty of the FBI Laboratories to which the forensic anthropologist makes frequent reference and which plays a major role in providing evidence of a crime and determining means of death in bone cases. Most of the FBI's techniques and criteria in tool-mark identification were developed in connection with other media than the human body.

One aspect of this expertise is the analysis of marks in wood for evidence of the tool used to cut it. Sometimes characteristic marks become printed in an object from pressure or contact, either briefly or over time, and that impression can become a valuable forensic record.

There are few materials in which the life history of an object is

more readily accessible to scientific analysis than metals. FBI metallurgists can determine conclusively whether a metal item or surface was
formed by casting, forging, hot or cold rolling, extrusion, or any number of means. They can detect microscopic surface evidence and,
through optical and electron microscopy, details of a metal's internal
structure.

Because they are so durable and yet so accessible to examination,
metals can offer profound insights into the history of accidents and
crimes. FBI examinations of broken or deformed parts yield clues to
tampering, corrosion, design flaws, fatigue, misuse, sawing, abrasion,
milling, cutting, burning, electrical malfunction, crushing, and shooting. They can measure impact and identify the opposing objects in a
collision. They can reveal the direction and magnitude of an explosion.

Metallurgy is not merely the discipline of metal behavior. Skilled
metallurgists can sometimes match fractures in materials of all kinds—
ceramics, plastics, rubber—to connect objects and suspects to accident
or crime sites. They can tell why a machine stopped, slowed down, or
failed, and when. There are often indications of where a part or product originated, and even the kind of individual who worked on it: analysts can read clues to the relative skill or ineptitude of a mechanic, a
diemaker, a cutter, or an assassin, and sometimes which hand was
used in the commission of a crime.

It happens now and then that I will find metal fragments embedded in bones, even where there are no holes or splintering of the sort
usually associated with gunshot in the same area. Sometimes these
fragments are splinters of lead, copper, steel, or alloys from shattered
bullets or pellets. Other times they are evidence of something entirely
different, including conditions at the gravesite unrelated to the cause
of death. Metallurgical analysis can tell them apart.

In fact, with infrared spectroscopy, X-ray diffractrometry, emission
spectrometry, gas chromatography, mass spectrography, and other
state-of-the-art instrumentation, backed up by some of the world's
most extensive sample files, examiners can identify just about any
material on the face of the earth. From a single chip of paint, they can
name the year and make of any automobile built in America, and most
imports. Paint chips from safes, locks, and window and door jambs
can be matched exactly with microscopic traces of the same paint on
the tools used to open them. They can frequently identify the manufacturer from bits of timing mechanisms and radio controls used to
make bombs, and track the source of tapes that held bombs together,
tied hostages, or bound packages of drugs. They can come up with

make and model from polymer car trim torn off in hit-and-runs.

The FBI maintains the world's largest computerized film file of kidnapping and extortion notes, threatening letters, and other anonymous communications. Document examiners frequently match such notes and other questioned documents from different cases to prove they originated from a common source. FBI specialists in Questioned Documents can positively identify an individual through the analysis and comparison of handwriting and printing. As anyone knows who has looked back through checks or letters written during a period of illness or extreme stress, penmanship can vary over time and with physical and emotional condition. It may change with the deliberate effort to disguise handwriting or if the signer has been drinking. But even with those variables, if both the known and questioned samples are comprehensive enough, the FBI's skilled document examiners can usually reach a conclusive determination. Their scientists retrieve images and information from documents that have been erased, soaked with water, bleached or stained with age, charred by fires, corroded by acids, eaten by worms, ravaged by weather, or otherwise obliterated by human beings or nature.

The Bureau is also expert in every method of printing and duplicating and the technology of papermaking. Their scientists can read latent impressions from second sheets, indented (inkless) type, and disappearing inks. Under the right conditions, the FBI can tell which photocopier printed a sheet of paper. Scientists can also identify two sets of questioned copies as having come from the same machine. Ditto for other forms of printing such as offset and letterpress. They can connect a printed document with its press, with its ink source, and with its original artwork, film, and plates. They can tell where the paper came from, and sometimes can establish the true date of the document.

In fact, the FBI keeps track of almost everything that could have any possible relevance to the solution of a crime. Some fifty thousand items in the Pornographic Materials File in print, film, and video are used to prove illegal interstate commerce, the exploitation of children or unconsenting adults, and in determining channels of production and distribution. There is even a collection of Shoe Print and Tire Tread Standards.

Finally, the FBI's forensic scientists spend a fair amount of their time in support of the classic spy-catching and racket-busting cases that have kept the Bureau in the public consciousness from its earliest beginnings. Gambling, loan-sharking, prostitution, and drug running are still the stock in trade of organized crime, and espionage still features in the competition for world dominion through the theft of information related to diplomacy, defense, or America's commercial competitiveness. The examination of criminal records, usually assisted by computers and sometimes requiring the breaking of codes, reveals the scope and hierarchy of illicit enterprises of all types and sizes.

In Mario Puzo's book *The Godfather,* Don Corleone observed that a dozen men with machine guns are no match for a single lawyer with a briefcase, and he had a point. Far more crimes in America are committed with paper than with guns, and many more times the amount of money and power change hands illegally through a stroke of the pen than through physical violence. Frequently a degree in accounting can be important in becoming an agent of the FBI, and being able to hit a moving target with a pistol or machine gun is far less of a factor in the solution of most crimes than the ability to follow a complex paper trail through to the crooked bottom line.

6

IS IT HUMAN?

In January 1978, a sanitation worker in a small city in Nebraska was investigating a stoppage in the grinding blades of the municipal sewage treatment facility when he came upon the decomposed remains of what appeared to be a human baby. The physician who examined the small bundle at the local hospital concurred that it was a full-term Caucasian infant, perhaps two weeks old, and it was assumed the child had been flushed down a toilet, perhaps as an abortion or within two weeks after birth. A quick canvass of area hospitals revealed no missing child of that age, however, so the remains were preserved in formaldehyde and forwarded to the FBI, along with a request for a determination of age, nationality, time since death, and any other information that might then be used to establish identity.

Even before we tipped the remains out of the plastic bottle, we could see that the outer epidermal layers had sloughed off the body, the result of immersion and, despite the time of year, the elevated temperatures within the sewer system. Once we recognized that this was what had happened to the body, we also realized that what we were looking at were not layers of white outer skin, as the physician had assumed, but the glistening white endodermis, the inner skin tissues, which are basically the same in appearance in almost every kind of animal. The head and feet had been forcibly removed, probably by the grinding blades, which further confused its appearance, but we could tell from the mangled bones that the remains were not those of a human infant at all. Within a few more minutes we located the top of a tufted ear.

By comparing the ear and the bones against some of the tens of thousands of samples in the Smithsonian's collections, we were able to determine that the body had belonged to an immature small dog, probably a beagle. Because most sewers are closed systems, we thought it likely that one of the original assumptions had been correct, that the body had been flushed down a toilet, which may or may not be a criminal act in Nebraska. As far as I know, authorities there were satisfied that it was not a case of murder, and let it go at that.

One of the first things we ask on examining alleged forensic evidence is whether it is of human origin. This may seem like the kind of question that could be answered by any competent medical examiner far earlier in the process, but often that isn't the case. Physicians expect to deal with people, not animals, and very few of them, even pathologists and medical examiners, have ever been trained in distinguishing human body parts, especially bones, from those of other species.

Between 10 and 15 percent of the presumed human skeletal remains sent to the FBI turn out to be something else. Most of the non-human referrals are quite obvious to a properly educated eye, but some are more subtle. Context can often play an important role in confusing even the best of us.

One bone the FBI received a decade ago from Alaska still fools almost everyone who looks at it. The fragment had been recovered from a campground near Anchorage, and probably the only reason it was spotted at all was the deeply imbedded metal prosthesis. The device was a plate which had been screwed into the midshaft to correct a pseudoarthrosis, a result of cartilage cells proliferating at the site of a compound fracture and forming a false joint. The subsequent remodeling around the metal and along the plane of the old break clearly indicated the passage of months or even years between surgery and the time of death. Carnivores obviously had been chewing on the bone and probably would have destroyed it, but they could not chew into the metal plate. The fragment made the rounds of virtually every orthopedic surgeon in Alaska, but not one of them was able to identify it as his work.

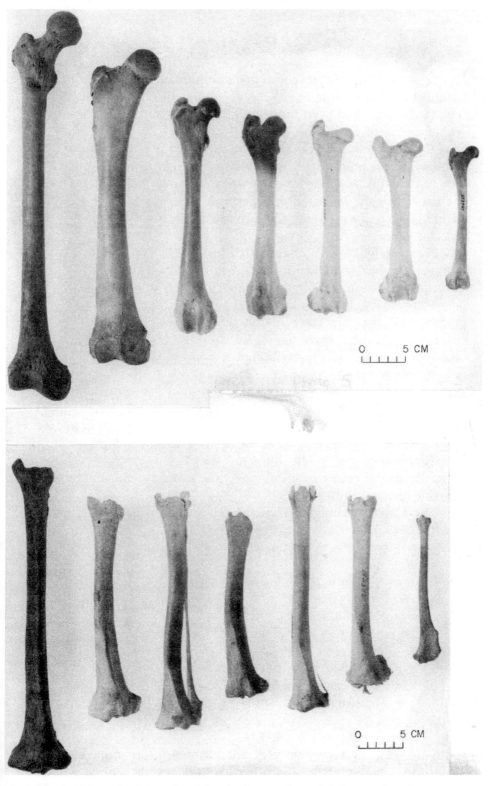

Is it human? From the left to the right, the bones of an adult human female, a black bear, a large dog, a hog, a deer, a domestic sheep, and a small dog. The top row is the femur; bottom row is the tibia.

When the bone finally got to the Smithsonian, in my initial examination I made the same mistake as everyone else. The gross morphology of the bone had been influenced by the initial trauma, the events connected with death, the effects of carnivore gnawing, weathering, and the wear and tear associated with the many prior stops on its long journey, to the point that it was almost unrecognizable. I also have to admit that this was one case in which my own assumptions were influenced by the long trail of paperwork that came with it. It simply didn't occur to me at the outset to challenge the basic premise that this was human.

Fortunately, I was later contacted by Dr. William Payton, chief of surgeons at the Public Health Hospital in Anchorage, who had submitted the bone to X-ray. From the pattern of the grain, which was far more discernable in the radiograph than from surface observations, he commented that the taper of the specimen was not what he had expected to see in normal bones. He also was the first to remark that the type of surgery was not typical of orthopedics.

To follow up on Dr. Payne's suggestion, we removed a sample of bone from one side of the fragment, away from the fracture. We then prepared a ground, thin section from the sample for microscopic analysis. In particular, we were looking for the pattern of osteons in the section. Osteons are small, circular bone structures that form continuously throughout life. In humans, they are randomly scattered throughout the cortex of the bone, while in many animals they frequently line up in rows.

The Alaska specimen clearly revealed the animal pattern. No wonder the orthopedic surgeons couldn't identify the specimen: the work had been done by a veterinarian, and the bone probably originated from a large dog.

Later, we learned that most veterinarians use the same surgical appliances as orthopedic surgeons, so the type of appliance by itself is no guarantee of a human origin.

Among the human skeletal parts received from a murder case from a remote Pacific island was a large bone that clearly did not belong with the rest of the body. It was easy enough to determine that it was non-human, but it took a lot of specialized knowledge from elsewhere within the Smithsonian to identify its actual source as a Pacific sea turtle.

Although the average non-vegetarian American encounters bones from fish, chicken, cattle, and other livestock several times a week at

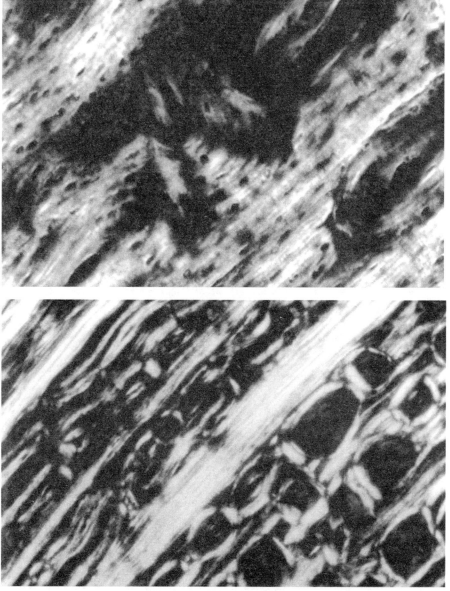

Microscopic examination shows the characteristic differences in the pattern of osteons in human bone *(top)* and animal bone *(bottom)*.

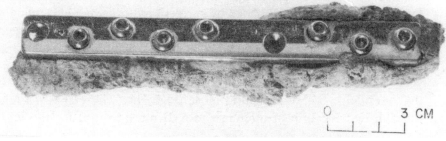

Because of the surgical plate, this animal bone found in Alaska was mistaken for human before microscopic analysis demonstrated otherwise.

the dinner table, the discovery of such familiar food debris in an unfamiliar context can result in confusion, apprehension, even horror. Like my own initial erroneous supposition that any bone with a prosthesis is human, the finder's reaction has a lot to do with what he or she assumes and expects from the setting.

A couple of years ago an amateur archaeologist turned up some bones while combing through topsoil at a construction site on what had been a Civil War battlefield in Virginia. He had previously recovered numerous spent bullets from the same area, and other searchers had even found Indian arrowheads there, so when he saw the bones, his expectations were already leaning in the direction of relics rather than trash. The man took the artifacts to the police, which added another context by the time the local newspaper heard about it. A police spokesman acknowledged all of the assumptions that attach to each context when bracketing the possibilities for a reporter: "We don't know whether they're Civil War, a murder, or somebody's cat."

Had he been absolutely candid, he might have acknowledged that the police had already ruled out the possibility of a cat. The remains included a fragment of mandible containing teeth, and these particular teeth obviously belonged to something bigger. Moreover, they were the kind that are used for grinding, not tearing. And one of them contained some silver imbedded in the crenulations on the biting surface. There were eighteen packages of bone fragments in the evidence box, but none of the fragments, not even the grinding teeth, was of human origin. The mandible had belonged to a pig. What appeared at first to be a metal filling in a pit on the occlusal surface proved to be aluminum foil; most likely it had been wedged there when the pig was foraging in garbage.

Because the remains had been handled sensibly and no one had gone out on a limb, it was retired quietly and without the slightest cause for embarrassment. A case from a city in the Midwest proved to be a horse of a different color.

The bones in this instance had been found near a dump in an area that was used as a cemetery up to the end of the last century. The first small fragments were unearthed by accident by someone who thought they might have been debris from a disturbed grave and turned them over to the authorities. However, police went back the next day and began digging in earnest when a local woman told them a thirteen-year-old girl who had been missing for over a decade was buried at that site. Once the police found more fragments where she had told them to dig, the lure of inference proved too powerful for the local prosecutor, and he announced to the press that the bones were those of a murder victim. The announcement got a lot of attention, and for a little while he was famous.

The bones clearly represented only a small part of a skeleton, and they had been burned, so the local medical examiner didn't have much to go on. He told the police that he didn't know whether they were human or non-human, and that he lacked the resources to make the distinction. On his recommendation, the fragments were sent to the Smithsonian. By that time, through no fault of the examiner, the prosecutor was already sitting well out on the leafy end of the branch, and I imagine he gladly would have forfeited his brief celebrity when the pathologist showed him my report. The fragments were not human; they all originated from the single lower leg bone of a horse or cow.

I don't know of any cases in which entire skeletons have been recovered in good condition and it was not possible to tell just by looking at their shape whether they were of human or non-human origin. People don't have four legs and a tail, or horns and hooves. Deer and cows don't have fingers, and most of the time they don't have the spherical braincases typical of a human head. That last rule isn't without a tiny number of exceptions, however, and in unraveling the mystery related to one of those exceptions, I was able to draw on my boyhood experience on a Kansas farm.

On June 30, 1988, I received two calvarium skulls (skulls without bones of the face) from Dr. Larry Balding at the Office of the Chief Medical Examiner in Oklahoma City. One of the skulls had just been recovered from a dog who was found gnawing on it in his front yard in the central part of the state, and the other had been brought up by a fisherman from a freshwater lake fifteen years earlier and several miles away. Dr. Balding told me they had been variously identified as belonging to an owl, a dolphin, and a deformed child. I turned them over in my hands. In both, the vault was very high and bulbous, in a humanlike pattern, but the occipital in the one that still had that surface was distinctly non-human.

My colleague Hugh Berryman, director of the regional forensic center in Memphis, Tennessee, told me he had examined a similar cranium from Mississippi that had come to him as a possible human forensic case, like these two from Oklahoma. We traded observations on our specimens.

Beyond the ambiguity of their partly human, partly animal appearance, there was something familiar about all three items. Although

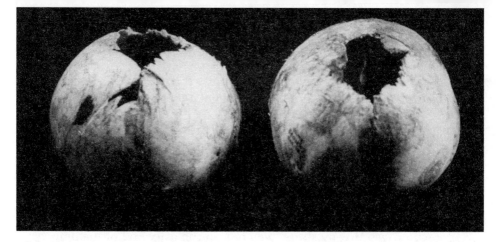

Preliminary examinations of these two crania from Oklahoma produced a range of suggested origins, from human child to owl and dolphin. Below, left to right, are crania of a human child, an Oklahoma specimen, a normal immature calf, and an immature hydrocephalic calf, viewed from above and below.

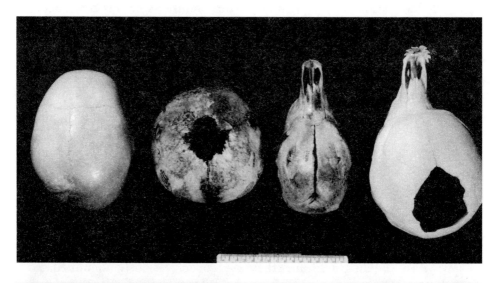

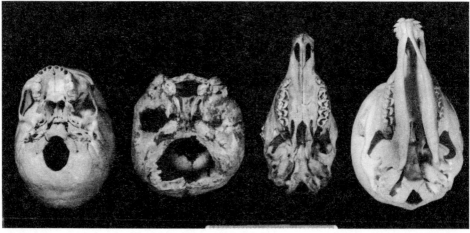

they were far too high-domed to be normal calf skulls, the possibility of such a connection was suggested by a number of other features—particularly the form of the occipital condyles, the presence of what appeared to be horn buds on Hugh's specimen, and characteristic grooves above the eye sockets of all three. I remembered from my time as a dairy farmer that every now and then a cow would produce a calf with a greatly enlarged braincase (the calves were usually stillbirths or died shortly after delivery), and I wondered if that could be what we were looking at here. We removed small samples of desiccated tissues from the two Oklahoma calvaria for immunological assessment. The tissue from one of them was too dry to produce a definitive result, but the other reacted positively with bovine antibody. Once we confirmed they were from calves, our next obvious assumption was that they were hydrocephalic.

Hydrocephalus is a fetal defect found in a number of animals, including people, in which the buildup of cerebrospinal fluid within the skull causes the cranial ventricles to expand with a corresponding enlargement of the skull itself, especially in the forehead, producing atrophy of the brain. I learned that a Professor G. W. Rieck at the Institut für Tierzucht und Haustiergenetik in Giessen, Germany, had made a study of this phenomenon in calves, and I sent him a letter describing our three specimens. Several weeks later a package arrived from Germany. To my astonishment and delight, it included a perfectly preserved specimen of a hydrocephalic Holstein-Friesian calf which Professor Rieck was donating to the Smithsonian's collection. In addition to being a wonderfully generous gift of a valuable research and reference resource, it provided tangible confirmation of our findings and completed the solution of three erstwhile forensic cases.

All three of those cases resolved the way they did because the medical examiners were smart enough not to settle for a quick judgment based on appearances. In similar situations where just the upper portion of such a skull from a calf has been found in a possibly forensic environment, it has more than once been mistaken for a human calvarium. I'm sure such mistakes will continue to be made by pathologists, vertebrate zoologists, and physical anthropologists, even though skulls can be identified correctly by immunological examination of soft tissue, microscopic analysis of hair, and comparisons of their general shape with clinically documented specimens.

Sometimes the physical evidence in a murder case, even the organic evidence, can involve the possibility of mixed media. My Smithsonian colleague Doug Owsley made a forensic examination on the body of a middle-aged woman that had been found on a bank of the Mississippi River. Although decomposition was well advanced, it was immediately apparent to the police she had been shot in the head and chest; a large portion of the skull had been blown away, the second blast had destroyed her right breast, and pellets were found in the surrounding soft tissue and in the humerus of the right arm. The body had been further mutilated by long incisions in the abdomen, both upper legs, and the upper back; it was not possible to determine whether the cutting had occurred before or after death, but local forensic pathologists assumed the gashes were intended to ensure that the body didn't float when thrown into the river.

The lower portion of the skull was relatively intact, and the victim was identified from a match with the dental records of a missing person from that area. Later the same evening, the police also identified a suspect, and they began putting together the case. The woman had been shot while sitting in the front seat of the killer's Jeep, and her body was thrown into the river at a nearby ferry landing. The murderer was seen by a witness at a gas station later, as he was apparently washing away the evidence of the crime. There was still some blood on the floor mats, so police impounded the car and went over it with a magnifying glass. Four small bone fragments were found in the dried blood. Two more chips were recovered from a search of the oil-pit trap at the gas station where he had done the cleaning. The largest piece of the six was two thirds of an inch long and one third of an inch wide. The defendant claimed the blood and bones were from a deer.

The easy way to prove he was lying would be to fit any one of the chips into its original place on the skeleton, but that did not prove possible; although they were the right cortical thickness to represent missing sections from the center of the blasted bone, none of the recovered chips was from the edge of the puzzle.

The hard way was by matching the histological structure of the bone. This wouldn't prove the fragments were necessarily from the murdered woman, but it might make a strong argument they came from a human being. The state police obtained the foreleg of a recently killed deer, and cross sections were made from it and from the victim's humerus. Under the microscope, Doug compared the two sections with each other and with a section of the largest recovered fragment from the car.

This class of animal bone differs most markedly from human bone in the uniformity and symmetry of the osteons, which are the channels through which they receive their blood supply. By microscopic comparisons of the shape of those osteons and other known variables, and supported by painstaking measurements, Doug demonstrated that the fragments resembled the section of the woman's humerus in every particular and that they were dissimilar in those same respects from the section of the deer leg. He used those comparisons to identify the bone fragments as human. On the eve of the trial, having been informed by his attorney what forensic data were awaiting him in court, the suspect confessed to the killing.

7

SEX, SIZE, RACE, AGE AT DEATH

The folklore of forensics is filled with tales of innocent people who were condemned for the wrong reason—including one case, in New York State, where the supposed victim turned up alive just in time to stop the execution of her alleged murderer. The remains which had convicted the innocent man proved, on closer study, to be those of a pet dog. That case is an extreme example of why no responsible forensic anthropologist accepts someone else's assumptions about age, sex, race, or stature.

An examiner properly trained in forensic anthropology wouldn't be fooled by an animal, but many forensic cases are more subtle. It would not be difficult to imagine the circumstances in which the remains of a fifteen-year-old girl, say, were mistakenly identified as those of a woman of thirty, especially if the examiner were told in advance what to expect. In forensics, unlike classical anthropology, the fate of the dead is often closely connected to the future of the living.

For that reason, when skeletal remains are delivered to my office, I make a practice of protecting myself from any more knowledge of such assumptions by others than is minimally necessary to log in the evidence.

My examination often begins with a look at gender. As a rule, it's very easy to determine sex in adults if the remains include bones of the pelvis. The pelvis of a woman is generally broader than that of a man; this difference is particularly noticeable in the bone of the anterior pelvic area called the pubis. The lower margin of the pubis forms the border of the subpubic angle; this has to be wider in females because it surrounds the birth canal, and during delivery, a baby's head must pass between these two bones. There are several other anatomical features of the pubis which can also be used to determine sex, sometimes from only a fragment of the bone.

If the police don't have the pubis, the probability of making a correct call declines. Generally it comes down to size differences—males being larger than females—but there's a certain amount of overlap in the middle, which is one of the reasons transvestites and transsexuals can sometimes be so successful in appearing to be something other than what they were born. Skulls are good indicators, perhaps as high as 90 percent reliable; the other 10 percent are the robust females and gracile males in that confusing middle ground.

Some forensic experts see less ambiguity than others in that middle ground, and are correspondingly more willing to make the call. In one case I inherited from Larry Angel, for example, he had no problem estimating that a small skeleton was female. In looking at the same evidence, I was only willing to say that I recognized a number of characteristics which were consistent with that sex, but I stopped short of stating that any one of them was definitive.

Determining sex in children can be even more elusive. Most of the skeletal differences, even in the pelvis, that distinguish the sexes don't fully define until early adulthood, and the differences that do exist in children are often not of the magnitude that permit a confident estimate.

One of the best indicators of sex in a child is the teeth. In determining gender, the indicator is not in how dissimilar they are, but in how alike. It is well known that in general males tend to be a year or two slower than females in their overall body development. But although girls' long bones grow earlier and faster than boys' do, for some reason that same advantage is not as extensive in the development of the teeth. Accordingly, it is possible to estimate the sex of a child's skeleton by comparing the extent of skeletal development with the level of dental maturation. The older the child, the more accurate the technique. However, we usually do not attempt to estimate the sex of immature skeletons because the rate of accuracy reaches only about 80 percent even in older children. In a forensic case, 80 percent is not good enough; we can estimate with 50 percent reliability just by guessing.

To estimate how tall someone was from their bones, we usually turn to bone measurements and regression equations. These mathematical equations, developed from studies of the bones of people of known stature, allow us to predict stature by measuring individual bones. For example, we can measure the length of the thigh bone, multiply it by a certain number, add another fixed number, and *voilà*, we have the approximate stature. The techniques are usually accurate to within a few centimeters, and can even be used on fragmentary bones, although with reduced accuracy.

We have learned that different sexes in different racial groups have different body proportions: one can't apply the formula for a black male, for example, to the femur of a white female. So, sex and race come first, and then stature follows.

In determining stature, certain allowances also have to be made for age. After a point, people tend to get shorter as they get older. Part of this process can involve kyphosis, which is an abnormal curvature of the spine, and wedging of the vertebrae.

An alternative approach to the determination of stature, not widely used today, was developed by a Frenchman named Fully, but this technique requires a complete skeleton. The investigator measures all the factors that contribute to stature, starting at the heel with the height of the calcaneus, then moving upward through the tibia, the femur, the vertebrae, and the skull. A variability factor is added in and the investigator then computes the total size of the living body. One obvious reason this approach is not widely used in forensic cases is that frequently some of those necessary parts are either damaged or missing.

Another problem with stature is that not many people know exactly how tall they are. In modern times, the document of record is the driver's license, but when you think about how license information is generated, its reliability can be open to reasonable doubt.

Even when the applicant is standing right in front of the registry employee, the process almost inevitably relies on the applicant's answers rather than direct observation. "What color is your hair?" is often answered by the color it used to be—and marked on the license accordingly. Weight is frequently understated, and the numbers given for height can be wrong for the same reason: the answers are wishes.

There have been several studies of how those wishes vary from the realities, and they indicate some interesting patterns. Extremely tall people often shrink a bit, and very short ones often add as much as several inches. The studies show that reporting discrepancies also vary with sex and age. In general, it is men who tend to exaggerate their stature, and women who more often err in the opposite direction. And in old age, when people shrink as the result of physical changes in their bones and in the ways they are connected, the differences between actual height and the numbers on the license can become even more remarkable.

Military records, by contrast, are far more reliable. In most cases, those numbers are based on actual measurements.

Race is one of the questions almost always asked of forensic anthropologists, but it can be a very difficult thing to determine with certainty because of the nature of race itself. The peoples of the world have far more in common than they have differences. The groupings that we know as race are largely defined by culture; although they have some biological/ancestral attributes, they also reflect cultural and historical factors that shape self-perceptions. When the police investigator asks us, "What race is it?", we try to use biological observations on the bones to estimate which ethnic group the individual probably would have been identified with during life. It isn't easy.

Some characteristics of particular populations are apparent in the skeleton, but there is a lot of variation even within groups that historically have had little admixture with others. Even without population amalgamation, people are not finely divided up into neat categories labeled "white," "Hispanic," "Asian," and so on. For example, most people who consider themselves to be "Mongoloid" do exhibit some skeletal features that are different from many of those who think of themselves as "white" or "black." Yet these groups strongly overlap in physical characteristics. There is a continuum of variation among them. Many individuals who consider themselves to be Mongoloid are indistinguishable skeletally from others who think of themselves as being black or white. Add to this the fact that many racial minorities in the United States are products of the melting pot, an environment in which racial characteristics tend to blur even further with the diversity of the mix. Because of these variables, the anthropologist looks for several extreme characteristics clustered together before suggesting affiliation with a particular major ethnic group.

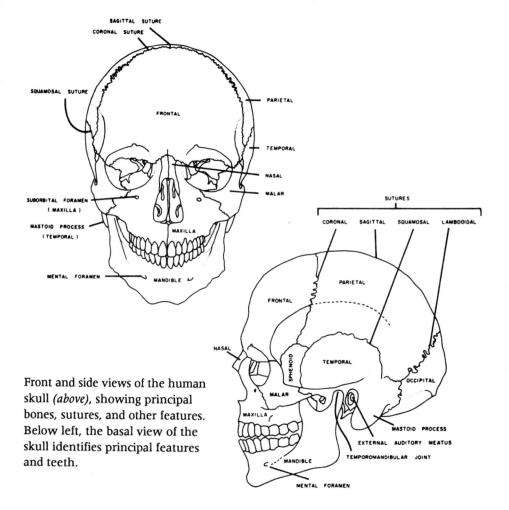

Front and side views of the human
skull *(above)*, showing principal
bones, sutures, and other features.
Below left, the basal view of the
skull identifies principal features
and teeth.

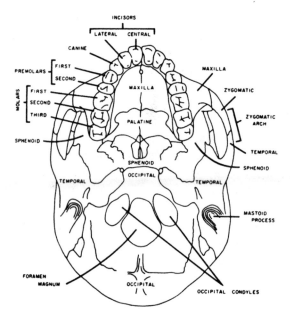

In general, such characteristics show themselves most immediately in the face. There are visual as well as mathematical criteria for making the call.

The skulls of Mongoloids (Eskimos, American Indians, the peoples of Asia) tend to have very forward-projecting cheekbones and comparatively flat faces. The nasal aperture is moderate in width. The eye sockets tend to be more circular than those of other groups, and the palate is moderately wide. Especially in American Indians, the suture line where the cheek joins the upper jaw tends to be straight.

Black or African skulls, by comparison, usually show little or no projection of the cheekbone. The eye sockets tend more toward rectangles, and they are usually wider apart. The nasal aperture is very broad. The palate is usually wide and somewhat rectangular. The part of the face below the nose tends to thrust forward in a trait called prognathism, giving the maxilla (upper jaw) and mandible (lower jaw) more prominence than among other populations. Many black skulls also exhibit a slight depression in the top area just behind the crown.

White or Caucasoid skulls are characterized by markedly recessive cheekbones, with the result that the faces are "sharper" or more pointed than among other groups. The nasal aperture is much narrower. The palate is also relatively narrow, and triangular. The seam between the cheek and upper jaw is usually curved. Also more common among whites is the persistence of another seam (called the metopic suture) extending from the top of the nasal arch to the junction of the coronal and sagittal sutures at the top of the head.

Teeth can provide clues to ancestry, but individuals vary so widely that they can sometimes be misleading. Mongoloid populations, especially American Indians, have excellent dental occlusion, with a near-perfect edge-to-edge bite. Most Caucasoids not treated by orthodontists show an overbite, where the upper teeth project further than the lower. Occlusion among blacks is intermediate and variable.

Wear on the biting surfaces is generally highest among ancient populations, especially those that grind their food on stones, releasing a lot of grit. By the same token, most hunters know that the teeth of coastal ruminants wear down faster than those further inland because of the presence of sand and grit in the forage. But dental attrition rates do not usually provide a clue to the ancestry of most modern populations.

Size, on the other hand, can suggest such clues in very rare instances. In general, the teeth of aboriginal Australians, Melanesians, American Indians, and Eskimos are among the largest, while Lapps

Three crania showing population variability. From left to right, an individual of European descent, an individual of African descent, and an Eskimo.

and Bushmen tend to have the smallest teeth. In the vast middle ground within those extremes, variations in tooth size between populations have been measured and catalogued, but without other evidence they have little value in establishing ethnic affiliation.

The same is true of shape, with a handful of interesting exceptions. Many Mongoloid maxillary incisors—the four shearing teeth in the center of the upper jaw—have prominent marginal ridges on the side nearer the tongue, giving them a "shovel shape." In extreme instances, the ridges also occur on the front surface in a pattern known as "double shoveling," and occasionally these ridges even meet, giving the incisors a barrel shape. American Indians and Eskimos have particularly high frequencies of this characteristic, but it's far from foolproof. Some Mongoloids don't have it at all, and it sometimes occurs in non-Mongoloids.

Even in cases where the skull is not available or its racial characteristics do not appear to be definitive, more clues are often available in the curvature of the long bones. In particular, blacks tend to have relatively straight upper leg bones or femora, with very little twisting of the neck or head. In Mongoloids, those same bones are usually quite curved, with considerable torsion at the neck, and among American Indians frequently show flattening of the upper front surface. The bones of whites are intermediate in both curvature and twisting.

In 1962, a couple of anthropologists named Giles and Eliot introduced a scoring method to estimate racial affiliation based on their studies of blacks, whites, and American Indians in skeleton collections from Missouri, Kentucky, the Gulf states, and the Southwest. Eight measurements of the cranium are multiplied by a determined factor, and the results are added or subtracted to produce a score that can be assessed for racial affiliation.

The system may work well enough within the populations from which the functions were derived, but a lot of archaeological skeletons and forensic cases derive from populations that are quite distinct from those studied by Giles and Eliot. A serious problem in physical anthropology is that the techniques described in the scientific literature have been developed from studies of particular population samples. Most of those samples, even such "modern" ones as the Terry Collection at the Smithsonian, represent people who lived some time ago, and many were formed for specific purposes which did not require a true cross-section of the general population, but rather were limited to various aspects of that population. One of the obvious factors distinguishing the Terry Collection is that the average members of the population from which the collection was drawn did *not* will their bodies to science, and therefore they aren't in it. Willing one's body to science is more likely to be the act of an older, better-educated member of the population, and these are not necessarily the kinds of people who wind up as forensic cases.

I once conducted a study in the Dominican Republic to test the applicability to black and Hispanic populations of the microscopic method of aging developed by Ellis Kerley. The Kerley method was based on a study he formulated in 1965 on a relatively healthy—albeit dead—military sample at the Armed Forces Institute of Pathology (AFIP). There was a question whether the technique would be as reliable for, say, an urban drifter who had died after a long history of alcoholism, or a middle-aged Hispanic immigrant, as it was for the younger and generally healthier group at AFIP. My own research focused on a population of black or mulatto individuals, all of whom had recently migrated to Santo Domingo from the rural countryside, and it showed that the Kerley technique generally underestimated the age of the Hispanic population by an average of five years. This meant that the rate of remodeling or bone turnover in my sample was different from the rate measured in the sample from which the technique was developed.

Another way of increasing the applicability of forensic data is through an ongoing project at the anthropology branch of the American Academy of Forensic Science, which maintains a databank at the University of Tennessee in Knoxville. The bank is dedicated to improving our scientific information on skeletal characteristics in all levels of society, particularly in those areas which statistics show us are more likely to be involved in crime, incorporating data from a large forensic sample of individuals from all parts of the United States. Forensic cases of known identity are fed into the system by anthropologists, and all relevant information on the skeletal remains as well as the personal history of the victim becomes available for future comparisons. The bones seldom stay with us in such cases, but the databank assures that the information they contain will be available indefinitely to supplement the museum collections and clinical literature.

The databank also offers the potential for developing custom techniques to analyze particularly difficult cases. I had occasion to use that capability recently. The skeleton in question was incomplete, and I was unable to determine with certainty either the sex or population of origin from the material in hand. After taking all the measurements I could on the partial skull, I contacted the databank. Working with the Knoxville staff, we devised a custom mathematical approach based on discriminate function analysis that compared those measurements with applicable data from other forensic cases, and then predicted sex and ethnic origin.

Although we have learned from experience that certain telltale population characteristics are present from birth, anthropologists agree that a lot is still to be learned about how children of different ancestry differ from one another. The reason for this gap is that there are no collections of children's skeletons; very few are willed to science or otherwise made available for study, so our principal sources remain archaeological digs and forensic cases.

The correct assessment of age at time of death, based on skeletal remains, is often an important factor in establishing identity; in forensic cases it sometimes plays a role in determining the nature of the charges.

When trying to estimate age at death, I look first at all the age indicators throughout the skeleton, comparing my observations on morphology with changes recorded for recent populations of known age, and then estimating any variable likely to exist between the remains and the information in the database. This third step—figuring in advance what factors are likely to be different—is seldom recognized or discussed in bone studies, but it can be of great importance.

That first, comprehensive look at all the age indicators of the skeleton draws on the anthropologist's knowledge of how certain bones change over time. These changes occur at different ages and different rates.

In trying to establish a specific age range, we start with indicators of relative age to determine whether the specimen is an infant, child, adolescent, or adult. If the skeletal remains are those of a fetus, we look first for the development of teeth, if any are present. Usually no teeth are found in fetal cases, and we look instead to the length of the bones, comparing our measurements with clinical data that are available to determine the number of months since conception.

In most states, abortion is illegal after a certain number of fetal months, so fetal cases are the most obvious example in which age at time of death can determine the charges, and sometimes whether the case should go to court. We begin by identifying the bone fragments that are still present, get an accurate measurement of them, and compare them against the charts developed for that purpose.

For children ranging from newborn into the teens, the best age

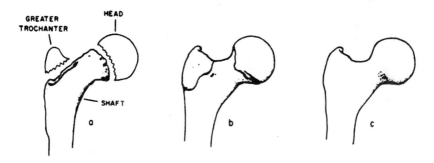

The degree of ossification or joining the femur is an indicator of age. In the above diagram, the epiphyses are united but their junctures are still clearly defined by lines. In the completed union, the junctures disappear.

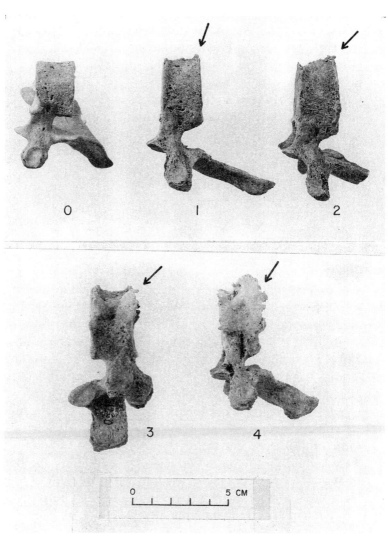

Pronounced bony outgrowths on vertebrae are an indicator of advanced age.

indicators are the stages of formation of the teeth, as seen in X-rays. Even in newborns, teeth are forming underneath the gums, although in forensic cases they are frequently so small they are overlooked and not recovered. If the teeth are not available, we look at the size of the long bones, the union of epiphyses (bony caps on the ends of the long bones), and other factors.

By the time a person reaches age twenty, most growth is complete, most epiphyses are united, and most teeth have erupted and are fully calcified. For the aging of adults, the best approach in my opinion is a broad one: looking at all the available age indicators and forming a general impression, rather than making a case on one or two of the most obvious criteria. Overall, adult aging landmarks are provided by the continued knitting of the skull plates to the point where the suture lines joining those bones eventually disappear; in addition, changes in the appearance of the pubis, degenerative changes such as osteoarthritis or dental attrition, and microscopic alterations in the structure of the bones and teeth are all important.

Criteria that are relevant to age in one stage of maturity are often totally irrelevant to another. Information on the eruption of the teeth through the gums can tell us whether a child is six or eight; it doesn't tell us a thing about whether an adult is thirty-five or seventy. But once we have determined the general stage of maturity, we can then select those criteria that allow for greater precision. The choice of methods depends not only on the reliability of one approach over another but also on the state of preservation of the bones and teeth, the availability of time and equipment, and the precision required by the problem being investigated. The greater the number of procedures employed, the more accurate the estimate is likely to be. It doesn't make sense to prepare microscopic slides when the analysis of the remains in a burial pit calls only for a general separation of young and old adults; it does make sense when you only have a femur and are attempting to determine whether it originated from a person who was thirty or sixty years old.

For adults, the criteria used include microscopic bone studies, examinations of the pubic symphyses (where the two pubic bones join in the front) and the bony surfaces of the sacroiliac joint, surfaces of the ilium, degenerative changes, the condition of rib ends (also variable with age by sex), and wear and loss of teeth.

The reason that sex, stature, race, and age are all combined in this chapter is that they are combined in life; each of these factors is commonly relative to the others, and it is sometimes impossible to infer

When the owner of a music store near the University of Wisconsin investigated a leak in his heating system, he discovered a human skull at the bottom of the flue.

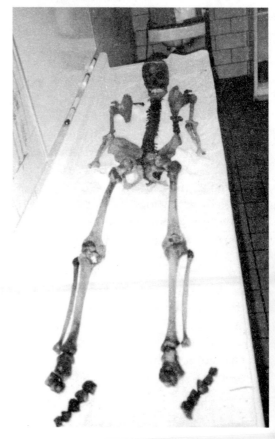

one characteristic without reference to them all. A dramatic example of that relationship was a 1989 murder case from Madison, Wisconsin.

The case began when the owner of a music store near the main campus of the University of Wisconsin tried to trace the source of water seepage from the chimney for his building's heating system. He went down to the cellar, pulled the vent pipe away from the brickwork, and found a human skull and some long bones in the chamber at the bottom of the flue. Shortly afterward, detectives and fire inspectors who dismantled the base of the chimney found a complete human skeleton, including a relatively intact clump of reddish-brown hair about six inches long. Although the flue was a ceramic pipe only one foot in diameter, the body had apparently been shoved feet-first down the chimney from the building's roof.

It had been there long enough to lose all the skin and soft tissue, but when the remains were laid out on the cellar floor it was obvious that the victim was of relatively small stature. The body was dressed in a sleeveless frock with a paisley print, a dark shag sweater, a pair of ankle socks, and women's shoes with a medium heel. Despite the hellish scenario that springs to mind from such a discovery, the only signs of trauma were compound fractures in the pubic bones. Many women are widest at the hips, and one obvious possibility was that the fractures were associated with the cramming of the body into the chimney opening.

The remains were examined by an anthropologist, a forensic pathologist, a forensic odontologist, and the Wisconsin State Crime Laboratory. Even though their findings generally agreed, they seemed so inconsistent with the rest of the evidence that Detective Jim Grann of the Madison Police Department requested an additional opinion from the FBI. Based on my examination of the skull and pelvic bones, I was able to confirm the conclusions of the other specialists: that the body was not that of a woman but a man.

A tentative new scenario emerged as a result of the forensic findings. The victim, who was between the ages of twenty-two and twenty-seven, may have been engaged in prostitution. The pubic bones could have been broken as the result of having his pelvis stomped by an irate customer on discovery of his gender; considering the location of the fractures, that may be a likely explanation. There is no way to tell from the remains whether he was alive or dead when his body was forced into the chimney for the drop to the cellar. Either way, it has to be one of the most horrific crimes I have ever encountered.

Detective Grann also requested facial reproductions, and we gave him those as well—one a computer-assisted sketch, and the other modeled in clay. Despite a slight overbite and a minor asymmetry which gave the face a certain distinction, neither reproduction produced an identification. It may have been that the victim was a transient; every large university has people living on the fringes who put down their roots in shallow soil, unnoticed when they arrive, unmissed when they leave. Students themselves are transient; in the years since the probable time of his disappearance, more than half the school's population would have turned over. It's also possible the reproductions failed to produce a match because we showed the victim as a man.

Finding the victim a lot sooner after the crime is still no guarantee a murder will be solved, or even that the body will be identified. In the summer of 1986, a garbage truck was being emptied at an eastern landfill when the operator caught sight of a severed human leg among the cascading debris. He called the police, and when the rest of the contents were removed, a headless, armless torso with the second leg still attached was found wedged against the rear wall of the truck. A long, careful search through other recent drops at the landfill failed to produce the missing head or arms. Saw marks were identified on the severed femur.

An attempt was made to identify the female victim, based on the sex, size, and race data collected at the autopsy, and on age characteristics inferred by an examiner at a local medical school. The attempt failed, and a year later I received the femur from the unsevered leg and was asked for a second opinion as to age. After a microscopic examination of a section of the bone, I came up with an estimated age of around twenty-two. That still didn't yield a positive result from the National Crime Information Center database, so several months after that the medical examiner asked me to do another aging estimate based on my examination of the pubic bone. These two approaches to aging, from different techniques applied to different parts of the body, produced the same numbers. But the fact that my two estimates agreed didn't improve the outcome, and she remains unidentified today.

It's a lot easier to identify a body part when you have some idea where it came from. That same year, I was asked to examine a partial skull that had been recovered near a local cemetery. The letter from the police said that a crypt had been desecrated five years earlier, and at that time a body had been found decapitated with a knife. Now, there was no way to match the skull with that body directly; the family felt it was inappropriate to reinter the remains after such a serious desecration, so the body had long since been cremated. The portion of the skull that was recovered was only the braincase, lacking a mandible or any upper teeth. If the skull was to be connected to the earlier mutilation, it would be on the estimates I was asked to make of sex, age, time of death, and time since death. I was able to tell the police the skull was a male aged between thirty and sixty, and probably of European ancestry. Though far from a positive identification in themselves, those observations agreed in every particular with the data on the desecration case and greatly increased the likelihood that was where the skull had originated.

Sometimes illness or abuse can alter signs of aging. A couple of assignments from Tennessee, on which I worked with Bill Bass, illustrate some of the other factors that may have to be considered in estimating any of the basic parameters from bones. The first was a torso that had been partially dismembered with a chainsaw.

Both legs were missing from just below the middle thigh, and the hands had been cut off as well, but the long bones of the right arm were sufficiently intact to permit a rough estimate of the stature from the length of the ulna. The murder was quite recent and it was possible to tell from the skin and body hair that the victim had been Caucasian. Using the Trotter and Gleser formula for white males, Bill estimated a height between 5′4¼″ and 5′8½″.

As for age, a general estimate of between thirty and the early fifties was made in Tennessee based on observation of a slight arthritic lipping of the lower lumbar vertebrae. My own specific estimate in Washington, based on microscopic analysis of the osteons from a cross-section of the femur, was about fifty-seven years. I used the osteon counting method developed initially by Kerley in 1965, but revised by Kerley and me in 1978 after we reanalyzed his original data.

The technique is based on our knowledge of the growth and rebuilding process in human bone. A bone increases in width by new deposits from a layer of tissue called the periosteum. Added layer upon layer like rings of a tree, these periosteum deposits are known as circumferential lamellar bone. Parallel with this process, beginning early in childhood and continuing for the life of the individual, the small, partially filled-in tunnels called osteons are formed throughout this bone to carry nourishment and nerves. There are three stages to the development of these tunnels. The first is the creation of the hole, or resorption space, by cells that destroy bone, called osteoclasts.

(Sometimes, especially in old age, these spaces do not fill in properly, which can contribute to the condition we know as osteoporosis.) In the second stage, the tunnels are partially filled in by other small cells called osteoblasts to form osteons. In the final stage, the osteons house blood vessels and nerve fibers, and are mainly responsible for maintaining the life of the inner bone. This entire process of internal bone change is known as remodeling. With increasing age, there are more and more osteons and less of the original circumferential lamellar bone. To calculate age at death, we count the osteons as well as the percentage of remaining lamellar bone.

In the case from Tennessee, there was evidence of extensive remodeling, with little circumferential lamellar bone remaining. I called in my estimate of age on a Friday afternoon; and as it happened, the body was identified that same day. The technique had permitted me to come within two years of the man's actual age at death; he had been nearly fifty-five. My accuracy in this case was not surprising, as we know from experience that estimates using this technique usually fall within five years. We also realize that a significant percentage of the estimates will fall outside that range, so even this technique has its limitations. When applied to unknown forensic cases, there is no way to tell where that estimate falls on the curve of probability.

The other Tennessee case was a skeleton in an advanced state of decay found at about the same time, complete except for the left leg below the knee and part of the right foot. I used the same technique to estimate age, but this time the microscope revealed two sets of apparently contradictory evidence. The osteon count showed that it was a man, about fifty years old, while the section also displayed a tremendous number of resorption spaces (the unfilled tunnels of stage one), usually characteristic of a much greater age. I decided the osteon count was the more reliable basis, and that the high resorption level was premature, a condition perhaps resulting from the abuse of alcohol. This is one case where we probably won't find out how close we came with our estimate. The body was never identified.

By contrast, it happens sometimes, although far less frequently, that anthropological studies of age, sex, and so on, are performed on subjects about whom an enormous amount is already known. Consider the case of Penpi. In 1884, in what may have marked the beginning of a laudable, still-flourishing tradition, this distinguished but little read writer arrived in Ithaca, New York, amidst considerable fanfare and ceremony, to take up residency in the sheltering groves of academe. Penpi's name may be nearly forgotten today, but he was one of the best-known Egyptian literary figures of his time, and he settled into his new home at Cornell University for what promised to be a long, comfortable sinecure.

Like many an academic celebrity since then, very little was expected of him except, to paraphrase Woody Allen, that he show up. No one seriously thought Penpi would ever write another thing, he didn't have to do much teaching, and as long as he was dutifully on hand for the university's major social events, his future seemed secure. But writers and other athletes share a sometimes devastating susceptibility to changes in fortune, and several years later Penpi found himself in the cellar, both metaphorically and literally. Ultimately the great scribe was subjected to dissection by one of the Cornell faculty archaeologists, this final indignity occurring in the 1960s. By then, Penpi was about 2,700 years old.

Happily, he was rescued, if only after the fact, by a team of anthropologists headed by the celebrated scholar Kenneth A. R. Kennedy, who also happens to be a diplomate of the American Board of Forensic Anthropology. Kenneth tidied up the mess created by the earlier examiner, who had never been trained in dissection procedure, and then availed himself of this nearly unique opportunity to conduct a comprehensive morphometric analysis of Penpi's mummified remains. I say nearly unique because the Egyptian scribe is one of the few ancient cadavers whose names and professions have traveled with their bones down through the millennia. Penpi could not have gotten a better, more thorough forensic examination if he had been shot behind the ear and dumped on the steps of the FBI.

The morphometric study revealed a slightly built man, about 5'9" in height, which was somewhat taller than average for his peers and probably reflected dietary advantages as a child. Ancient Egyptians were great chewers—of flavored seeds, resins, reeds, and gums—and beyond the wear to Penpi's teeth (he lost four to the tooth puller), that habit was reflected in the robust musculature which had helped shape his jaw. The attrition on the remaining teeth was also indicative of diet; like the deer on Martha's Vineyard whose life spans are limited by the same factor, ancient Egyptians ingested a lot of sand and grit with their food, and their teeth often gave out faster than the rest of their bodies.

For most of the years since death, the scribe's mummy had been interred in the great necropolis at Thebes, and was exhumed by archaeologists in 1883; just a year later, Penpi was packed off to college in New York. Despite the obvious fact that he had achieved sufficient social stature to warrant embalming and interment at the Forest Lawn of ancient Egypt, Penpi probably didn't live to be more than twenty-five. Certain cranial alterations and the bent long bones of his legs (the latter condition called saber-shin tibia or "boomerang leg") suggest he may have suffered from a treponemal disease such as yaws. He also showed signs of porotic hyperostosis, a form of anemia thought to be largely caused by iron deficiency. For all that, his life was not exceptionally short for the Dynastic Period; Kenneth points out that by the age of thirty, half the adult population of that era had already died.

Forensic anthropologists like to relate skeletal evidence to occupations, and it was common for laborers of ancient Egypt, as in many cultures elsewhere and even today, to develop facets on certain bones from long periods of squatting. Scribes, by contrast, sat cross-legged on the floor and used the tightly stretched skirts of their garments for a desktop on which they did their writing, so there was no such faceting on Penpi's remains. His skeleton may have exhibited signs of his profession, however. Kennedy's careful analysis detected modifications of the palmar surfaces of the phalanges of the right hand, which could reflect Penpi's long-term use of the stylus. Based on clavicular and upper extremity bone lengths, it appears likely he was right-handed.

Penpi may have been unique in some respects, but as anyone knows who pays attention to the current media, he was not the only eminent personage of the past to achieve even further celebrity in modern times from the forensic anthropological examination of his remains. These modern studies are performed for the same reasons as any other forensic examination—to confirm identity, to search for evidence of crime, to provide insights into how people lived and perhaps how they died—that would not be available from any other source. In addition, eminent remains sometimes hold the potential for resolving historical conflicts and unraveling ancient enigmas.

8

GRAVE CONSEQUENCES

A smart detective knows how much may be learned from the environment in which a body has been found, especially in cases involving advanced decomposition. One of the smartest is Kenny Martin of the Fingerprint and Photography Section of the Massachusetts State Police. In 1985, he investigated some skeletal remains discovered in the grass beside the interstate highway which passes through the town of Fairhaven. The skeleton was in wet ground and had become intricately embraced by a wild network of shrubs, weeds, and vines, and Martin realized that to extricate it for examination would risk the destruction of potentially valuable evidence. A metal detector was brought in: careful probing within the frame of bones produced four bullets. After the scene was photographed in detail, he divided the body in two at the top of the legs, then lifted each half—bones, shreds of clothes, soil, plant life, root systems, and all—in two huge blocks, which were packaged in heavy shipping crates and sent to Washington.

The crates were delivered across the street, in the laboratories of the FBI. A short time later my phone rang, and I heard, "You won't

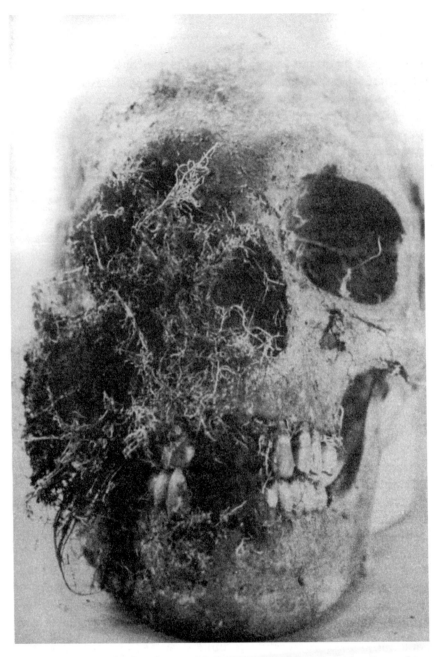

Roots growing in the facial area of the cranium found at the side of a road in Massachusetts.

believe this one. Along with the bones, they've sent us a couple of acres of Massachusetts real estate." I rushed right over, afraid I'd miss the opening.

When the sides of the crates were removed, we all saw the body almost exactly as it had first been found. It was an unforgettable scene. The two huge cubes of earth, like great chunks of chocolate cake, were topped with ornate burdens of twisted vines, shrubbery, twigs, dead grass, roadside debris, and human bones. Corners of the cubes crumbled quietly onto zinc and Formica surfaces of the pristine, sterile laboratory room, and the FBI examiners who surrounded them moved back, allowing my assistant and me to begin our initial examination. I felt a bit like Mohammed contemplating the mountain on his doorstep.

As we started to untangle the evidence from its setting, one or two of the FBI examiners commented on the problems of dealing with such a huge puzzle this way, and there may have been some implied criticism of the shipment as excessive. But if this kind of challenge was daunting to scientists in a laboratory setting, how much more difficult it must have appeared to the detectives who faced the task of separating evidence from its intricate context in the field, without the advantages of our collective specialized training and without the time and space to approach it systematically. By addressing it in this manner, we had a unique opportunity to see the remains in the laboratory in exactly the same relationship they had to each other in the field—and once that relationship was disturbed, it could never be re-created with complete accuracy. I thought Kenny Martin had done exactly the right thing, and that his solution was inspired.

Another great advantage in seeing the body in that context was that it allowed me to distinguish between trauma at the time of death (perimortem) and the effects of postmortem vegetable growth. When a root penetrates a bone, it keeps growing, and the expansion can ultimately break the bone into fragments, mimicking other forms of trauma; it would have been very difficult or even impossible for me to identify the sites of bullet impact, as I did, if they had been allowed to get lost among the similar destruction related to later root growth.

In addition, careful study of root systems can provide very valuable data on time since death, such as how many seasons have passed since they began their progress through the victim's clothing and skeleton. In this case, examining the body *in situ* also permitted me to interpret the relationship between the bones and associated clothing as they had been left at the site by the killer, and to infer the trajectory of yet another bullet which we recovered from the body in the FBI Laboratory.

One of the first questions the police ask a forensic anthropologist is how long a subject has been dead. It is also one of the most difficult to answer. Until fairly recently, the knowledge traditionally used to interpret what happens to skeletons after death has been derived largely from circumstance. Forensic specialists recorded the impact of various environmental factors—rain and snow, sunlight, plant growth, heat and cold, water, insects, larvae, corrosives and solvents—as they found them at the discovery site, and their observations associated with the recovery of bodies from thousands of field locations comprise much of the collective wisdom from which we have developed our forensic standards.

Even in less spectacular cases than the body in the root system, in the absence of choice there's nothing wrong with relying on empirical evidence. But in most branches of science, the preferable alternative to circumstantial data is planned research, and there has been a long-standing need for controlled experiments to understand and record more exactly and more reliably what happens to a decaying body after death. The earliest experimental work in this field was done on arthropods, mainly fly larvae, observing the patterns associated with their feeding on dead pigs, which were either buried or placed above the ground in various situations. The insects that came to feed on the pig flesh were carefully monitored, and a documentary record was kept of the order in which they arrived, how long they stayed, what happened to them while they were there, and the stages they went through. These patterns were then applied to observation of arthropod and insect activity on human remains; as a result, inferences could be made on how long the bodies had been where they were found, and sometimes what had happened to them during and since death.

The problem with those experiments was that pigs, as a sage once said, is pigs; the need persisted for controlled observations of these same patterns in humans. Bill Bass had recognized this need for a long time, and after his transfer to the University of Tennessee he began to work on it in earnest. In the late 1970s he organized ARF, the Anthropological Research Facility, at Knoxville and commenced studies of decay rates under carefully monitored conditions with bodies donated from the Medical Examiner's Office that were either unidentified or unclaimed at the time of death. The skeletons later became part of a reference collection for the future recovery of data as the need arose. (Bill told me recently that local lawyers and forensic specialists

Bill Bass doing field work in 1965.

have added his name to the facility, so it is now known more familiarly by the acronym BARF.)

The decay rate facility was in a wooded area behind the medical center, and at first Bill's studies proceeded in relative peace and privacy. Eventually, however, the center built a parking lot on two sides of the area where he did his work, and one day several of the construction workers happened to notice that there were a lot of dead bodies lying around in the woods. Bill's picture was on the front page of the local paper for the next few days, and he was afraid his research was going to be nipped in the bud. He defended his project, and the chancellor of the University of Tennessee responded heroically with the funds for a chain-link fence embedded in concrete and surmounted by three strands of barbed wire. Bill says the fence does provide security for his research, but he still is not certain whether it is intended primarily to protect the tenants of ARF's al fresco mortuary or the sensibilities of the medical center's staff who park in the new lot.

ARF processes between thirty and forty bodies a year, as well as a number of dogs obtained from the city pound. The remains are placed on the ground or on a concrete slab in their natural condition, usually without embalming. The only artificial aspect of the environment is its security; the fence precludes carnivore activity, which is not an uncommon part of the process by which many abandoned bodies return to nature.

Sometimes the skeletal remains of murder victims are found wrapped in plastic, so now and then an ARF body will be wrapped in plastic as well. Sometimes the ARF bodies are buried, although not very deep; most buried murder victims are recovered from fairly near the surface. Decay rates are compared: shallow grave wrapped vs. shallow grave unwrapped; or surface wrapped vs. surface unwrapped. Surface bodies are photographed at standard intervals to record the process graphically. Buried bodies are either exhumed at relatively short intervals for the same purpose or after longer fixed periods, sometimes spanning several years.

Changes in vegetation and in the composition of the soil are also noted and recorded precisely as a guide to the recovery of bodies in the field. Underbrush foliage can change color, becoming lighter when its root system has been disturbed by a burial, and surface loam is often displaced by lighter-colored subsoils when a hole has been refilled.

It is not uncommon for exhumed bodies to display maggot activity even when they have been buried at a depth of two feet, far deeper than arthropods penetrate under normal conditions. It's hard to explain with certainty, but probably fly eggs were deposited on the body in the short time between death and burial rather than the larvae migrating down from the surface. Whatever their source, there's no doubt that this activity in the controlled setting at ARF parallels what happens to bodies buried in the field, and the process is recorded in meticulous detail.

The facility operates year round, of course, so some of the observations have addressed seasonal differences in the rate and character of deterioration in cold months as compared to warm ones. In general, a body left exposed to the elements in the winter will decay more quickly from within, but with none of the surface larval activity that can consume the skin in summer. As another result, because the skin of a wintertime-killing victim lasts longer, it is more likely to stain and discolor. That is not to suggest that maggots are absent; they are often part of the accelerated decay process within the body cavities of pelvis, chest, or head, closed environments where they generate their own heat, but they are not likely to migrate to the outside where they would become subject to death by freezing. Cold weather greatly impedes the overall life cycle of the larvae and flies.

In hot weather, maggots will typically strip a body to the bones in two weeks, fall off, bore into the ground, and pupate; two weeks later they emerge as adults, resurface, and begin the whole cycle again. In the winter, the maggot stage can last as long as several months.

The primary cause of bone changes after death is chemical erosion. The rate and nature of the erosion can vary with the type and acidity of the soil, moisture, method of burial, and the condition of the remains immediately following death. If chemicals have been used to deliberately disguise the identity of a victim or to accelerate decomposition of the body, those processes will continue, in one degree or another, after the remains have been placed in the ground or otherwise disposed of.

Under natural conditions, decomposition occurs at different rates on different parts of a skeleton, and sometimes those differences can be misinterpreted as the results of pathological or environmental changes. Differences in kinds and degrees of these changes to various parts of the same skeleton often provide clues to their real causes. Another common cause of postmortem change in the bones of murder victims is exposure to sunlight. Bones that lie on the surface for long periods become bleached and are more brittle than those that are buried. The effect is usually diffuse, without sharp margins, but the difference between exposed and unexposed surfaces can be dramatic; in cases where the remains have been disturbed, the pattern of those differences can often provide clear evidence of the original position of the remains during the period of prolonged exposure.

There may be a certain amount of poetic symmetry in the fact that at least one of the bodies whose deterioration has been recorded at the facility was that of a murderer. In the case I know of, it belonged to an old man who had died in prison after being convicted years earlier, and it had already been embalmed before the decision was made to donate the remains to research. It provided some useful comparative data on decay rates when chemicals are or are not used. Larval activity, for example, is greatly reduced in most embalming cases, and the decay pattern is not only slower but different in kind. In this particular case, after about three weeks of warm weather exposure the hands had shriveled and started to lose pigmentation, there was pronounced tissue loss on both legs, the hair had begun to detach, and the body cavity aspiration points in the groin and under the arm had begun to decompose. But the body was still fully articulated and retained most of its flesh, even though a non-embalmed cadaver would have already disintegrated.

After two more months, the tissues of the embalmed murderer's face had shrunk only slightly, and there was some attrition due to rodent activity around the ears, nose, and lips, but even the eyes were still intact, all of which underscores the difficulty of dating the death of a preserved body. It was still intact after another four months, and by then the process of deterioration had gone about as far as it ever would. Some of the embalmed bodies at the facility have been left outdoors for several years, with no marked alterations after the first six months.

By contrast, a woman of seventy who was embalmed after dying of a heart attack deteriorated in a markedly different way. On the fifth day, her face had all but disappeared, largely due to maggot activity. The pattern of the leg deterioration was the same, but all the fatty areas of the body had broken down far more quickly than those with muscles or sinewy tissue. The preservation procedures were identical, but the nature of the two bodies was different. As a rule of thumb, the less fatty tissue in a body, the greater the effect of the embalming.

A far more remarkable contrast is in the comparison between decay rates for bodies that have been embalmed and those that have not. The process of natural disintegration can be astonishingly swift. One series of ARF pictures, taken in the heat of a Tennessee summer, chronicles what happened to the body of a dog that had been left outside on one of the facility's concrete slabs. A couple of years ago a Bass student named Bob Mann used this series in the Smithsonian's annual week-long forensic seminar for medical examiners and police, and he invited guesses from the audience for the time between death and the nearly total skeletonization of the head. Following the usual questions about climatic conditions at the time, most of the estimates ranged from two weeks to two months. The correct answer was seventy-two hours. Even among professionals, no one came close. The same thing can happen to a human, under similar conditions, with the same speed.

The rate of decomposition of a body also can vary greatly with the type of trauma associated with the death. One of Bill's forensic cases in Tennessee was a drug murder in which the victim had been struck repeatedly in the head with a hammer, hacked with a machete, then doused with combustibles and set afire in a field. A couple of drunks happened to be sleeping in the field at the time, and when they woke up, the body was still smoking. Because of their own condition, the witnesses' reaction may have been a bit laggardly, but by the time the police arrived the body was already swarming with larvae. Just a few hours later, by comparison with any reasonable expectation for the rate of decomposition, it would be hard even for a professional to tell the body had not been dead a week.

As invaluable as his work has been, Bill Bass knows that his observations are still a long way from setting a universal standard for the patterns followed by all human remains after death. What happens to a body in Tennessee may not be applicable to patterns in such other climates as the desert of the Southwest, the tundra of Alaska and Canada, the tropical marshes and grasslands of Florida, or the arid wastelands of southern California. Because of the success of his work in Knoxville, however, Bass's pioneering efforts contributed in large measure to the development of other research facilities for that same purpose in the Southwest, including California and Texas, and other areas. Through all of these programs, anthropologists continue to build up our understanding of the process of decay, disarticulation, and disintegration, and how it works in different environments.

9

SCAVENGING

When police recovered a skeleton from the woods of southern Virginia last year, I found clear evidence of a gunshot wound to the right first rib, just below the neck, with radiating fractures. Two bullets had been recovered from the ground directly under the body, and a third was found in the waistband of a pair of women's black bikini underpants. It was unlikely that the bullet causing the hole in the first rib would have ended up halfway down the body at the waistband; a more likely candidate was one of the other two bullets, recovered from outside the skeleton at a site on the ground just above the remnants of a brassière.

There were several other bones that could well have contained evidence of injuries similar to the bullethole in the first right rib; broken areas on the sternal end of the right second rib and the head of a lower right rib, in particular, could have been the result of a passing projectile, as could the shattered thoracic vertebra. But the only positive evidence that the victim had been shot was the hole just below the clavicle. Even when examining the other bones under a microscope, it was impossible for me to distinguish between such possible trauma and the gnawing on the bones by carnivores.

There were tooth marks on bones throughout the body. The right shoulder blade had been gnawed, as had both sides of the lower jaw, two vertebrae in the upper back and one in the lower, the heads of two right lower ribs, the lower end of the bone from the left upper arm, both sides of the pelvis, and a third of the upper bone of the right arm. But there was no way to tell whether they were hiding gunshot injury or mimicking it.

Animal activity is one of the most frequent sources of skeletal alterations in murder cases, and it can be one of the most confusing, especially to the inexperienced examiner. I have seen numerous examples of carnivore damage mistakenly associated with cause of death, and I have also seen cases in which the real cause of death was hidden among the tooth marks of a rat or dog. In the case from Virginia, the bullets were of a low caliber and apparently had not had enough force to pass through the whole body. But in cases involving extensive carnivore activity where there is no spent bullet, I am certain that the evidence of such perimortem trauma is often hidden or destroyed by the gnawing.

Animal chewing can destroy far more than evidence of the probable cause of death. In one case, the body of a victim had been subject for a prolonged period to cold, dry conditions and had become mummified. The temperature was too low for flies or larval activity, and many parts of the corpse were nearly intact when recovered by the police some five or six weeks after death. But if there had been any hope of identifying the remains from the face, they had disappeared with the rats that had eaten away the lips, cheeks, most of the nose, and all the soft tissue for a diameter of four inches around the empty orbits of each eye.

Rats and dogs aren't the only sources of misleading evidence and the loss of valuable forensic data. All kinds of animals, from burrowing insects to grizzly bears, can create damage to skeletal remains that ranges from leaving easily misinterpreted microscopic marks in the bones to the strewing and destruction of entire skeletons. One colleague, Dr. Ted Rathbun of the University of South Carolina, reported on a human leg bone removed from the belly of a great white shark, and I have heard of other cases in which a large shark devoured an entire body—including, possibly, a late prime minister of Australia.

On the micro end of that spectrum, it is more common for the activity of insects, larvae, and mollusks to be mistaken for pathology than for trauma. I examined the internal surface of a skull from the Dominican Republic and found extensive pitting that could easily have been explained as parasitic disease. However, the specimen had been found in sandy soil near the ocean, and there was far greater likelihood that the destruction had followed long after death.

In the more readily visible range of such evidence, I have encountered the gnawing of rodents in fragments of the shafts of long bones recovered from burial urns in Ecuador. The irregular, linear notches are the result of rodents seeking calcium or protein residues, and are far more commonly found on skeletal remains that were either exposed on the surface or buried at shallow depths. They are also found in the majority of forensic cases in which the body has become skeletonized. The rule of thumb for distinguishing such animal activity in archaeology is that knife and other man-made instrument cuts are usually found near the joints, as they are most often the results of intentional disarticulation or defleshing of the body. That rule doesn't apply in homicide cases, where the cut can come from more random stabbing, or in archaeological cases involving ritual torture or human sacrifice.

To the trained eye, most knife marks can be readily distinguished from tooth damage, regardless of the size of the tooth. Cuts from sharp instruments have sharper borders, are narrower, straighter, and usually more widely spaced. In the macro range, large animals such as dogs, coyotes, and wolves tend to gnaw at the ends of long bones, destroying the articular surfaces and epiphyses. Bears tend to break the diaphyses of long bones and may clamp down on bones, leaving telltale imprints of their canine teeth. Many forensic cases depend on nothing more than that ability to separate the signs of animal predation from evidence of human violence. A referral to the FBI from an island in the Caribbean offers a dramatic example.

In the winter of 1986, fragments of human bones and scraps of clothing were found in a cane field. In the tropics, bodies deteriorate far more quickly than in colder climates, and the materials were thought to be the remains of a sixty-eight-year-old black woman who had disappeared two months earlier, just before Christmas. A preliminary examination of the skull by local police noted unusual conditions of the brow ridge over both eye sockets. The FBI was requested to examine the remains for approximate age, sex, race, and time since death, and in particular for whether the conditions of the skull represented trauma that could have been related to death.

I had no trouble telling the island authorities that the sex, age, and race of the remains were all consistent with the missing woman. As for signs of trauma, the bones had undergone considerable attrition and there was evidence that every one of them had been chewed by a large carnivore, probably a dog.

But a wound in the back was different from the other damage, and had been caused by some other instrument than the teeth of a dog.

The 6 mm incision behind her left shoulder had probably been produced by the violent thrust of a sharp-edged instrument. And it had probably occurred at or about the time of her death.

There was also strong evidence that the woman had been smashed—perhaps lethally—in the face. The two fractures on the front of the skull that extended from the interior wall of the left eye socket to just right of the midline of the skull, about 26 mm above the junction of the frontal and nasal bones, were probably the results of blunt force.

Forensic examiners seldom learn the results of their findings when the examination is related to a crime in another country, so I don't know how this case turned out. But at least I know it got a proper start, and that surface appearances weren't allowed to conceal the evidence of murder. And I also had the satisfaction of knowing this was one time when the forensic examination didn't let a killer get away with giving a dog a bad name.

I'm not going to give a dog a bad name either, at least not any of the dogs that found ten-year-old Charity Powers. Charity was a fifth grader in a suburb of Richmond, Virginia, who disappeared in early October 1990. Her mother had a date with friends that evening, so she hired a baby-sitter for her two younger children and dropped Charity off at a skating rink five miles from their house at 9:30 P.M. She had 75 cents, part of which was to call the baby-sitter when she was ready to be picked up. At the rink, Charity skated with two girlfriends, aged ten and twelve. The friends were picked up by the older girl's father when the rink closed, and a half hour later Charity walked into a nearby Hardee's restaurant and asked an employee what time it was. "Past your bedtime," the woman answered. The little girl walked back out onto the highway.

At quarter to three, Charity's mother returned home from her date. The baby-sitter was asleep on the sofa. One of the younger children had apparently knocked the telephone off the hook, and the sitter had slept through the expected call. Charity's bed was empty. The mother called the police.

Weeks passed. More than twenty thousand fliers with Charity's picture and description were distributed around the country, and her mother spent over a thousand dollars on telephone calls following up on leads. Police collected several leads of their own in the first couple of days after the disappearance, but none stood out. That changed a couple of weeks before Christmas, when they learned that a marginal suspect whom they had interviewed the second day of the case, an unemployed laborer named Everett Lee Mueller, aged forty-two, had a long history of violent criminal behavior.

Mueller had been committed to a California mental hospital in 1972 after raping two women, one of whom he kidnapped off a street at knifepoint, but he was released after two years of psychiatric treatment. In 1976 he raped a third woman while holding a knife to the side of her head, and for that he served twelve years in prison. Mueller had been reported to have been seen in his car at the restaurant, watching Charity as she sat out front on the curb at 1:00 A.M. on the night she disappeared. But that wasn't much of an accusation, and until police checked his record, they had no reason to doubt his denials that he had ever seen her.

Even with his history, they couldn't just go out and arrest Mueller. A task force of local police and special agents of the FBI went back to work around the clock. In February 1991, with the help of dogs trained in the recovery of dead bodies, a fastidious search began of a 75-acre tract less than half a mile from Mueller's house. The police had searched the area once before with no result. This time the dogs sniffed out Charity's decaying body two feet below the surface.

Mueller confessed he had raped the girl and then strangled her, and I examined the bones just three days after the report of his confession was published in the newspapers. In strangulation cases, one indicator with adult victims is whether the hyoid, a small bone associated with the windpipe, has been broken by the pressure of the killer's thumbs. However, the unity of this same bone can also be one of the indicators of age; the hyoid starts off in three pieces and doesn't merge into one until near the end of the growth process. In the case of a child of ten, its disunity was not a sign she had been strangled, but of her youth.

But there was more, and it was more to the point: a section of the occipital bone in Charity's skull was slightly separated from the surrounding bone, especially at the base. This was a possible indication of trauma in the neck area, which would be consistent with Mueller's own statement of what had happened. But even by itself, Mueller's confession was probably enough.

He was eventually sentenced to die in Virginia's electric chair.

It is very common for dogs to find missing bodies, even bodies that have been buried for months or years, and they are used regularly for that purpose by police all over the country. I have examined several skeletons from Bristol County, Massachusetts, which were recovered by Crime Prevention and Control (CPAC) detectives with the help of search dogs, in connection with the Roadside Murder series. The body of Barbara Raposa, the second victim in a three-part Bristol County mini-series in 1979 and 1980, was also found by dogs, although in that case they were freelancers who had the same natural talent as police dogs specially trained to the task.

Just a few months ago I examined a case that started when a dog strolled into his yard and dropped a skull, complete with bullethole, on the front lawn. He then led police back to the rest of the skeleton of a murdered woman.

A little earlier I was sent another skull (of considerable antiquity) that was originally delivered by another family dog to his doctor-owner's homestead in Missouri. That story didn't have as strong a second act. The dog went out again that same day, perhaps to prove he wasn't just a flash in the pan, and returned with another bone that the doctor and the police also thought might be human. This time it was an old soup bone, however, so the gesture proved to be something of an anticlimax.

It's easy enough to figure out why dogs are so successful at this line of work. First of all, dogs are attracted to smells which many humans find repulsive. Second, dead bodies are often deliberately hidden in remote places, and often those are the very places dogs like best.

That second point applies particularly to the types of bodies that end up at the Smithsonian. Looking back at the ways in which an anthropologist's forensic cases materialize, the largest common denominator in the several hundred in my own experience has been that they were discovered out in the countryside. Even though the great majority of murders and deaths by misadventure take place in cities, we are not as likely to get cases from more populous areas for the simple reason that discovery in such places would normally occur sooner. Most bodies we see are from rural sites with dense vegetation, or from locations where the remains have been hidden. Those are places dogs love to go.

So do people, but nowhere nearly as frequently. In most parts of the country, people spend less time in the forest during the summer than in the fall; the woods are most often hot, sticky, and filled with bugs, vegetation is thick, visibility is limited, and access is more difficult. But in fall and winter, two things occur which affect the detection and recovery of human remains. One is simply that the leaves drop, which greatly increases visibility in deciduous forests. The other is the hunting season. Discoveries by hunters may well be the most common starting point on the journey that leads to the laboratory of the forensic anthropologist.

One of the first forensic cases to come my way, in early 1979, consisted of a human skull with a bullethole in the right temporal. I determined that it had belonged to a young adult Caucasian male, that the time since death was probably several years, and that the 11 mm hole appeared to be the entry point for a projectile that had fractured the left frontal and left parietal without exiting. I wasn't able to add much that the referring authorities in Wyoming didn't already know; the skull had already been identified from dental records as the remains of a twenty-three-year-old ex-Marine from neighboring South Dakota, and a deformed bullet had been found in the mud imbedded inside the braincase. What impressed me about this killing was the length of time between the man's disappearance and the recovery of his body.

The victim had left his home on October 11, 1956, and a week later his abandoned car was found hidden in a grove of trees at the bottom of a steep ravine. There was a brief search in the immediate area but nothing was found, and the young man was carried on the books as a missing person for the next twenty-one years. In September 1977, two local elk hunters came across his remains only three miles away. The body was in plain sight, right out in the open, and I can imagine there was some distress among his family that he wasn't found in the initial search. However, some simple mathematics reveal the magnitude of the effort that would have been required for the police to cover the same area two decades before.

Assuming the search were in a quadrant, which is the normal way of doing these things, in order to reach the body, each side of the square would have measured six miles. That produces a total surface area of some 24,000 acres, more than one and a half times the size of Manhattan Island. The thousands of man-hours required for such an effort didn't appear justified by the evidence, which was nothing more than an abandoned car. It would have made a lot more sense to issue a few extra elk licenses in that same area for the season that started a month after he disappeared.

Some hunters use dogs, which suggests the possibility that dogs are also in the woods more frequently during the fall and winter. Again in my own experience, dogs run a close second to hunters in the recovery of lost or missing bodies, although in their case I haven't noticed any particular seasonal patterns, and there is no doubt that dogs find many times more bodies than they bring home. In all the cases of this sort which I have investigated, it is my impression dogs retrieve human remains for the same reason they bring back any other kind of bone: not to show off a trophy, but to seek out some comfortable place, frequently under the back porch, to settle in and enjoy a good chew. Sometimes that process is interrupted when someone says, "My God, look what the dog brought home!" Perhaps even more frequently, because most of what goes on under porches is not observed by human eyes, the chewing takes its normal course, as with any other bone, until nothing recognizable is left.

A couple of years ago, State Police Detective Kenny Martin came down from Massachusetts to participate in a seminar on forensic anthropology. I have known Kenny for several years, having worked with him on the notorious New Bedford Roadside Murders as well as numerous other bone cases in the area of New Bedford and Fall River, and I have come to appreciate how much he knows about how bones are found. In the seminar I had talked about the role of hunters, dogs, berry pickers, and highway maintenance workers, and as we walked together down the long hallway toward my office, between the tall rows of sliding wooden shelves that contain the Smithsonian's collection of human skeletons, I asked Kenny if he had anything to add to my short list of primary sources for the recovery of forensic remains.

He didn't have to reflect on the question; without hesitation he said there should be a place on the list for drinkers. "Beer drinkers in particular," he said. "One of the principal reasons people pull over to the side of the highway is a full bladder. If enough people do it enough times, it's bound to happen that a few of them are going to find themselves standing in the exact same spot a murderer stood sometime earlier, and they discover what he left there."

Although a good many forensic cases start with the household pet, Bill Bass had one in Tennessee that reversed the pattern and ended up there instead. Unlike most rural forensic cases, it involved a wealthy victim, a woman who lived in a large home on an elegant estate a few miles south of Nashville. She had two German shepherds and a collie.

The woman was a relatively private person, but when her neighbors realized that as much as two weeks had passed without any of them seeing her, one of them decided to call the county sheriff. The deputy drove up the long driveway, got no answer when he knocked at the door, then took a look around the outside of the house.

At the rear, he observed a screen door with a hole in the mesh where the dogs could pass in and out of the house. The inner door was open, so he called a few times first, and getting no response he pulled back the screen door and went inside. The floor of the kitchen was a mess, littered with clumps of hair, bone fragments, and other material apparently strewn about by the dogs, and there was evidence they had been roaming unattended through the rest of the house as well. The deputy called for support. Subsequently the police swept up some of the debris into little plastic bags and sent it over to Knoxville for analysis. As they had feared, it proved to be human.

There was no sign that the dogs were vicious, so it was assumed the woman had died of natural causes and they had eaten her afterwards, when there was no one to feed them and they were faced with starvation.

As is often the case in situations involving dogs, only the shafts of the bones were recovered; the ends are softer, more chewable and less prone to splintering, and they are also where the marrow is concentrated. However, a section of the cranial wall was discovered relatively intact, and because the owner of the house had recently undergone a series of CAT-scans, by comparing tomographic sections Bill was able positively to identify the skull fragment as belonging to the missing homeowner.

About a week later, Bill received a call from a young woman at a Nashville bank. The caller said she had heard of Bill's identification of the remains, and she asked him if, while examining the debris, he had noticed a diamond ring. Bill laughed and said he would have reported it if he had seen something of obvious value, and in turn he asked her why the bank was interested in the case. She told him the ring was part of the victim's estate, and if it was missing the bank would have to report it as an insurance loss. He thought for a moment, and asked the caller if she were aware that the deceased woman had been eaten by her dogs. Yes, she said, she was.

Bill thought about it a moment longer. "Well, I'll tell you what I'm going to do. I'll call the sheriff's department and ask them to send someone back out there to pick up all the dog droppings they can find on the property. If the ring passed through one of the animals that ate her, that's where it would be, somewhere out in the backyard."

The banker said she would be very grateful for any help Bill could give her. Accordingly, two days later a couple of large plastic bags of dog feces were delivered by an obviously disgruntled deputy to Bill's office in Knoxville; one weighed 10 pounds, and the other 11.

The request had not won any friends at the sheriff's department, so before the deputy left, Bill did everything possible to assure him that his efforts were appreciated and that the scientist/students in Bill's

Department of Forensic Anthropology were not going to get off any easier than the police in dealing with the unappetizing task before them. He announced to all within hearing that the feces would have to be placed in trays and allowed to soften in water overnight, and the following morning the whole staff would sort carefully through the delivery by hand. The policeman smiled in grim satisfaction. But when the deputy left, Bill knew he had traded one bad situation for another as he found himself facing a roomful of sullen graduate students. "Come to think of it," he said, "maybe a better way to handle it would be to use X-ray."

So that's what they did, just as he had intended all along. When the film was processed, the material that showed up on the X-rays surprised even Bill: paper clips, bobby pins, hairpins, nails, three teeth that matched the dental record of the owner, even a painted toenail still wrapped in a section of pantyhose. It was an amazing testament to the feeding zeal and digestive capability of three hungry dogs.

He went back to the house twice afterwards with his graduate students and collected even more droppings, but the ring was never found.

Bill never tells this story without adding a postscript. The woman had two daughters who lived in another part of the country, and when her estate was finally settled, it turned out that neither of them was particularly anxious to take home the three dogs who had eaten their mother. This presented a quandary as they had been family pets for a long time, so a decision was made to advertise in the local newspaper and put them up for adoption.

"There were no takers there, either," Bill says. "Everyone in the county knew these were the dogs who had eaten their owner. I guess people figured it would be hard to have any one of them look at you, even when his tail was wagging, without wondering if he was sizing you up for his next meal."

Maybe so. But unless the dogs' digestive systems were X-rayed along with their droppings, I should think there was a slight chance one of them might be worth $7,000.

10

HEADS WILL ROLL

The first forensic case on which I ever testified in court was in Pensacola, Florida. Even if it hadn't been a personal landmark, it would have stayed with me in vivid detail because of the terrible tragedy behind the case, and the bizarre turns it took in its course through the Florida system of criminal justice.

The victim was a young woman of twenty from Massachusetts. She was last seen alive walking near a shopping mall in mid-September 1977, and although there was no solid evidence she had been abducted, there was even less reason to believe she had disappeared voluntarily. The question appeared to be settled six months later when a man walked into the County Sheriff's Office carrying her head in a plastic bag.

The man, a bartender aged twenty-seven, said he had found the skull, and the rest of the body, just over the state line in Alabama, and that he had been led to the site as the result of having witnessed the murder of the young woman in a dream.

Dreams can play a major role in police work, especially in the solving of murders, but almost never in the ways depicted in *The Twilight Zone*. People who are burdened with terrible guilt often feel the need to lay that burden down. Since the consequences of an outright confession are likely to be nearly as awful as the crime, they may try to get out of that double bind by inventing a proxy. The police refer to these stories as "dream confessions," and even in the absence of more substantial admissions by the accused, juries have been known to convict the "dreamers" on the evidence inferred from their testimony that they were present at the crime. In this case, no such inference was necessary; just a short time after floating his story, the bartender admitted to the girl's abduction, rape, and murder.

In due course, the rest of the remains were recovered from Alabama and sent up to Washington. Inside the cardboard carton were several paper sacks containing most of the skeleton. I laid out the bones on my examining table, setting aside a separate package containing the hair, along with a fragment of an unrelated animal rib.

One of the first things I noticed was evidence of a gunshot wound in the skull. The apparent entry point was a circular perforation 12 mm across at the junction of the right occipital and temporal bones; the exit point was a larger, more irregular hole in the left parietal bone near the front of the left parietal, with fractures radiating from both sites—a pattern suggesting the bullet entered the lower right side of the skull and exited through the top left.

Except for a bit of soil adhering to the left shoulder blade, a pine needle on the skull, and some adult and larval-stage arthropods feeding on the strips of soft tissue, the bones were relatively clean. Some had become separated from the rest of the skeleton, but a good number were still articulated. There was evidence of animal activity, but beyond the bulletholes the only other indications of trauma were a slight, well-remodeled fracture line on one left lower leg bone and some minor distortion on the other, signs of a probable fracture of the left ankle several years before death.

After determining from my own observations that the remains were those of a female, about twenty-one, Caucasian, 5'4", dead more than a month and less than a year, I compared those results with information furnished by the Florida police on the missing girl. There was only one discrepancy, and that was between the skeletal teeth and the missing girl's dental record. The records showed that the maxillary left third molar had been extracted a couple of years earlier. Although that tooth was not present in the skull, the sharp borders of the alveolus in that area were signs the extraction was unhealed, suggesting that the tooth was lost either postmortem or shortly before death. However, the tooth directly opposite it on the other side of the mouth was missing as well, even though it was not marked as missing on the girl's dental charts, and the extent of bone remodeling suggested it had been extracted a long time before death, possibly several years. I suggested the discrepancy was explainable by the dentist having made a common error in distinguishing left from right.

The victim's file also contained hospital records showing an ankle fracture consistent with the alterations I had observed on the back of the left distal tibia and fibula. It was an unusual spot for a break, the kind of thing that can result only if the foot is in a particular position such as stepping off a curb. Larry Angel examined the remains as well and agreed with my conclusions. There was little doubt the skeleton was the missing girl.

At the time of this murder, there had been only one execution in the United States since the Supreme Court lifted the moratorium on the death penalty in 1976. By the time the case came to trial in 1978, however, the number of condemned murderers in Florida jails was accumulating faster than in any other state but Texas. If the reinstatement of capital punishment was clearly doing nothing to reduce the number of murders in those states permitting it, it certainly appeared to be cutting down on the number of confessions. The man with the head in the bag changed his mind about what he had done and entered a plea of not guilty. Subsequently, despite objections from the prosecution, the judge decided that the confession could not be used against the defendant in court.

Accordingly, I was invited down to Florida with two other forensic scientists: an old FBI Laboratory veteran named Fred Wallace, for many years a special agent with the Hair and Fiber Unit and the Bureau's liaison with the Smithsonian; and Dr. Marie Nylan, a specialist from the National Institute of Dental Research of the National Institutes of Health who had made further matches for a positive identification from the victim's teeth. Our testimony had nothing to do with innocence or guilt. We were called upon simply to testify on the identity of the victim, and to prove that she was the missing girl.

Florida does not allow a defendant's confession to be admitted into evidence until it has been demonstrated that a crime was committed, and that requires three things: proof that a victim is dead; proof of the dead person's identity; and proof that the death was caused by a criminal agency or resulted from the criminal act of an individual. The prosecution won on the first two tests. But regardless of the bulletholes in the skull, Escambia County Circuit Judge William Rowley decided the evidence of criminal agency fell short of proof of murder.

Despite the "dream" that had led the police to the body, despite the confession, despite the forensic proof that the victim was indeed the missing girl and that she had suffered a gunshot wound to the head, the case was dismissed by Judge Rowley on a technical interpretation of the law. The man who confessed to the crime walked away, and the case can never be brought against him again.

The moment that stands out most clearly in my memory was the scene in the courthouse anteroom where we and other witnesses were waiting to testify. There was a young man pacing back and forth at the back, and even though this was my first case in court, it was clear to me he was suffering from something far more serious than a case of pretrial jitters; the strain on his face and everything else about him spoke of a barely controlled rage. Someone whispered to me that the victim had been his fiancée, and that she had been murdered shortly before they were to have been married.

I glanced over at the young man from time to time as I continued to wait, thinking that by contrast my own involvement in this case was so dispassionate, so removed from consequence or sorrow. I found myself wondering how long it takes before the turbulent wake that rises to the surface behind a crime like murder is made calm, before the fury and the heartbreak are washed away and none of its victims is still in pain, before the waters close again with forgetting. I hoped for this young man's sake that it might happen in his lifetime, but in watching him I doubted that it would. When I heard the outcome of the trial, that doubt became a near certainty.

Not all dream confessions lead to the same result. A couple of years later, when a middle-aged handyman named Andy Maltais was questioned in the murder of a nineteen-year-old prostitute in Fall River, Massachusetts, it's remotely possible he knew how successful this ploy had been for the bartender in Florida. On a bitter cold winter's day, Maltais led a small parade of law enforcement officials to the field where the body had been found several days earlier. Maltais began to share his dream vision of the killing. Playing to an all-star audience, which included the district attorney, an assistant DA, detectives from both the state and local police, and two stenographers, he reconstructed the murder in lurid detail.

"I could see this man standing on the ground. I was up high in the sky. She kept saying, 'Forgive me, Andy.'... It was cold out, like today. He had a leather coat on. After the first hit, she couldn't talk anymore.

He was constantly hitting her with what he had in his hands. He kept hitting her.... The Devil's got the best of her. I hope she goes to heaven."

No one present at Andy's recital was indelicate enough to suggest they didn't believe this was a dream; they were playing out the line, hoping he'd tell them more details of the murder, details that would have been available only to an eyewitness. But the bitter cold was working against the mutual charade, and apparently Maltais misinterpreted the desire of the police and the DA to get back inside a warm place as signs they doubted his story. When he sensed he was losing his audience, in a last-minute bid for credence he walked over to a pile of concrete curbing blocks. "The rock [in the killer's hands] was square at the sides."

Every policeman there immediately forgot how cold it was. The best-kept secret of the case was that it was one of those curbing blocks, and not a rock, that had been used to kill the girl. To verify the findings of the autopsy, several chunks of concrete recovered from the murder site had been sent down to the FBI Laboratories, and scientists there had identified pieces of the victim's hair, samples of her blood—and pieces of her fingernails, from when she had defended herself against the blows—imbedded in the crushed, powdery aggregate. Maltais lingered at the rock pile, then turned back to his interrogators. "I sense a murder weapon here," he said. "It might have been a piece of concrete."

Maltais dreamed himself into a life sentence. He died in prison four years ago.

The killing of which Maltais was convicted was one of three related Fall River murders that took place in the winter of 1979–80. All the victims were young prostitutes but, unlike Andy's case, the other two involved elements of ritual torture and Satanism. The last of the three was a girl named Karen Marsden. Her partial skull, which is all the police ever found of her body, was delivered to my office by Fred Wallace and another agent in the early spring of 1980.

At that point, there was still some question about the identity of the victim. Despite strong circumstantial evidence, including the hair and scalp that had been pulled from her head before she died, as well as clothing and some items of jewelry, provably Karen Marsden's, recovered from the murder site, police had no direct connection between this severed head and the missing girl. Everything below the eye orbits had been carefully and deliberately broken away and disposed elsewhere. There was no mandible, no upper or lower teeth, no eyes, and little skin. The technical term for a fragmentary skull of this sort is a calvarium.

The police and the district attorney had an obvious stake in proving the identity of the victim, but at that point the best I could say was that the skull had belonged to a female between fifteen and thirty-five years of age. Most of the soft tissue had already been removed by medical examiners in Massachusetts, including the brain and meningial membrane, but there was still some evidence of moisture in what remained. The remnant had been found in a deeply wooded area near the coast, and even though it was May, I knew that the seasons change more slowly beside the ocean and the process of decay and drying was not as predictable as in places further inland. I said only that the murder appeared to have been relatively recent, but that an estimate of time since death would not be possible.

It was clear that all the disfigurement represented an attempt to conceal the identity of the victim. Almost everyone knows a body can often be identified by its teeth, so all the teeth had been removed. More sophisticated criminals also may be aware of the arts of facial reproduction and photographic superimposition; since so many of the facial bones had also been deliberately destroyed, it appeared unlikely that either technique would produce enough evidence to convince a jury, or even for me to offer a reasonable opinion. But if the calvarium had been left behind to taunt the police with the impossibility of linking it to the suspected victim, there was a remote chance the killers had made a big mistake.

If there had ever been an X-ray of Karen Marsden's head while living, I felt there was a good chance I could match the frontal sinus with the same pattern in an X-ray of the calvarium skull. The frontal sinus is a filigree butterfly embedded in the bone behind and above the brow ridge, and it is as varied and unique in each of us as a snowflake or a fingerprint. The technique had been used in court a couple of times to establish identity in estate cases, although to the best of my knowledge that kind of a match had never been admitted in a capital trial. When I returned the skull to Fred Wallace with my report, I told him a comparison X-ray would be helpful. A short time later, the chief medical examiner of Rhode Island told Massachusetts police the same thing.

The likelihood of anyone needing a skull X-ray is very low, especially an apparently healthy young woman of twenty-two, and after an initial canvass of local hospitals and clinics proved fruitless, the district attorney decided to go to court with just the evidence then in hand. The murder trial of Karen's principal alleged killer was set for March 1981. I marked the date on my calendar, but not with any deep conviction that my meager testimony would add much to the case. Over the intervening months, as I was caught up in the rush of work on digs in Ecuador and new responsibilities as chair of the Department of Anthropology, this case and the coming trial settled even lower in my horizon.

All that changed dramatically in the week before the trial began. The Rhode Island medical examiner's suggestion had been given a lot of weight by the Massachusetts police, and particularly by the ME's counterpart in neighboring Bristol County, where the skull was discovered. The day before I was to leave for Boston, I received word that a medical X-ray of Karen Marsden's head had been located at the last possible minute; it had been taken just months before her death in the same hospital where her ravaged skull was subsequently autopsied. Comparison X-rays were now being taken in Rhode Island at the same angle and focus, and I could expect to see both sets of radiographs—of the sinus pattern in the living girl and in the calvarium fragment— when I arrived in the central Massachusetts city where the trial was being held.

That city was Fitchburg, picked because the location was far enough from the murder site to escape the taint of publicity that had attached to this case, by now the most spectacular Fall River killing since the trial of Lizzie Borden. A number of the witnesses were billeted in a motel on the outskirts of town, and when I arrived I learned that Paul Fitzgerald, the state police detective in charge of the skull, had still not arrived with the X-rays. It was not until long after supper that he finally pulled in from Rhode Island, bearing the freshly developed radiographs in a large manila envelope and the slides for projecting them in a pair of circular trays.

We walked into the bathroom of my motel unit and turned on the light over the sink. Holding the X-rays side by side, I saw it immediately: the frontal sinus in each radiograph was distinguished by an anomaly unlike any I had ever seen before. In both the medical X-ray, which was marked "Karen Marsden," and the forensic X-ray of the skull found in the woods, the butterfly had only one wing; where the other wing should have been, there was only a smudge. "They're the same skull, no doubt about it," I told the eager detective. "You've identified your victim."

The next day I made the same positive identification in court. That killer, too, was sentenced to life without parole. The story of all three

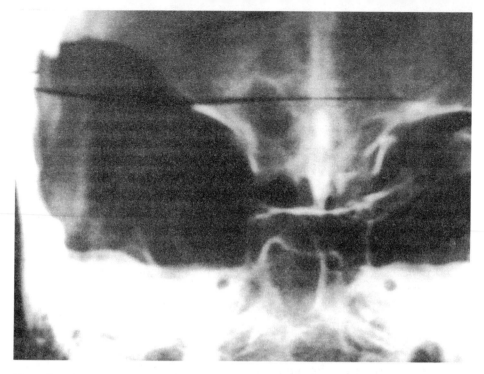

Though police suspected the calvarium above was all that remained of Karen Marsden, it could not be proved until an x-ray taken of Marsden during life (below) showed the same unique configuration in the sinus area. This identification was crucial evidence in the trial of Carl Drew.

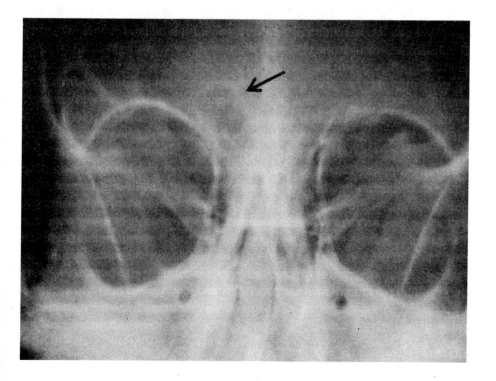

Fall River murders supplies the plot of the book *Mortal Remains*.

Marsden's was a case in which a little luck rewarded the hard work of investigators—a mere fragment of a body, apparently totally fragmented in an effort to disguise the identity of the victim, had been enough to prove the victim's identity. But another case in Texas proved that identifying characteristics can lead nowhere.

This was a severed head, partly protruding from a ripped garbage bag. It was discovered by three teenagers in the middle of a horse pasture in southeast Texas. A local pathologist concluded that it was a black male between twenty-five and thirty-five years old who had been decapitated at the fifth vertebra with a hacksaw. When it arrived in my office a month later, I disagreed with all the pathologist's conclusions except for the sex.

The morphology of the skull suggested the victim was white, with a probable admixture of other racial groups. The degree of suture closure and the condition of the teeth pointed to an age of thirty to forty. The vertebrae showed clear signs of sharp-force injury, as from a cleaver, hatchet, or large knife. A variety of cut marks on two contiguous vertebrae revealed at least five separate cutting actions and maybe more. The sixth cervical vertebra had been sheared completely through its horizontal axis, which probably resulted in nearly complete severance of the neck.

On the skull itself, there were other indications of trauma which may have been related to cause of death. There was an irregular perforation about 8 × 6 mm in the occipital bone, with fractures radiating out toward the base of the brain stem and across to the right margin of the occipital bone, causing the bone surrounding the right inner ear to separate from the rest of the skull. Other fractures extended forward across the right side of the face to the floor of the right eye orbit. A lifting or bending of the bone in the perforated area indicated the trauma was inflicted at about the time of death. There was no tissue adhering to the bone, no odor, and the skull had been bleached white—indicating that it had been exposed to the sun for a considerable length of time, despite the fact that it was partially inside the split garbage bag when found.

In particular, there were two aspects of the skull which seemed to hold promise for an early identification. The more obvious was the extensive dental restoration, including three teeth with gold alloy crowns and a fourth with stainless steel, which would provide proof positive if they could be matched with dental X-rays by a forensic odontologist. The second was subtler. There was evidence of a slight overbite, and associated asymmetry in the lower margin of the nasal aperture, which meant that in life, the left side of the victim's nose would have been slightly lower than the right. But eight years later the skull sits enigmatically on the desk of a detective who will not give up the case. It still has not yielded up its secret.

The bleaching of a skull from the sun can often supply useful insights to a body's postmortem history, and the process can occur in unlikely places. In one case from Nebraska, the bleaching took place while the body was at the bottom of an unused cistern.

That story began in 1975, when a young woman of nineteen, last seen at a party hosted by a Hell's Angels motorcycle gang, was reported by her family to be missing. Police immediately assumed foul play, and over the next several years dug for her body on one unsuccessful lead after another. Nine years later, it was recovered by chance, when authorities at an airport near Omaha happened to raise the lid on the cistern. After a positive ID was established by a local dentist, the skeleton was turned over to the FBI.

When the body had made its way across Pennsylvania Avenue to my examining table, I immediately noted two unusual features, both on the skull. There was a whitening and deep etching of the bones in the facial area, with bone loss in the middle of the forehead producing a roughly triangular hole of about an inch on each side through the exterior of the frontal sinus. The eroded area was confined to the outer table of the skull, and the interior sinus wall was intact. The margins of the eroded area were very distinct, covering much of the face and lower left side of the cranial vault, as well as extending down across the upper jaw, the occlusal plane (where the teeth overlap), and over the front of the lower jaw. The condition of the teeth was unusual as well: it was as though the enamel had decalcified. Dr. Norman Sperber, chief forensic dentist for San Diego, who also examined the skull, said that clinical decalcification is commonly seen near the gums and between the teeth. It is a condition that shows up from time to time with people who eat too many lemons, or don't follow proper techniques of oral hygiene, but not to the extent seen here. All of the teeth were a curious, chalky white. Sperber and I agreed that the corroded condition of the skull, mandible, and teeth was inconsistent with a body lying undisturbed for nine years. It was obvious that a corrosive agent had been applied while the body was still fleshed.

The second unusual feature was two whitened circles on the frontal and upper parietals near the midline, well outside the area affected by the acid. The one on the frontal had very even margins and

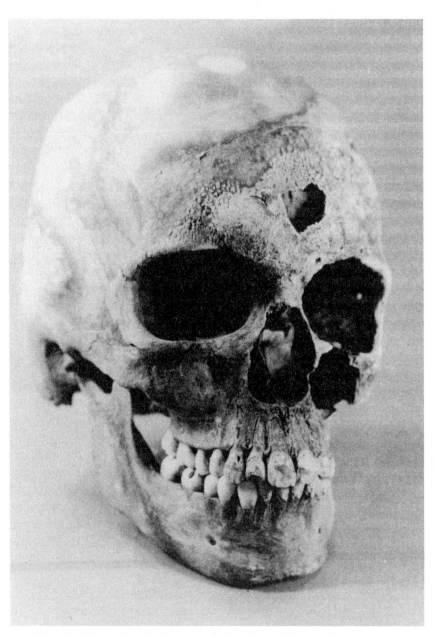

The skull from the Omaha cistern, showing evidence of corrosion.

was about the size of a quarter, and the other was about half that in diameter. The bleaching did not extend through the bone to the inner surface, and there were no signs of erosion or abrasion.

In early 1986, a biker was brought to trial for the girl's murder. As in the Marsden case, an attempt had been made to hide the girl's identity: a witness suggested that lye or a similar substance had been poured on her face after she was killed.

Because one of the heaviest parts is supported by one of the most fragile, when a body disarticulates, the head will often fall off of the neck and go its separate way. Sometimes, when the remains are at the top of an incline, for example, it travels so far that it is the only part to be recovered. The path traced by the caustic substance on the skeleton of this victim provided courtroom evidence of a phenomenon associated with decaying bodies that has been long known by anthropologists: if the corpse is left in a certain position, the head eventually will roll.

In this case, witnesses testified that the body was laid in the cistern shortly after death, and it was evident from photographs taken at recovery that it was lying on its back with the legs extended and the head propped up against the cement wall. Predictably, once the supporting soft tissue had decomposed, the skull had rolled off the skeleton and separated from the lower jaw. By matching corrosion patterns on teeth in both the upper and lower jaws, it became clear that the acid had been applied while the body was all in one piece.

While the bleaching of the facial bones was caused by a corrosive agent, the circular white spots proved to be another matter. But once again these were a record of the same pattern of disarticulation. The cistern had been capped with a heavy metal lid, a manhole cover, which had a number of circular perforations to permit the flow of air and water once the cistern was in use. Two of those holes were in a position to spotlight the skull for a few minutes every clear day, when the sun was in exactly the right alignment for its rays to strike directly. After many months, the sun bleached spots on the top of the skull. The slight asymmetry of the larger circle probably represented a shift in the position of the skull as the process of disarticulation continued; it even could have recorded the slippage that resulted from the falling away of the mandible.

I remember when the deputy county attorney, Sam Cooper, brought the skeleton to the FBI for examination. He impressed me with his concern for the victim, explaining how she had come from a well-respected family and had certainly done nothing to invite the

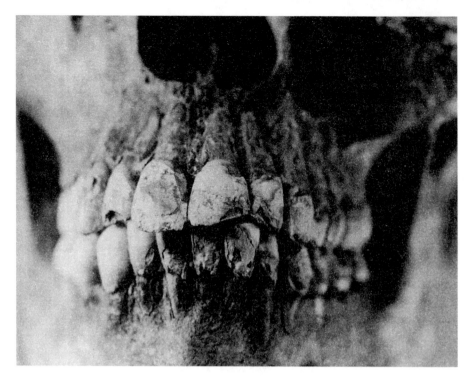

Details of the Omaha skull, showing decalcification of the teeth and bleached spots on the cranium.

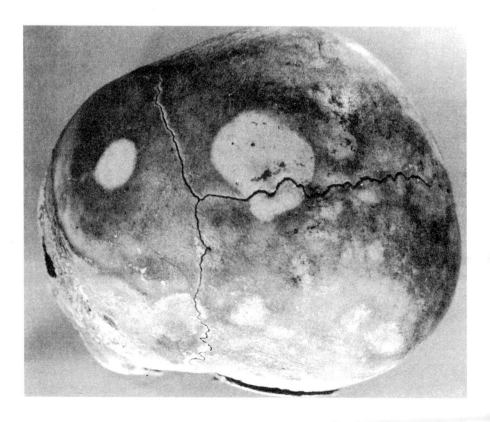

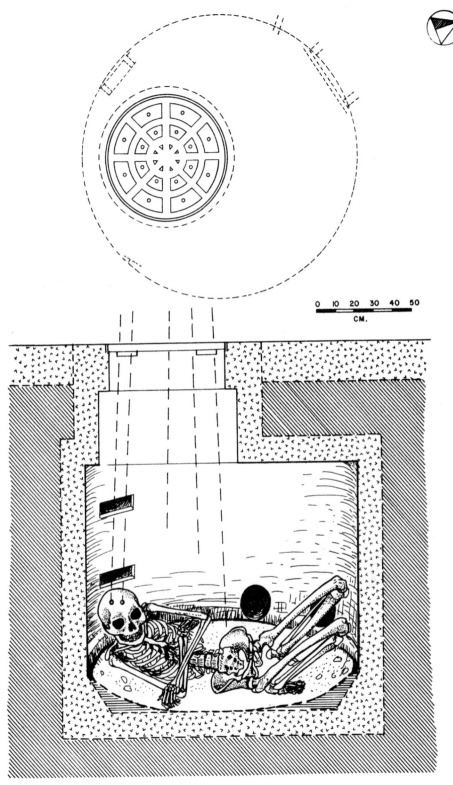

An artist's conception of the skeleton resting in the cistern with the manhole
cover above. The dashed lines represent light striking the skeleton.

tragedy that had befallen her. He also described a tentative scenario which the local police on the case had worked out to explain some of the skeletal changes, particularly the pitting of the facial area and a blackening of the bones of the legs. (That theory is described in Chapter 11.)

I remember that the state sent me a first-class ticket, which was just about the only time I can remember that happening, and I felt very important during the course of the elegant trip out to Nebraska, all the more for finding myself in the company of Jesse Jackson, who was just across the aisle during the leg from Washington to Kansas City. But despite the splendid setting and favored treatment, I found my thoughts traveling back to the case and the vague, persistent unease that attached to the prospect of confronting a courtroom full of irate Hell's Angels.

That unease swiftly descended to a short moment of more tangible anxiety when I stepped out of the entry gate and into the airport lounge in Omaha. Right in front of me was a group of obvious bikers, complete with scuffed black leather jackets, chains, bandanas, patches, lots of facial hair, and sullen demeanors. I was seized by the thought that this was a welcoming committee. But by the time I got to the baggage claim, I found myself smiling, partly at the small rush of adrenalin, and partly in comic relief. I had passed by without attracting so much as a glance.

The facts in this case proved to be just as potent as the suppositions. On the evidence presented in court, Thomas Nesbitt was convicted of first-degree murder.

One final skull story is an unsolved 1978 case from Wisconsin, included here mostly in the hope that a reader might recognize the victim. The skull, complete with mandible and the first cervical vertebra, was recovered that summer near the town of Knapp, in a rural area about 100 yards from the road in the woods. Some 10 yards away police found three plastic garbage bags in which the skull had been wrapped before animals pulled it loose. The bags were bound in light chain and wire, and a machete, probably the instrument of decapitation, had been left sticking into the ground. There were no clues to the victim's identity or what had happened to the rest of his body.

A colleague estimated that the skull belonged to a white male over forty-five years old who wore a small stud-type earring. No other part of the body was ever found, and no one recognized him as a result of our reproduction. Here's one last try.

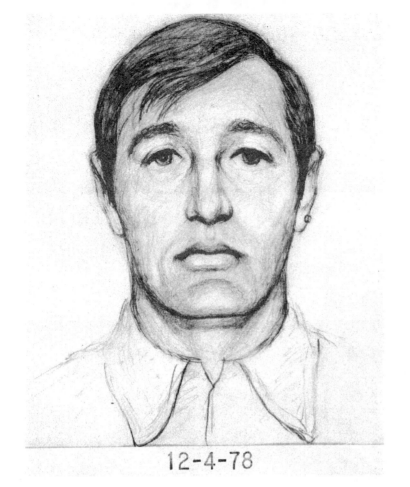

12-4-78

11

BURNING QUESTIONS

Fire may be the nearest thing to magic in the natural world. It is one of the few metaphors—for ardor, for rage, for irreversible change—whose nature is itself metaphorical; that is, it changes the shape of what it touches. Anyone who has sat at hearthside on a winter's night or by a bonfire on the beach in summer knows the hypnotic effect of flames. There is something endlessly astonishing about solid matter disappearing as we watch, its molecules reorganizing themselves into gases and ash, releasing the heat of the sun that gave the matter its substance, undoing the effects of time, consuming the tangible past.

Fire is so efficient at erasing things, it is very popular as a means of hiding the evidence of murder. The precise degree of that popularity will have to remain a matter for speculation; this is not an area with a lot of testimonials or in which success is inclined to advertise. But it would be my guess, educated by examining dozens of cases in which the attempts to hide a murder by this means failed, that it is considerably overrated as an aid to criminals. I have never known of a single cremation, not even the most professional one, that has succeeded in consuming all the remains of a human body. And far from disguising a murder, in many non-professional attempts the cremation itself provided the first clue that a crime had been committed.

Conversely, probably the first reason fire succeeds in an illicit purpose is that investigators are certain to miss a lot of the evidence unless they have been specially trained in what to look for. Bill Bass had a case recently in Tennessee which proves both those points and which stands as a masterpiece of forensic detective work.

Bill was called to the scene a week after the fire, based on a tip to police by neighbors that the owner had not been seen by anyone in the time since the rural home had burned to the ground. When Bill and his team arrived, all that was left of the house was the foundation, filled with charred debris. They carefully worked their way down through the ashes, and by the time they had excavated to the cellar floor they found the charred remains of a skeleton.

In cases like this one, where the incineration is nearly total, the remains are usually very fragmentary. The firing process produces dramatic changes in the size and shape of each bone. We know from controlled experiments that the amount of shrinkage varies from 1 to 25 percent, depending on bone density and the temperature and duration of the fire. We also know that most bone shrinkage occurs in the temperature range between 700 and 900 degrees C.; little occurs below that minimum, and after the progression within those brackets, little occurs when the heat goes higher. We also know that extensive shrinkage is accompanied by changes in color, first to black, then gray, and then on to white. When it comes to identification of remains, examiners working with white fragments of bone must allow for shrinkage of up to 25 percent; this is also important when sizes of bones are used to infer sex and age.

Also on the cellar floor, still associated with the whitened remains of the spinal column, Bill's forensic crew identified the flat, melted residue of a bullet. But as they excavated further, they found that they were dealing only with the lower half of the skeleton, ending at about the middle of the chest. There were no arms, no shoulders, no scapulae, no cervical spine, and no skull.

This is a situation that sometimes occurs in a house fire, when a body that starts off on an upper floor breaks apart as the burning upper structure collapses to the ground floor or, when one exists, to the cellar. But that was not what had happened here. The body had literally cooked onto the cement floor of the basement, with no debris in between.

"The only other explanation we could think of," Bill says, "was an explosion."

When he offered his theory to the police, they verified that neighbors had reported hearing a large blast just before the start of the fire. The forensic crew continued digging. About eight feet from the thoracic end of the charred lower half, they found the skull and shoulders, still connected to each other, and similarly welded to the cellar floor. The source of the explosion clearly had been under the victim's chest: it had blown the body apart at the same time it ignited the fire that burned down the house.

Based on these discoveries, the police developed a solid case against a local handyman who had been hired to redecorate the victim's house and had killed him after stealing his savings.

It is highly unlikely that either the discovery of the cremated body among the debris from this conflagration, much less the reconstruction of events from the evidence revealed there, would ever have been possible were it not for the specialized skills that Bill Bass and his crew of forensic anthropologists brought to the investigation. When the suspect began to talk, Bill's scenario proved to be astonishingly accurate.

The man had indeed been shot. The killer had then blown up the body with a stick of dynamite and burned down the house to hide the crime.

Dynamite and fire had been the last resort. The only part of the story Bill had missed was one he couldn't possibly have predicted. The case of the old woman near Nashville who died at home and had been eaten by her hungry pets was well known in Tennessee. After the shooting, the killer had brought in some dogs and left them in the cellar without food. In this instance, the dogs balked.

"There are two good things about this case," Bill reminisced later in an interview with the BBC. "One is the sequence being exactly what we had arrived at with the scientific evidence. The second, and the thing that really touched me the most, was that after I had testified in court, the family came to me outside the courtroom and thanked me many, many times—for my expertise, and for getting involved in helping convict the person who had killed their son. What this says to me is that as an academic person I'm doing a service to the public that really is of value."

One of my own earliest cremation cases was that of a body discovered in a burned automobile in Macedonia, Ohio, in 1982. The fire was so intense that the automobile had been almost completely destroyed, and most of what was left of the corpse were parts of the liver, lungs,

Cracking and longitudinal splitting in these cremated bones indicate that they were dry when burned.

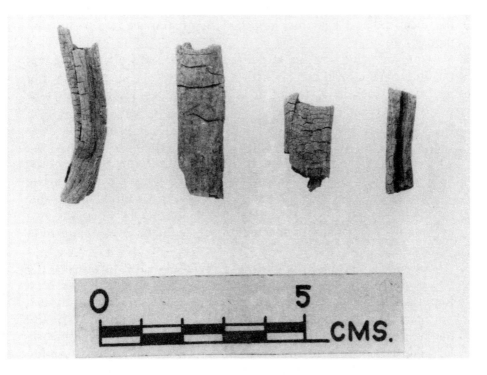

Pronounced warping, transverse fractures, and irregular lengthwise splitting indicate that these remains were cremated while the bones were still covered with flesh.

heart, kidney, bones, and some charred tissue, an aggregate that weighed in at the autopsy at 63 pounds. Even the hottest fire consumes a body unevenly, however, and some parts were in far better states of preservation than others.

The police thought the remains belonged to an ex-convict who had had several teeth extracted while serving time in a state reformatory back in 1953, while still in his teens. The history was useful, because the charred skull contained an admixture of real and artificial teeth. The dentures, furthermore, appeared to be made of a porcelain consistent with the materials employed years earlier in the reformatory dental clinic.

Even though this was a neat match between two bits of a larger puzzle, it wasn't enough for a positive ID. And it didn't tell the police how the victim had died.

The only part of the body that was sent to me for examination was the right femur, the long bone of the upper leg. It was well preserved, compared to what I read of the rest of the remains, with a fair amount of charred and moist soft tissue still adhering. I inferred from its condition that the time of death was fairly recent—certainly within a month. The reason I was asked to look at this particular bone was that the local medical examiner hoped it might provide a clue to perimortem trauma.

One such clue was the fact that the lower third of the bone was missing, having been cut off with a shearing action of some kind of instrument such as a cleaver or an ax—although in special circumstances a violent automobile accident could produce similar results. But there was more: the bottom portion of what remained was badly charred and blackened. The charring was superficial, but covered the whole sheared surface. By contrast, the burning in that portion of the body had not been sufficiently prolonged to destroy a commensurate amount of the associated soft tissue. Based on that contrast, I was able to advise the police of the temporal relationship between the two events: the bone had been sheared off before the body was exposed to the fire.

The letter accompanying the bone did not describe how the car fire had been started, but on inquiry I learned that the vehicle had been found in the parking lot behind Forepaugh's restaurant and had not been involved in any kind of collision. Police determined the fire had been set. This information greatly increased the likelihood that the leg bone had been severed in a separate violent act, and that the fire had been intended to cover the crime.

The police accepted my estimates of sex, stature, and the use of microscopic techniques for getting at age (between forty and sixty-eight, probably around fifty-four), coupled with dental data and the history of the case, as proof of the victim's identity. Based on that same information, they also determined that he had been murdered. But that's as far as it went. There has never been an arrest, and although the case is still open it is no longer active. Just about the only thing that's changed is that Forepaugh's restaurant is no longer there. It too burned to the ground in the summer of 1990.

Sometimes fire is secondary to some much larger event, such as a plane crash, and plays a relatively minor role, compared to the trauma of impact, in disguising or obliterating potential forensic data. In 1984, when federal agents found skeletal remains scattered 60 feet across an area of dense undergrowth in Mississippi near the site where a drug plane had crashed a year earlier, it was assumed that the body parts may have represented all three of the plane's crew. There was charring on the left frontal and left parietal bones of a skull, and on a left femur, but despite the burning I was able to estimate sex, age, stature, and race, and to determine that all of the bones which had been collected were likely from one individual.

Conversely, fire can play a larger role in some situations than may be obvious at first glance. In a case from a national park in the Rocky Mountains, some hikers found what appeared to be a concentration of bone fragments at an altitude of 12,500 feet, along with some dental debris, which they gathered together and presented to an anthropologist at the local university. The pieces were identified as skull and rib fragments, probably human, and an almost complete set of old and worn human false teeth. The examiner said they appeared to have been left in the open, exposed to extremes of weather, for several years.

In that time, however, the park had no lost climbers, hikers, or campers, and there were no reports of missing persons from any of the surrounding area that could possibly match the remains. The hikers returned to the recovery site with a park ranger. They found more fragments in three concentrations over a strip of ground about 18 inches wide by 5½ feet long, and after the ranger photographed the area overall and in close-up, the remaining materials were collected as well. A National Park Service police investigator examined the combined finds. He thought he detected tiny metal fragments on some of the bone chips, and requested that the FBI check them for evidence of gunshot.

After unwrapping the package, I weighed out the bone fragments at 340 grams, or about three quarters of a pound. They ranged in size from dust to a length of 31 mm, small enough that if it weren't for the teeth and metal, they almost certainly would have escaped detection in a rocky setting. I recognized fragments of the skull and long bones, and they appeared to be human. Two of the cranial fragments showed open sutures; although they were adult, they argued against extreme old age at death. Beyond that, there was no way to estimate age, sex, stature, race, or cause of death. I found no sign of metal in the bones.

Beyond a certain point, bones crack when they are burned, and the cremation of dried bones produces different fracture patterns than cremation of bones with flesh around them. Burning of dry bones causes cracking or "checking" on the surface and longitudinal splitting, but little warping or twisting. Burning of "green" or flesh-covered bones frequently creates curved transverse fractures—an appearance that Bill Bass has characterized as "a stack of wooden nickels"—along with irregular longitudinal splitting and marked warping. If the bones have undergone extreme combustion, their fracture patterns can reveal whether the individual was cremated in the flesh.

All the fragments from the mountainside showed advanced calcination, the whitening which results from prolonged extreme heat. Where they could be seen, tiny fracture patterns suggested that the individual had been burned in the flesh, which ruled out the possibility that somehow a collection of bones had been thrown into a campfire or otherwise ignited at that high altitude. I looked carefully at the photographs of the recovery site, but could find absolutely no evidence of open burning anywhere in the area.

What these tiny fragments suggested, supported by the picture of the scatter pattern on the mountainside, was not a crime at all. To me, they were evidence of the last faithful act of a friend or spouse, following a professional cremation, in offering the ashes of a loved one back to nature.

Another possible instance of such an offering took place in a cemetery, this time in the Midwest. A maintenance worker noticed freshly disturbed sod above two old graves, and he called a policeman to be his witness while he probed the soil. In each plot, about two feet below the surface, he found a sealed plastic bag containing what appeared to be burned bones. No one had been given permission to bury a body at either of the gravesites, but the packaging and the shovel marks on the disturbed surface areas suggested both burials had been recent and from the same source.

I opened the bags in my office and found a mixture of fragmentary bone, soil, organic debris, dust, and associated materials. Close examination of the bone fragments showed that they were human, and I could tell from their fracture patterns and twisted shapes that they had been burned with flesh attached, usually an indicator of professional cremation. Differences in coloration and fragment size also indicated the two burials represented separate burnings, and that two individuals were involved. That reduced the likelihood of a prank, but deepened the mystery. My guess would be that both were cases in which the bereaved wanted a cemetery burial for a family member or loved one, but couldn't afford the burial plot. Even with guesses, the study told us nothing at all about who they had been, and the cases are still open.

Not every calcined or blackened bone got that way as the result of fire. There are numerous man-made and natural circumstances which create a condition of pseudoburning, and some of these false clues have misled forensic examiners. One that had the potential for such a result, but was recognized instead for its true cause, was the Hell's Angels murder victim described in the previous chapter. The acid had burned the exposed portions of bone and in some respects mimicked the effects of fire. The knee areas of the femora of this individual were almost black, and at first glance they too looked as though they had been burned. There was some evidence of a fire in the basement of the house from which she disappeared, and some wooden steps were missing from the cellar stairs. Authorities speculated the killers might have used the cellar steps to fuel a fire designed to destroy the body. It was a good theory, but the body hadn't been burned. Even natural processes as mundane as mildewing can be mistaken for charring. The black color had been produced by fungal organisms growing in the moist environment of her cistern grave.

One way to eliminate doubt in such matters is for the forensics specialist to examine the remains while the body is still smoking.

Bill Bass has had a number of cases in which the victims have been delivered direct from fires, and others in which he has conducted his examinations on the site of the conflagration. Because of his experience in this area (among many others), I have been fortunate in obtaining his participation in our annual week-long seminars on forensic anthropology at the Smithsonian, and he has advised a number of police and fire departments around the country in what to look for in searching a fire's aftermath.

The most common cause of death in fires is not flame but smoke inhalation; frequently the bodies of victims show little if any effect of heat or burning. When a body has been exposed to sufficient flame to cause charring, even though it seldom is enough to consume more than a fraction of the soft tissue, the effect of the heat can be shrinkage of the tendons and connective tissues. When that happens, it clenches the hands into fists and draws up the arms and legs into flexed postures which are variously characterized as the pugilistic position (flexed to 90 degrees, so the arms are held out like a boxer's), or the fetal position, which is more acute. Firefighters searching burned residential structures look first for upraised knees and forearms amidst the debris of a blaze. In more advanced burning, the flexure relaxes and unless something else is in the way the body returns to an outstretched posture.

I frequently see burn victims as well in archaeological material, but as a rule after a considerably longer time since death, usually several hundred years. Even my forensic cases involving fire tend to be relatively ancient, but there have been some memorable exceptions. One of them that stands out in particular was a body delivered in 1990 from the Midwest.

The victim was a young mother whose corpse was found in a stack of burning automobile tires in the woods five miles from her home. Authorities had suspected foul play when she was reported missing on New Year's morning, but apprehension had increased more recently when a dog dragged some blood-soaked women's clothing into a neighborhood yard. The discovery of the fire, which police estimated could have been burning for two days, came a week and a half after her disappearance and one day after the dog incident. She was identified by county medical and dental examiners, and an attorney from the prosecutor's office determined to waste no time in bringing her to Washington for an examination at the Smithsonian. I agreed to the urgent request, having no idea from the telephone call that the cremation was superficial and the soft tissue was still relatively intact. I expected a smallish box of bones and ashes.

Soon afterward, the prosecutor and a pilot arrived with the remains by private plane at National Airport, and I got a second call asking how they should get to the Smithsonian. I suggested the easiest way would be to just take a taxi. So they did. The cabbie apparently assumed the bag which his two passengers laid out carefully on top of their overnight bags and briefcases in the trunk was a garment bag. I didn't realize how complete those remains were, even after they had arrived at my third-floor office, until we moved some piles of papers, they laid the bag down on a table, and one of them opened it up....

12

SOAP

On August 26, 1979, Dale Willes, his daughter Debbie, and two friends were digging for relics deep in an old lava-tube cave in Clark County, Idaho, in the hills north of Dubois. This combination of spelunking and relic hunting is illegal in most areas, and the very thought of descending into the earth may be offputting to people who suffer from claustrophobia, dislike bats, have problems with dampness, or are afraid of the dark. By the end of the day, the Willes family had found yet another reason to stay out of caves.

They were digging in packed, sandy soil exactly 212 feet from the mouth of the cave when their shovels came in contact with something soft. Lowering their lights for a better view, they carefully scooped back the soil to uncover their trophy. It wasn't what they had come looking for. Instead of arrowheads or pot shards or the remains of an ancient fireplace, they had found a human body, fully clothed, lying on its back. And it was hardly ancient. The part they uncovered first was wearing a pink shirt with blue pinstripes and mother-of-pearl buttons, a maroon woolen sweater, and black wool pants attached to a pair of suspenders. The diggers recovered enough from the initial shock to brush back the soil which they assumed covered the rest of the body. The surprises weren't over. There were no legs below the knees. There were no arms below the elbows. There was no head.

A few hours later, when the coroner lifted the torso out of the 18-inch-deep grave, other artifacts were found beneath it: pieces of burlap, a handkerchief, scraps of clothing that had apparently been cut off at the same time as the lower limbs. Diggers from the sheriff's office excavated further in their search for the missing parts, but another foot below was nothing but bedrock.

Two weeks later the remains arrived in my office, along with the fabrics and a report from the sheriff. In addition to requests for the usual data, including the stature of the victim when he was still alive, this particular referral asked if we could determine whether death occurred after or before (i.e., as the result of) dismemberment.

There was nothing difficult about the preliminaries. The torso had belonged to a white male of about forty. There were no unusual marks or perforations, but without the missing parts, especially the head, I had no way of telling whether he had been hacked to death or had died in some other way before being chopped up. The police report indicated the body had been shot, but there were no signs of any sort on the torso to indicate that this had been the case. As to when he had died, that was even trickier.

Except for the baseless inference about shooting, the report from the sheriff's office was laudably exact. It said the air temperature in the cave was 43 degrees, the humidity was 66 percent, and the temperature of the sand from which the body had been exhumed was 37 degrees. The soft tissue was leathery and mummified, well into a process known as adipocere. While dissecting out the pubic area I noted a considerable odor, and under ordinary conditions that might have indicated the time since death was only a few months. But I knew enough about this particular process of natural preservation, thanks largely to careful studies by Bill Bass and Dale Stewart, to understand that even with the odor, the body could have been dead for many years.

Adipocere—a word derived from the roots for "fat" and "wax"—is a waxy, brownish substance resulting from chemical changes in soft tissues which have been buried or immersed for long periods in moisture, such as a bog or pond, a cave, or a damp grave. For a long time it was thought to be the result of the body turning literally to soap, and that is nearly what happens; chemically, it consists of fatty acids formed by the hydrolysis and hydrogenation of body fats after death. Depending on conditions, the skin of an adipocered body can become as hard and leathery as bacon rind or an old boot, and eventually the remains take on many of the properties of a mummy.

Dale Stewart reported on this phenomenon in detail after encountering adipocere while examining deeply buried bodies of American soldiers killed in the Korean War. In *Essentials of Forensic Anthropology* (1979), Dale cites what may be the first scientific reference to adipocere by a man named Wetherill, who made his observations while supervising the relocation of a cemetery in Philadelphia in 1860.

It may have been another seventy-five years before adipocere made its way to court. Perhaps the earliest forensic reference to the process is in Sir Sidney Smith's *Studies in Identification,* published just before the start of World War II in England. Smith described a forensic case based on his examination of a skull recovered from the bank of an English canal, where it had been partially buried in mud. "There was no scalp or hair, no tissues of the face, and no lower jaw. A quantity of whitish, firm substance, identified as adipocere, was adherent to the base of the skull, and embedded in this substance there were four small pieces of bone."

That was the entire extent of the evidence. Working with nothing more, Smith determined that the skull belonged to a woman between twenty and thirty years old, that she had suffered from torticollis, an abnormal twisting of the neck associated with muscular contracture and known in those days as wryneck, that as a consequence of her condition she had specific peculiarities of appearance that would make her easily identifiable from his description, and that her head had been buried in the damp earth for several months. He also determined the cause of death.

Smith's last two insights—time since death and cause of death—were related in part to his observations of the adipocere. He determined that the small fragments of bone embedded in it were the two horns and the body of the hyoid. The hyoid is either a bone or a complex of bones, depending on the age of the subject, located at the base of the tongue and supporting the tongue and its muscles. He wrote:

Fracture of the hyoid is so commonly produced by manual strangulation and results so uncommonly from any other form of violence that its identification is of great importance.... [In this case] The horns had not united with the body, and there was a fracture of the right horn.

In the fractured ends adipocere had been deposited, showing that the fracture was present before the body or head was buried, and from its presence we may assume that strangulation was the cause of death.

Armed with Smith's inferences about the woman's appearance, police had no trouble identifying the skull as the head of a woman missing from a nearby village. Further inquiries led to the arrest and trial of the woman's husband, and his conviction for her murder. I recommend this story to any modern forensic scientist in need of a little quick humility.

Smith was right when he estimated the skull had been in the canal for several months, but in the absence of other factors, it could as easily have been several years. When a body has turned to soap in this way, beyond a certain point it's just about impossible to be certain about the time since death. Bill Bass discovered the risks of dating an adipocere case the hard way.

In 1977, just two years before the case from Idaho came my way, Tennessee police told him they thought they had uncovered a bizarre method of disposing of the bodies of murder victims; at the bottom of a disturbed grave from the time of the Civil War, they had found a partially decomposed body which they believed had been there only about a year. When Bill examined it, he agreed with them, based on the amount of decay. However, after he and some graduate students came back to do some additional work on it, he concluded that the body was exactly the person named on the headstone, a Confederate colonel who had died in the Battle of Nashville. "You can imagine how embarrassed I was," Bill recalls. "It wasn't exactly a small mistake; I had missed by 112 years."

Accordingly, I was very careful to underline that it was strictly my *guess* when I suggested that the body from the Idaho cave had died between six months and five years earlier. It was pretty obvious from the clothing that the body didn't date back to an Idaho event contemporaneous with the Battle of Nashville, but I wasn't taking any chances.

For several weeks after the discovery, police and search teams dug elsewhere around the cave, but with no result. It took another father-daughter team and the passage of another twelve years before most of the missing parts were finally located.

In the spring of 1991, Lynn Thomas of Dubois was digging for relics with his daughter, Lynette Rogers, and her two children when granddaughter Anna, eleven, thought she saw something strange.

Anna may have been a little nervous because the family had been talking just a moment before about the grisly discovery of 1979. To put her mind at ease, she aimed the beam of her flashlight directly toward whatever the thing was. It proved to be a human hand, sticking up out of the ground.

I don't know what effect the discovery had on young Anna. It's hard not to believe the reaction was extreme and long-lasting, either in the direction of traumatizing her against caves and handshakes for the rest of her life, or of so desensitizing her that she will laugh her way through every horror film she ever sees. But from my limited experience, especially with my own son Max, who is about the same age, it's far more likely she'll look back on the event as a great adventure. I hope so.

Thomas went over to examine the find and saw that the hand was still attached to part of an arm, which in turn was covered by the sleeve of a sweater. It looked as though the whole limb, clothing and all, had been cut off from the body with a saw. They left the cave and headed for the nearest telephone.

Sheriff's deputies found the second arm in the same hole with the first. Beneath it, wrapped in what was left of a burlap bag, were the two legs.

Within a few days, the cavern was swarming with student archaeologists from Idaho State University, as well as members of the Clark County Search and Rescue Group. They started by lining up across the 90-foot width of the cave and driving a steel probe into the ground every 10 centimeters. They then crisscrossed the cavern for most of its length, which was about a half mile, without once hearing the telltale thud of an empty skull below the surface. Plan B called for the digging of intersecting trenches over the distance between where the torso was found and the hole with the limbs, some 100 feet nearer the entrance, and it was equally non-productive.

So far, the head has not been found and the case has not been solved. Newspaper accounts of this second discovery cited my earlier examination, saying my report "concluded the man had died from six months to five years before" the finding of the torso in 1979, which goes to show what can happen to a guess even when it's labeled a guess. The point is, sometimes there's just no way of telling.

And other times, despite adipocere, you can tell a lot. In 1979, a man was cleaning up the yard behind his house in Metairie, Louisiana, and found a paper bag containing a human skull. A month later, three weeks before Christmas, it arrived in my office, bag and all, with the usual questions from the police. It was clearly the head of a child. The next thing I noticed was that a portion of the brain was still intact, preserved in adipocere.

The child appeared to have been of European ancestry, but that was an inference more from the hair than the bones; ancestry and sex are not easy to pin down with children from nothing more than the skull. I was able to estimate the age fairly precisely from the teeth at between three and a half and four years. On the upper right frontal were two parallel cut marks, about 8 mm long and 3 mm apart, made by a sharp instrument at or near the time of death.

It wasn't much to go on, but there were other clues that the drama had been played out over a period of time. Even minimal evidence can provide inferences into unseen events. There were no soil particles adhering to the bones, which said the skull had not been in direct contact with the ground. The lack of bleaching told me the bones had had little or no exposure to the sun. Based on the extent of soft tissue preservation, the formation of adipocere, and the absence of odor, I made another clearly labeled guess that the time since death was greater than a year and less than five years. Even if the minimal estimate was too low, which I seriously doubt, it was obvious from the condition of the paper that the bag was a lot newer than the skull inside it. In my report I concluded that the remains had been transferred from some other type of container long before it was discarded in the backyard. That case, too, remains unsolved.

Rivers are also good adipocere breeding places, and because river water moves, the mystery of adipocered remains recovered from their shores is sometimes compounded by great distance. I once examined a case from eastern Ohio, in which a boot was found along the banks of the Ohio River by a man searching for old coins. Inside, held together by adipocere and the shredded remains of a tube sock, were the bones of a foot. The letter from the detective who forwarded the find to the FBI said it was not uncommon for his department to pull "floaters" from the river, or to recover beached bodies along its edges which had entered the water in West Virginia or as far away as Pennsylvania. In this case, there was a strong possibility that the foot was from a boy who had fallen through the ice a year earlier near a town northeast of Pittsburgh, many miles upriver from where the boot was found in Ohio.

By the time I examined the foot some six weeks after it was recovered from the water's edge, the adipocere had dried to the consistency of soft chalk. There wasn't much to go on. The size of the bones suggested an age at death of between nine and sixteen, and the extent of adipocere formation and tissue loss told me the foot had been in the water for at least a month. There was no clue to sex or ancestry, and with adipocere I knew the time since death could have been several years. The age range meant it was possible the foot was part of the remains of the missing boy from Pennsylvania, and his stepfather, who was a policeman, said he thought he recognized the boot. But the mother said the boot was the wrong shape. She was committed to the notion that her son had been kidnapped, and the foot in the boot was not enough evidence for her to give up her theory, and her hope.

Because adipocere can prolong the structural integrity of human remains, in some instances for many years beyond normal expectations, in 1990 another Kenny Martin case from Bristol County, Massachusetts, raised the brief, false hope that an adipocered body discovered in a granite quarry might represent the solution to a decade-old mystery.

The quarry had fallen into disuse and filled with water. The body was floating some 18 feet below the surface in a plastic sheet; it was largely disarticulated, but some sections were remarkably preserved in adipocere. The sheet was like a spectral, semi-inflated dirigible suspended underwater, tethered by a length of heavy chain to a cement mooring block on the pool's bottom. It was discovered by divers on a Sunday afternoon in April, and by the time a recovery team was assembled, the decision was made to wait until the following morning to bring it to the surface. A detail of state and local police was assigned to guard the site.

Throughout that night, speculation was rampant around Fall River that the body in the plastic sheet was the long-sought remains of Karen Marsden, the young prostitute whose skull had been found in the woods of nearby Westport, Massachusetts, ten years before. I had identified the victim from her frontal sinus pattern at the trial (see Chapter 10), and for that murder Carl Drew was serving a life term in Norfolk Prison. If news of the quarry discovery reached as far as Drew's cell that night, he may have been the only person to hear about it who knew for a certainty that the body was not Karen's.

At 9:00 A.M. on Monday, according to Kenny Martin's report, the police divers returned to the scene, and ninety minutes later they brought to the surface the larger portion of the body, from the waist down. Standing at the edge of the quarry, before the load cleared the water, Kenny could see that the lower half of the victim's legs were tied with rope around the calf area, and that a pair of sweat pants was caught up with the rope. A swirl of silt, stirred up from the bottom as the parcel was lifted from the water, slowly settled. There on a rock ledge several feet below the surface, Kenny and the divers could see the victim's skull.

The suspense was over. A mystery had been solved, but it was the mystery of a girl who had disappeared only three years before, not ten. The question of what had happened to the rest of Karen Marsden's body remained unanswered.

13

BEYOND SOAP

few years ago, the body of a young woman was found in a wooded area not far from the District of Columbia. The police observed no immediate evidence of foul play, but in the normal course of things, photographs were taken of the corpse as it was found. It was late summer, and the dead woman was wearing a tube top and slacks. The clothes were intact, which reduced the likelihood that there had been a sexual assault.

Despite the relative tranquility of the scene, it wasn't the kind of case a medical examiner looks forward to receiving. The body had been lying out in the open for about ten to twelve days, and there were larvae—the polite word for maggots—in the eyes, around the nose and mouth, in the chest area, and on the palms of both hands. The dead woman was identified almost immediately, and because of the decomposition there was a certain amount of pressure on the authorities to release the body for a speedy burial. After a limited autopsy, the cause of death was recorded as unknown and the body turned over to the undertaker.

In most such situations, that would have been the end of the mat-

Going back for a second look.

ter. But one detective on the case couldn't get it out of his mind. The thing that bothered him most was a question about the time of death. He knew her disappearance had been reported a few days before the body was discovered along the trail, but the autopsy was superficial due to the advanced degree of decomposition, and he kept wondering whether there might be a meaningful disparity between the time she was reported missing and the time she had died. Finally, three years later, he got in touch with a forensic anthropologist, showed him the photographs, and asked if there was any possibility of a second opinion.

The anthropologist, a colleague of mine named Bill Rodriguez, looked at the pictures thoughtfully, asking the normal questions about the surrounding circumstances. Then he told the detective that considering the time of year, the larval activity in the photographs was consistent with the medical examiner's estimate of time since death. As he started to hand back the photos, Rodriguez asked if the police had a suspect. The detective shook his head; there was no evidence of foul play, so they hadn't bothered looking.

"Of course there's evidence," Rodriguez said, pointing to the pictures. "You just showed it to me." Because of his forensic training with Bill Bass, he had recognized immediately the significance of the larval activity in the palms of the hands. Although the remaining surfaces of both arms were clearly free of any maggots, the flies had laid their eggs in deep lesions across the width of the palms, signifying the kind of injury he knew from his experience at the University of Tennessee was often associated with defense against a knife.

"But how can you be sure the hand injuries aren't just something that happened when she fell?" the detective asked.

Rodriguez shook his head and pointed to the chest area in the top photo. "This pattern of decomposition is also suggestive of perimortem trauma. It's the same thing you see on her face and the injured hands. Maggots don't swarm like that unless they have something to feed on. If you take another look at the body, I think you're going to find she was stabbed in the chest."

Several more months passed before the detective was able to convince officials to request a disinterment order from the courts, but finally the body was exhumed by lantern light in the middle of a snowstorm. This time the examination was more thorough. The soft tissue was gently simmered away for a clearer view, and unmistakable blade patterns were found in the bones of the hands and in the chest. A new death certificate was issued, and the manner of death was reclassified as homicide.

* * *

From back during my more formative years, I recall someone telling me once that we all get the friends we deserve, and we deserve the friends we get. Maybe some of that same philosophy applies to forensic anthropology: I can only guess at the number of murder cases that have gone undetected because the killer's best friend was a small, carnivorous arthropod left behind by a passing fly. Or, more exactly, an army of such arthropods.

Maggots are repulsive to almost everyone. The most seasoned medical examiners have learned to tolerate the associated odor, but less experienced examiners instinctively arm themselves with a few deep breaths and annoint their upper lips with oil of camphor or tiger balm before approaching a death scene in which maggots are still at work. No matter how many such cases they see or how fascinated they may become by the process of translating the mysteries to which they may provide the key, there is still an element of shock in seeing one of the lowest forms of life at feast on the remains of the highest. Because of that shock, and because it is very difficult to see below the surface state when the soft tissue is dry or in advanced composition, some medical examiners turn away sooner than they should, and murder goes unnoticed.

A couple of years ago, police entered an apartment in an abandoned building in the densely packed slum section of an eastern city, following a request that they investigate an overpowering odor apparently coming from inside. In the doorway to one of the bedrooms they found the body of a black male. The next day I read the police report describing the scene: "The body is fully extended face down with the face tilted left. The right cheek and entire body is stuck to the floor. There are no body fluids visible and the body is dried out. It appears to have been chewed and the bones are exposed. The fire department responded and assisted with shovels in prying the body from the floor."

It was a difficult case to work on. Although much of the body was desiccated, as the report said, some of the soft tissue was still moist; there was still some maggot activity, and the odor was overwhelming. Based on the time of year, the degree of odor, the presence of empty pupal cases, the desiccation of some of the flesh, and the number and size of larvae still feeding, the time since death appeared to be about three months. I verified that the body was that of a black male, and based on observations of the pelvis, long bones, rib ends, and spine, I estimated his age at between twenty-six and thirty-six years. No lacerations or other evidence of foul play were detected on the remaining soft tissue, although I noted in my report that the extended state of decomposition prevented examination of all surfaces.

What we found below the surface was a different story. We stripped off as much of the desiccated and rotting flesh as possible, cleaned up the maggots, and tried for a reasonably clear look at the bones. When we got to the skull, we observed a depressed fracture and radiating fractures in the left temporal/parietal region, evidence of blunt-force trauma which clearly suggested murder. Another oval-shaped depressed fracture was found along the inferior border of the skull, indicating that the victim had been struck repeatedly by an oval object.

In examining bodies in that condition, the soft tissue has to be carefully removed from those areas most likely to show trauma. This can be done by teasing the tissue away with instruments, by simply simmering it away, or through the use of chemicals or bleaches. In the first case especially, care must be taken not to make marks on the bones that could later be confused with evidence from the time of death. In the use of liquids, removal can be accomplished with hot water, and sometimes with bleach, oxidizing agents, and/or anti-fat enzymes.

It is not unusual for active arthropod feeding to continue in the moist tissues of bodies that are otherwise dried up, even in cases where the body appears to have become mummified. In another case four years earlier from that same city, a body was found in a wooded vacant lot in the late fall, lying over a log. The skin had not gone into adipocere, which might have been expected from the damp environment, but was in a brown, leatherlike condition associated with tanning or ancient embalming. I had seen a number of forensic cases with skin in that state before, and would observe it later in a majority of the victims from the New Bedford Roadside Murder series, all of which were found in similar wooded settings. Yet despite the rigidity and thickness of the skin, there was a detectable odor and, beneath the surface, lots of fly larvae were actively feeding. Initial appearance not withstanding, it was another very messy case.

It also was filled with contradictions. Found in a predominantly black section of the city, the victim was a Caucasian male, aged forty-five to fifty, height about 5'7". The body was nude, and there was evidence of a major blow to the back of the head, but most of the larval activity was internal and the skin was relatively intact. The area around the lot was heavily populated, yet the body had remained undetected for several weeks and perhaps even a few months. Despite the invitation the body presented to birds, to the numerous rodents in the area, and to passing dogs, there were only a few small signs of gnawing activity around the smaller toes of one foot. And although the murder had happened during the hottest months of the year, the usual odor from the decomposing body was apparently not strong enough in this instance to attract the attention of passers-by. So far, the victim is still a John Doe and no suspects have been identified.

Last summer Bill Bass told me of another case, this one from a state adjoining Tennessee, in which maggots not only helped establish time since death but provided astonishingly detailed insights to what happened after the murder.

The story began when the victim failed to show up for work one morning and was reported missing by his employer. Eighteen days later, two dirt bikers driving through a rural area just a few miles away came across a burned-out car, and inside, slumped across the back seat, they saw the charred remains of a body. The police arrived, and in short order a call went out for the forensic team from Knoxville. Bill and his crew surveyed the crime scene, removed the corpse from the car, and on returning to their laboratory conducted an autopsy on the blackened cadaver.

Live larvae were observed throughout the surface of the body. But when they removed the top of the skull, cooked maggots were found inside the brain.

It takes a disciplined mind and a strong stomach to recognize the significance of that kind of discovery. The victim had been dead long enough for flies to leave larvae, for maggots to grow and eat away much of the decaying outer tissue and to enter the braincase. From precise measurement of the cooked maggots and comparison with his charts on larval growth, Bill was able to conclude that the maggots inside the head had died between fourteen and sixteen days *after* the victim himself had been killed.

"It was a very clear picture," he recalled. "The man was murdered and left in the back seat. Some two weeks later, the people who did it came back and set fire to the car, maybe in the hope of getting rid of the corpse or creating the impression he had died in an automobile accident. The fire eventually went out, and the body cooled enough for flies to come back and lay more eggs on the burned material. So what we found on the outside of the body were live maggots about two days old from after the fire, and on the inside were the cooked maggots about two weeks old from before. Taken together, they account for just about every day since the man was reported missing. The next thing we found were knife marks in the vertebra, so we also had the cause of death."

Different species of flies have different reproductive time intervals, and although most lay eggs, some lay larvae that are deposited alive on their food supply. Because larvae do not all come from the same source, in determining the time since death of a murder victim it is sometimes necessary to identify the specific type of maggot in order to recognize its stage of growth. Larval activity can provide a very exact benchmark, but only when the pattern for the particular species has been recorded. They are typically consistent in size with the flies they came from, and they usually have specific stages: they grow to a certain size, then split the outer shell and grow further. In the initial stage they migrate away from the body and go into the ground to pupate.

One way forensic entomologists verify such benchmarks is to remove the larvae and cultivate them until they hatch. By themselves, maggots are very difficult to identify with accuracy by species, but that is not the case with an adult fly, and the timing data from its life cycle can be applied precisely once it has been recognized. By digging up pupae from under a decaying body and analyzing the age of the cases, it is possible to determine the number of generations of flies (to a point), and that number can in turn be multiplied by the length of the cycle in order to determine the period since the laying of the first egg.

Another clue that larva can sometimes provide is whether the body has been moved since time of death—even whether the victim was killed indoors or out. The common housefly, which is easily identified by its three black thoracic stripes, is primarily an indoor animal. If a body is found in a wooded area and the larvae are predominantly of that species, chances are good that the murder occurred indoors and the body was then dumped.

Not all maggots pupate at the scene of their larval feeding. When the body of a murdered man was found at the edge of a mowed field near Chattanooga, Tennessee, there were three dark stains running out from the discovery site through the cut grass. To the unpracticed eye, the lines looked like they might have been pathways along which the dead body had been dragged, long enough after the murder that it left a greasy residue. That didn't make much sense, so again they called in Bill Bass.

"Not many people have our kind of experience, watching bodies as they decay and timing the rate at which maggots drop off of them," Bill told me later. "One of the things we had learned from that work was that maggots sometimes work like an army. The sergeant starts off at the head of the column, and thousands of maggots follow along behind him. As soon as I saw the paths, I said, 'Hey, these are maggot trails.'"

Bill told the other investigators at the scene to follow the trails and excavate the pupal cases they were sure to find just below the surface. Just as he predicted, every trail was marked with the empty, papery containers. Excavations to either side of the trail produced none. Scientifically, the observation and recording of this migration is of real importance to anthropology, and there was little in the literature prior to Bill's work in Knoxville. I have kidded Bill about the relative importance of his Trail of Grease in a state marked by another historic path—the tragic Trail of Tears of the Cherokee. Nevertheless, Bill's work has proven once again the rewards of patience, fortitude, a thirst for knowledge, and a powerful love of nature in all its forms.

The observation of maggots is a repulsive pastime on the face of it, but Bill's studies reveal new dimensions to a life cycle that is wonderfully complex. Whenever there is a smell of death, flies come in great numbers. They lay their eggs in the open orifices. The eggs hatch to form larvae, the larvae will feed until they get to a certain size determined by their species, and then it's time to pupate. In some cases, the maggots march off in the organized armies Bill has observed and search for a safe hatching place. Usually they dig into the ground, but in some cases Bill has found swarms of maggots hiding under the bark of trees as high as 15 feet up. They stay there until their outer bodies harden into exoskeletons and they metamorphose into adult flies. In turn, the flies break their way out of their cases and escape into the air, to begin the cycle once again.

Once the first generation of this activity is finished, at successive intervals in the process other species of arthropods will come in to feed on a decomposing body: beetles, other types of flies, other types of larvae. The stage of the process of decomposition largely dictates the host's attractiveness to these different species. By careful collection of dead animals and observation of larval animals on the carrion, a forensics expert can identify the stage of succession and through that can approximate the time of death.

Another approach to this same information has been developed by Arpad A. Vass, a graduate student of Bill's at Knoxville. (It's not just by chance that about half of the forty current diplomates in forensic anthropology in the world, including me, are present or former students of Bill Bass.) Through the analysis of various body components in the ground beneath the cadaver, Vass has been able to prove that there is a fairly steady rate of chemical breakdown of those constituents. Measurement of the chemical composition of the soil can be used as a third means, after general observations on the state of decomposition and study of insect activity, for estimating time since death. All three methods require many more experiments before they will reveal enough information about these processes to make consistently reliable deductions from them.

Traditionally, almost anything to do with increasing our understanding of the human body has inspired conflict, sometimes intense, in the continuous war between the sanctity of life and the need to protect ourselves against evil and death. Not too long ago in human history, it was a crime to give an anatomy lesson, to do an autopsy, even to touch a dead body. It was a major breakthrough in medicine when student physicians were actually allowed to examine cadavers in order to understand such essentials as the rudiments of anatomy, the effects of trauma, and the process of disease.

Although they less frequently erupt as open war, some aspects of that battle are still being waged in the field of forensic anthropology. As morbid as it may seem to put bodies out and watch what happens to them, it provides a tremendous amount of information useful to our science in helping solve some of the mysteries with which we are confronted almost daily.

This is another area in which there is a strong, two-way connection between archaeological inference and forensic science. In the case of our analyses of the ancient ossuaries in Maryland, forensic data gave us insights into the time interval over which each ossuary was in use, and from that we were able to infer population size. Often forensic studies feed directly into our understanding of more complex questions, such as what kind of cultural impact incoming Europeans had on native American populations. This was the case in our analyses of the remains from an early historic cemetery in South Dakota—the Leavenworth site—which had been visited by Lewis and Clark in 1804 and 1806. Even though the site was hundreds of years old, the soil preservation was so good that we were able to recover the exoskeletal remains of many insect larvae, mixed right in with the bones of the human bodies on which they had fed.

Our observations of open pupal egg cases provided evidence that the adult flies had emerged. Since these egg cases were found but we didn't find any adult flies, we could infer that the bodies had probably not been buried until after the hatching cycle had been completed. That told us that even in early historic times, these native Americans were keeping the bodies above ground for a period of probably ten days to two weeks after death before burial, which is a lot longer than we previously believed.

In material recovered from even earlier sites than the one visited by Lewis and Clark, we found the remains not just of flies but of a beetle called *Trox*, a genus which is attracted only to desiccated carrion that have been above ground long enough to become dry and sinewy. This told us that the aboriginal Americans of the earlier period had made a practice of keeping the bodies of their dead above ground even longer than was the practice later. And at locations we considered to be earlier yet—from approximately 1000 A.D. to 1550 A.D.—we found secondary burials where the bones were losing their articulation, which implied the possible use of scaffolding to keep the corpses in the open air until they had deteriorated further than in the middle period. Clearly the Indians were shortening the time period between death and burial, probably as a result of cultural pressure from the Europeans.

At all of these important scientific sites, it was primarily insect evidence that was used to chronicle the evolution of an important custom and to give us insights into the ancient human past that would otherwise have been inaccessible. The relevance of that evidence was established first in the subdiscipline of forensic anthropology.

14

THE FACE IS FAMILIAR

In the winter of 1984 a complete skeleton was recovered from a rural area a few yards off a Georgia highway. It was lying face up beside a small ditch, with honeysuckle vines growing through the remains. It appeared to have been there about a year. The body had been relatively undisturbed, and though the fabric had deteriorated, authorities were able to develop a very clear inventory of how the victim had been dressed. He was wearing a light, long-sleeved dress shirt imprinted with light and dark blue triangles, plus blue jeans, and a brown leather belt with the letter R on the silver buckle. A spent bullet was recovered from the area of the chest.

The only part I got to examine was the skull, which I was able to verify had belonged to a black male of between thirty and forty-five. I saw from the attached paperwork that the body had been about 6'2", and had a 36-inch waist; obviously there was no waist left to measure, and that number had come from a label on his underwear. It was estimated from other measurements that in life the man had weighed about 200 pounds.

One of the first things I noted in the skull was a feature that would

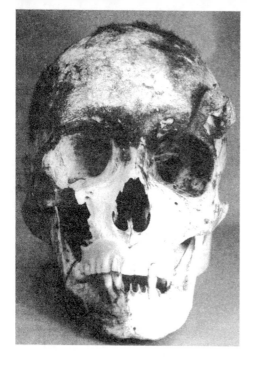

A sketch based on this skull found in Georgia, compared to a photograph taken during life. Despite the differences, the resemblance was enough to trigger an inquiry that resulted in a positive identification from dental records.

help a lot in the identification, assuming we could come close enough with the artist's rendition to find someone who recognized the likeness: he had a complete upper denture, and although all the maxillary teeth were therefore artificial, the two lateral incisors in that plate were gold. Apparently he had liked the look of gold teeth, or perhaps he felt they gave the illusion that the other teeth in the denture were real. We didn't attempt to show the teeth in the reproduction—the FBI artist sketched him with his mouth shut—but it was the kind of verifying detail that would help to clinch a positive ID.

On Friday, April 6, 1984, less than ninety days after the discovery of the remains, the conceptual drawing was shown on WSB Television in Georgia, on both the evening and late-night news. In response to the newscasts, a man called the reaction center of the Georgia Bureau of Investigation and identified the victim.

Sometime later, I received a photograph of the victim taken from life, and compared it with the reproduction. It impressed me far less with how alike they were than with how different. I'm sure that if a stranger had passed the man on the street after seeing that artist's rendition, he wouldn't have recognized him from the sketch. But reproductions are not intended for the eyes of strangers. The drawing worked because it obviously captured enough of the basic characteristics of the face to trigger a response from someone who knew the victim and thought it might be the same person. Even if the call had come in because the sketch had been a dead ringer, reproductions are still not positive proof of identity.

Most of us are familiar with the movie scene where the forensic artist, starting with little more than a skull, reproduces the face of an unknown murder victim with astonishing precision. Up through the 1950s, Hollywood's version of that process was pretty much limited to showing an artist's drawing on a sketch pad. The scene usually ended when a passer-by, often a reporter, took one look at the result, gasped, and said something like, "Good heavens! It's the Governor's missing daughter!"

Since that more innocent age, forensic technology and the public's appetite for the lurid have matured in tandem. In *Gorky Park*, the state of the reproductive art was demonstrated in three dimensions as police scientists rebuilt the faces right over the brutally peeled heads that opened the film. In *Terminator* and *Terminator II* we see the process unwind in reverse, starting with a human face and stripping away the layers of skin, muscle, and connective tissue to reveal the exotic metal core inside Arnold Schwarzenegger's dream monster.

In real life, there are occasional circumstances that may warrant attempting to reproduce facial appearance. When fossil remains of hominids are discovered, for example, anthropologists like to see how they compare with the appearance of our own species, and the pages of the *National Geographic* are filled with portraits of our early ancestors which have been scientifically extrapolated from the evidence of their bones. Now and then, police use the same techniques to help get an idea of the appearance of the victim in a forensic case, but real life varies from fiction in one important particular: no matter how accurately they may reflect the victim's appearance, in no court in the country are reproductions ever accepted by themselves as positive identification.

Even the most skilled reproduction artists know that the product of their efforts is at best an approximation. How approximate depends on how successfully they emphasize the surface features that can be reliably inferred from the skeleton: the overall outline of the face, the fold of the nose, and the distribution of the various facial components. In addition, an attempt is made to identify and highlight any aspect of the skeletal framework that suggests visible or unusual surface characteristics such as old fractures, asymmetry of the skull, or gaps between the teeth. Reproductive artists downplay those characteristics about which accuracy is difficult or impossible, such as the form of the hair, style of clothing, and the subject's characteristic smile or frown. As Dale Stewart observed in 1979 in *Essentials of Forensic Anthropology*, "Many artists have a hard enough time getting a sitter's eyes and mouth right when they are simply copying what is before them." And Dale should know, since he is an accomplished portrait artist.

Dale went further than that. He considered it "largely accidental" when a reproduction led to identification in cases where the artist and anthropologist had nothing more to work with than a skull. In forensic applications, the purpose of a reproduction is never to prove that the governor's daughter has been found, but rather to provide a visual reminder, conveyed through the media to the public, that someone with those same facial characteristics is dead and unidentified. In those cases where positive identification is established, it is because someone came forward with information that was linked to some other clue. No matter how breathtaking the likeness, the reproduction is never enough.

There are two approaches to facial reproduction: building the face

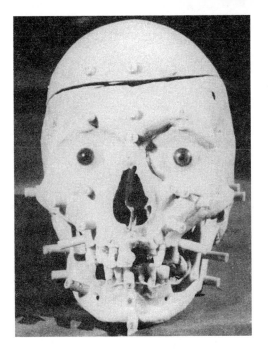

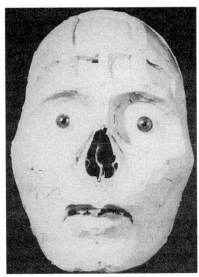

Three-dimensional reconstruction.
After tissue markers and artificial eyes are in
place (top left photograph), intervening spaces
are filled in with modeling medium. Lower
photograph shows the reconstruction to
the right of the actual death mask.

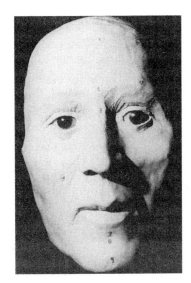

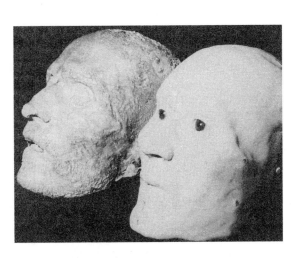

in clay directly over the cranium; and sketching the likeness from photographs and measurements of the skull, sometimes with the help of a computer.

Both begin with an estimate of the amount of muscle and other soft tissue that covered the cranium in life. In both approaches, tissue depth is usually mapped with the aid of small, cylindrical markers affixed to the cranium at specific points; their length corresponds to values derived from measuring males and females of the principal racial groups. For American Caucasoids, values have been refined according to body build.

In the sculpturing technique, after the tissue-thickness markers have been set in place, clay or a similar material is used to fill the intervening spaces. Artificial eyes are inserted into the orbits, lips and eyelids are fashioned from strips of the modeling medium, the features are refined, and in cases where there is sufficient evidence, the process may be completed by the addition of hair and clothing.

Sketching also begins with placement of the appropriate tissue-thickness markers on the cranium. The anthropologist then describes to the artist the aspects that should be highlighted. Police departments use identity kits for developing composite portraits of suspects from the testimony of witnesses, and the facial components in those kits can be helpful here as well: the anthropologist may select from them the appropriate chin type, nose form, or eye separation to guide the artist, based on the contours of the cranium and the markers.

Even in those parts of the face more likely to be defined by flesh and cartilage, such as the nose and lips, the adjacent bones and our knowledge of characteristics related to ancestry provide clues that guide our estimates. Some features, such as the shape and size of the ears, are far more speculative—and therefore are not emphasized in the reproduction. We stress the things we can see, and play down those we cannot.

Not all sketched reproductions are based on skulls and tissue markers. In 1986, Krogman and Iscan discussed a method in which the drawings were made from X-rays rather than bones, and the following year R. M. George described a procedure based on tracings over lateral craniographs (side views of the skull). Nearly sixty years ago, J. Gillman described a method of reproducing the appearance in life of a mummified body in which the soft tissue was still present.

For all the caveats, both three-dimensional reproduction and two-dimensional sketching have been used successfully in establishing identity. Rebuilding may offer a slight advantage in accuracy of proportions when executed by a skilled artist, but it requires much more time and effort than sketching and does not usually produce as lifelike an appearance.

One of the best forensic sculptors in the United States is Lew Sadler of the Department of Biomedical Visualization, University of Illinois at Chicago, and his three-dimensional work consistently comes close to approximating the subject's appearance in life. Even so, when Lew's name is mentioned for his work in our science a few decades from now, I believe it will be primarily for another reason. His most important contribution to the art of facial reproduction is not in his genius with modeling clay, glass eyes, and wigs, but with the computer. Among other things, he has developed a laser-guided system that predicts what a missing child will look like at various intervals on the road to maturity. It has been used more than once to recover children years after they were stolen.

One of the most dramatic new techniques permits the duplication and three-dimensional modeling of skulls from archaeological or forensic remains without disturbing or even touching the original evidence. It started with anthropological examinations of museum mummies with CAT-scanners, which reconstructed computerized axial sections of the target on film. The advantage of CAT-scanning of mummified skulls is that it allows a view of the bone without dissecting and thereby sacrificing the remaining soft tissue—and without being misled by distortions in this tissue that often result from the practice of binding the body for burial, or simply the passage of great periods of time. Just a few months ago, Lew left me with a plastic skull that had been exactly modeled from a mummy by a new system in which a CAD/CAM computer had been linked with the CAT-scan output. As a logical next step, it would be possible to use that plastic replica to reproduce the face of the subject with the same likelihood of accuracy as though it were the original skull—and all without having to dissect the mummy.

In the last few years, I have worked with Gene O'Donnell, a visual information specialist with the FBI developing a computer-based approach to facial reproduction. Based on equipment designed to show progressive aging on missing children and other missing persons, this system captures images of the skull and mandible, digitizes them, and allows us to select and add the appropriate components (nose, ears, mouth, etc.) and manipulate them until our estimate of facial appearance emerges. The computer stores the various stages of reproduction as well as the final product, so that any stage may be recalled if necessary. In using this technique, the skull and mandible are fitted with soft-tissue depth markers, properly positioned, and scanned optically. The anthropologist then selects the appropriate components, which are added by the operator and modified until the most likely appearance is achieved.

We used the technique to reproduce the face, based on the partially skeletonized head, of a severely decomposed young white female body found beside a North Carolina highway in 1990. A lot of restoration was apparent on her teeth, but there were no locally missing persons whose dental records could be successfully matched with the victim. I estimated her age at under twenty, and her living height at 5'3". We knew her hair was either brown or blond, and she appeared to have been strangled.

I suggested to North Carolina authorities that the skull and jaw be stripped and cleaned and sent to Washington for facial reproduction. My examination of these artifacts, after routine study by the FBI, agreed with the facts as they had been given to us—the age fell between fifteen and nineteen. Following the procedure described above, we produced the result you see below on the computer in about two hours, far faster than three-dimensional modeling, and with greater versatility and detail than through a strictly manual sketch.

As useful as reproduction sometimes may be in forensics, without a match even the most dramatic likeness has little value. A skeleton from Georgia, in which the skull contained some of the most salient clues to appearance in life I've ever encountered, is a good case in point.

The remains were found in a wooded area about 75 feet from the edge of a major highway. The soft tissue had mostly decomposed, and weeds were growing up through the bones. Most of the bones were still in their natural relationship, although a couple of them had been scattered, apparently by small animals. After photographs and measurements, the body was taken away in a rubber disaster bag. Examining the place where the skull had lain, detectives found an artificial brown eye and what they thought was a silicone implant, partially imbedded in the dirt. Later sifting of the same soil yielded a couple of teeth, a small bone, and an unidentified metal object. There were no bullets or other indications of cause of death.

The state crime lab said the victim was a white female between seventeen and nineteen years old, height about 5'5" or 5'6". The examiner commented on a major injury to the front of the face.

When I spread the bones out in my office, I saw considerable evidence of bleaching, indicative of prolonged exposure to the sun and

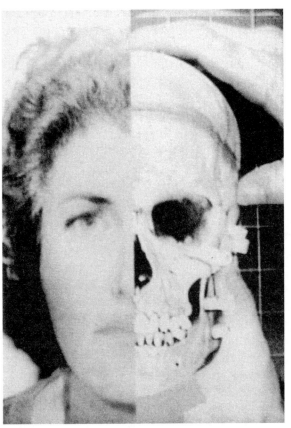

Using a new computer technique, this sketch of a young woman whose remains were found in North Carolina was achieved in only two hours, and with greater potential for accuracy than with a strictly manual sketch.

useful in setting the time since death. But although the bones exhibited a number of Caucasian characteristics, they were only part of the picture. The nasal area was narrow as in white populations, but lacked a nasal sill; the alveolus (the portion of the upper and lower jaws that holds the teeth) displayed marked prognathism, or jutting; and the lower leg bones were relatively straight—all characteristics of black racial affiliation. It would be difficult to guess whether the victim considered herself black or white.

I agreed with the previous examiner on gender, but the fusion of the osseous caps on the ends of the bones indicated an older age at death, between twenty and twenty-four years, and I estimated her height to be two or three inches shorter, at 5'3".

One important key to identity lay in the old injury to her skull, which included evidence of massive trauma to the right frontal and right facial region. There was an immense hole in the forehead, an old compressed fracture which had healed but not closed, traversing some 65 mm from the eye orbit to a place above the likely hairline. The right upper jaw just below the eye socket also had been fractured with a 3 mm displacement on the outside of that socket, so that one eye was lower than the other. A small wire (the unidentified metal device in the police report) extended through two natural canals in the right nasal bone. The glass eye, the wire insert, and the implant were almost certainly all parts of the surgical attempt to restore the face after that old trauma, which I estimated had taken place at least two years earlier.

No matter how artfully a plastic surgeon may have patched her up in life, there was no question the trauma would have produced massive scars on one entire side of her face. And if those scars weren't themselves unforgettable, she also had very distinctive teeth. There was one tooth lost before death, and it was a left bicuspid of the lower jaw, near the front where the gap might have been noticeable. More prominently, the teeth showed marked overcrowding and a pronounced overbite causing considerable prognathism. This combination of mixed racial characteristics, traumatic scars, and dramatic dentition made her an excellent candidate for facial reproduction. I couldn't imagine there was anyone else on earth with the same appearance.

The sketch was widely circulated in the area where the body had been recovered and throughout that region of Georgia. I felt our reproduction was reasonably accurate and highlighted many unique features. Out of professional curiosity and perhaps a bit of personal pride, I called the chief deputy a few years later to hear how the case had been resolved.

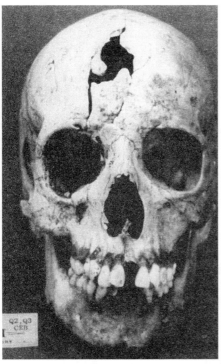

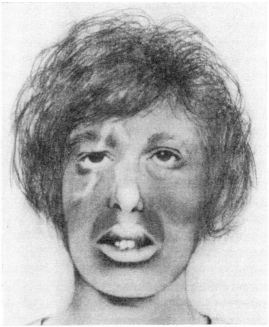

Even though this young woman found in Georgia had suffered massive facial injuries only partly corrected by plastic surgery, as of this writing she still has not been identified.

The reproduction hadn't produced a single lead. They still had no idea who the woman had been, how she had died, or who had left her body beside the highway, and the case was still open.

It would be callous to suggest that any forensic case has a happy ending, but I believe the truth does set us free—from doubt, from fear, from false hope, and from fearful imaginings—and by that standard there are lots of facial reproduction cases that end better than the one in Georgia.

When the skeletal remains of an eighteen- to twenty-year-old female were found near the campus of Lewis and Clark College in Portland, Oregon, on July 28, 1978, the police searched their file of Missing Persons, checked with authorities at the school, and even launched a program of highly visible publicity in the local media—all without producing a single lead as to who she might have been. Late that fall they sent the bones to the FBI for any clues I might find to the cause of death, and for a facial reproduction to be used as an aid in their continued search for her identity.

The body had been there long enough to lose all its soft tissue, but in hot weather that can happen fast, so I estimated the time since death as several weeks to several months. Along with the skeleton I received a pair of partially decomposed blue knee-high stockings, to which adhered small clumps of soil, moss, the pupal cases of flies, and a human toenail. Small particles of fabric, apparently the remnants of her other clothing, were attached in places to the bones. She was of European ancestry, stood about 5'4", and had probably given birth at least once. The skeleton was fairly complete, with the principal exception of several bones from her hands and feet.

I noted four characteristics in the remains which I was sure would be helpful in making a positive ID, assuming the availability of medical or dental X-rays from life. The most obvious was the teeth; all were present except one which was lost postmortem, and there were fillings in nine of them. Probably the most striking, however, was the presence of a sixth lumbar vertebra, which is one more than nature usually gives us. Another skeletal rarity, at the midline in the frontal bone of her skull, was a metopic suture where most people have no suture at all. And finally, the left capitate and lesser mutangular, two small bones of the wrist, were fused—probably since birth, as there was no other evidence of trauma in the area.

One other item found at the recovery site was a clump of hair. It was a bonus in that it told us about color and texture, but even though hair is one of the major components of a person's appearance, it is also a serious potential pitfall when used in a reproduction. The quickest way for anyone, especially a woman, to alter overall appearance is to change hairstyles. If you look carefully through the fashion ads in the Sunday supplements, it's not uncommon to find the same model impersonating a crowd—wearing six different outfits and fixing her hair differently each time.

This time, the reproduction led directly to the identification of the victim: police matched it with the photograph of a local girl with a history of emotional disorder. In the absence of any indication of foul play, authorities speculated she may have died of a drug overdose. Lieutenant Rod Englert of the Multnomah County Sheriff's Office told me they could see the resemblance immediately, but when they changed the hair in the artist's version to duplicate her real style, the likeness was astonishing.

Photographic superimposition probably first came into use in identifying victims of crime in about 1935, when two partial skeletons were recovered near Moffat, Scotland. They were matched with the photographs of a couple of missing women, Isabella Ruxton and Mary Rogerson. The matching was done by tracing an outline of the reassembled skulls and mandibles, then comparing them with photographs of the living women adjusted to the same size. The exercise produced nothing more than an opinion that the pictures and skulls could have been the same women, and the results were not offered as positive identification. But taken with the other evidence it was a contributing factor, and the husband of Mrs. Ruxton was hanged on the verdict.

The first report of photographic superimposition to establish positive identification was a case in 1960 in India. A full human skeleton was recovered on March 21 from a marshy *jheel* beside the Taratala Road, along with some personal effects believed to belong to the deceased. The skull and a passport-sized photograph of the suspected victim were sent to the state's Forensic Science Laboratory.

The criteria for the superimposition were based on data developed in controlled experiments on skeletal collections in the anatomy department of the Calcutta Medical College, and the technique held up a few years later when challenged in the Supreme Court of India. It was similar to the Scottish method in that salient features were marked out from a photograph, although in this case the photo was a negative and the markings were on glass. The skull was on an adjustable tripod, which allowed it to be aligned exactly with that of the face whose

When police compared the sketch of a young woman found in Oregon with a photograph of a local missing person, they quickly saw the resemblance. When the hair was redrawn to match her actual style, the likeness was striking.

salients were marked on the glass, and photographed. The two negatives were then projected over one another to determine fit.

The identity of the skull was established; it belonged to a missing man named Pancham Sukla, a subgunner of the Calcutta Port Commissioners. Sukla was thought to have been murdered, and a suspect was committed to sessions for trial. Based in part on the testimony of the forensic scientists who identified Sukla, the case resulted in a conviction.

In 1976, that basic technique was further refined: by using two video cameras, an electronic mixing device, and a viewing screen, an image could be shown on a television screen. This enabled scientists to compare computer-reconstructed cross-sections of the bone with soft tissue. A decade later, in the hands of the German scientist R. P. Helmer, this technique produced convincing evidence in the identification of the skeletal remains of Wolfgang Gerhard, who had lived quietly in Brazil for years, as being those of Dr. Josef Mengele, Nazi Germany's notorious "Angel of Death." Tests on DNA extracted from the Brazilian bones further confirmed the identification.

At first, the principal use of computers in this type of forensics was to analyze the degree of fit in the comparison of the two images of a skull and a photograph. Recently, however, some colleagues and I have developed a new approach for the FBI in which computer superimposition becomes an interactive process.

Recently, we applied the new technique in the case of the black woman, described in Chapter 4, whose skeleton was discovered by a hunter in rural Ohio back in 1978. The police strongly suspected the victim's identity, but in the absence of medical records had been unable to confirm it. They sent the FBI the skull, mandible, and a photograph of the suspected victim taken during life.

After logging in, the package was sent to the Microscopic Analysis Unit, where it was Q'ed and K'ed for other possible examinations. Then Special Agents Bob Fram and Joe Dizinno brought it across Pennsylvania Avenue to my lab at the Smithsonian. We knew from our own and previous anthropological examinations of the skull that it was from an adult black female. My assistant, Erica Bubniak, started by cutting depth markers equal in length to the depth of the soft tissues, based on averages for sex and ancestry. She then carefully attached each marker to the prescribed location on the cranium and jaw. When she was done, I called Bob and told him we were ready for an appointment with the computer specialist.

Over the years, I have worked with a lot of artists in the Special

Projects Section of the FBI in attempting facial reproductions. For the computer technique, however, I've worked more exclusively with Gene O'Donnell, who is a computer specialist. A few days after Erica completed her work, I carried the evidence back across the street, met Fram, was logged in at the reception desk, then proceded to O'Donnell's office down a long, familiar labyrinth of hallways. As usual, he was ready for us.

We began by placing the photograph on the copy stand below the video camera and watched as the image reassembled, line by line, on the computer screen. Gene had to adjust the distance of the camera so that the image filled about two thirds of the video screen. He then taped a plastic film over the screen, and began tracing such key anatomical landmarks as contour of face, base of nose, and borders of eyes and nose. This image was digitized and entered into the computer.

Next, the photograph was replaced on the copy stand beside the skull and attached mandible, with the appropriate tissue-thickness markers in place. The bones were then manipulated on a donut ring until their orientation agreed with that of the photographic image marked on the plastic sheet. During this process, Gene again continually adjusted the focal distance of the camera so the image size also agreed with the size of the computerized photograph. This is the trickiest part of the process, and often takes several tries to achieve the best possible alignment. The image of the bones is also digitized, then superimposed by computer on the digitized photo for detailed visual comparison on the monitor.

The software allows any desired combination of skeleton-photograph comparisons, including the removal of soft tissue to view the underlying skeletal structure. The images can be stored permanently in computer memory, and the system allows fast, easy, high-quality hard-copy printouts. All of this still requires the interpretive input of an experienced anthropologist, but in the hands of a skilled operator like Gene it can produce a finished product in under an hour.

We started with a complete superimposition of the two images, and our hopes for a match began to rise: they corresponded very closely, with no obvious points of dissimilarity. We then brought the screen back to just the skull. Gene entered new instructions, and on the right half of the screen, line by line, the image of the right side of the face in the photograph began to displace that of the right side of the skull. Slowly but surely, the points of comparison came into new alignment. On the right, the base of the chin in the photograph matched exactly with the marker which had been placed by Erica on the bottom of the

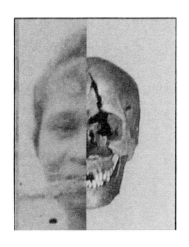
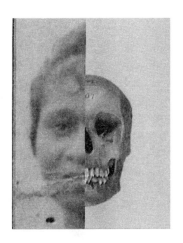

Computer-assisted photographic super-imposition. The skull of a black female found in Ohio matched a photograph of the suspected victim *(top left figure)*. The figures that follow are unsuccessful attempts to find another match in the Terry Collection—more than 1,700 skeletal remains on permanent loan to the Smithsonian from the state of Missouri. Each skeleton in the collection includes a full description of the living person, usually one or more photographs from life, and in some cases death masks. Not only does the Terry Collection bear witness to the unique physiognomy of individual human beings, it provides reproduction artists with an ideal resource for testing the accuracy of their work.

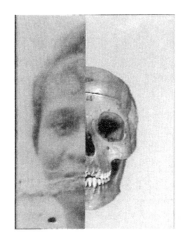

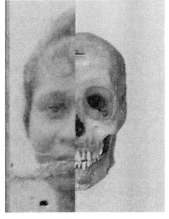

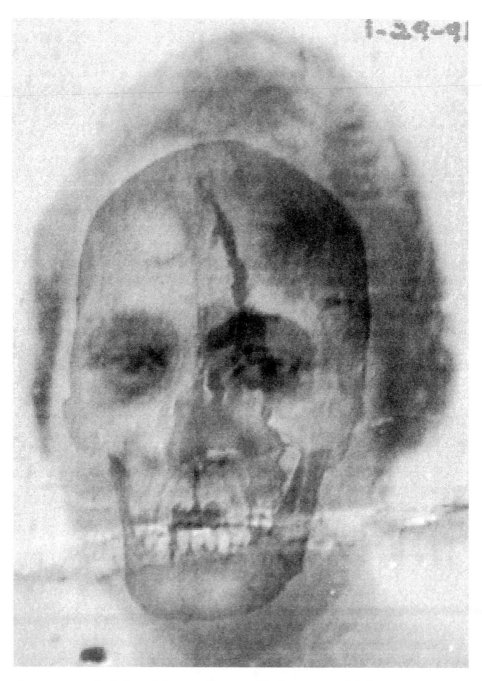

Computer manipulation of the two photographic images can simulate
an autopsy, selectively removing or replacing flesh to verify the match.

jaw on the left. The tip of the central incisors seen in the photograph agreed precisely with the same teeth in the skull. The base of the nose in the skull connected perfectly with the nasal base in the picture. The right eye was on exactly the same plane as the opposing socket. Finally, as the scan migrated upward across the brow and into the hairline, the correspondence was still impressive. I said to Gene, "This looks like it may be the same lady."

He nodded. "So far, so good."

"Let's check out the right lateral canthus," I said.

Part of the magic of the software in Gene's computer system is that it allows for selective manipulation of the superimposed images in such a way as to nearly approximate an autopsy. He moved the mouse across the control pad, and on the screen a section of the photographic image on the right side of the eye was stripped away to reveal the bone beneath. Below the flesh, exactly where it ought to be, was the image of Whitnall's tubercle, a small bump of bone, described as a forensic landmark by Dale Stewart in 1983, that marks the corner of the eye opening. "Okay," I said, "let's go for the ear."

He stripped away the photographic image of the ear and revealed the corresponding marker I had placed in the external auditory meatus of the skull, again just where it should have been. Gene studied the matches intently, still nodding and now smiling as well. "Pretty convincing," he said.

I agreed, but we both knew that was not yet enough. I returned to the Smithsonian and collected more skulls. Of all the skulls in the museum's collections, I chose those that most closely resembled the one from Ohio. Back at the FBI, we repeated the procedure for each of them, comparing their digitized images with the Ohio photograph on Gene's computer. In each case, although they agreed on one point or another because of how they had been chosen, serious disparities remained. If the chin was right, the brow was wrong. When the eyes agreed, the teeth did not. Not one of them was anywhere nearly as close to a total match as the skull from Ohio.

Our purpose in developing the system was twofold: to reduce the time required for this form of study and to improve its reliability. This technique is still a long way from being an absolute and positive means of identification. Some skulls are more unique than others, and at the lower end of the age scale there is insufficient data to validate even the most impressive alignments. Evidence collected by this method is not yet legally admissible as final proof in American courts, though it has gained limited acceptance in Europe. In this country,

The remains of this cross-dressing male were found inside a Madison, Wisconsin chimney in 1989 (see Chapter 7). This is the first time he has been depicted as both a woman and a man. If you think you have information about the case, write Detective James I. Grann III, Madison Police Department, 211 South Carroll Street, Madison, Wisconsin 53710, or call (608) 266-4368.

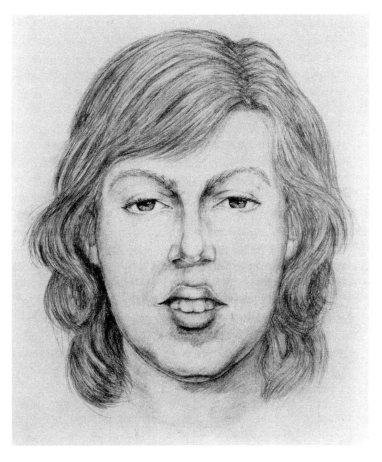

Only two bodies have remained unidentified in the state of Vermont over the past decade. This one was found on the Canadian border in Canaan, Vermont, in May 1988. She was a young white woman, probably in her late teens, short with a thin build, and had brown or blonde hair. Cause of death was one or more severe blows to the head. She most likely died between 1982 and 1987. So far, forty-five possible matches have been ruled out, mainly on the basis of dental comparisons. If you think you might know something about this case, contact the Vermont State Police, Troop B, St. Johnsbury Barracks, RD #3, St. Johnsbury, Vermont 05819.

The body of this Massachusetts homicide victim arrived at the Smithsonian in two large crates which also contained the soil and extensive root system in which it was embedded (see Chapter 8). Despite the advanced state of decomposition, FBI artists were able to produce this likeness based on anthropological measurements of the skull. He has never been identified.

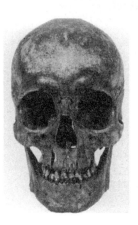

Sketch and three-dimensional reproduction of the man in the iron coffin. At first thought to be an intruder in a private family cemetery in Louisiana, he had been dead about a century when his unusual casket was accidentally unearthed in the early 1960s. Smithsonian clothing historians were fascinated by his period bow tie, black woolen broadcloth coat, knitted silk gloves, and the fact that he was buried in shoes—an uncommon practice for that period. His identity is still unproven, but the Smithsonian's Doug Owsley has built a strong case that he was affiliated with the family owning the plot. He died at about age fifty, between 1860 and 1870, was 5'6" tall, and had a distinctly robust 16-inch neck. Two facial reproductions from the skull, one in clay and one by an artist using composites, were done as a scientific exercise, not in any hope that they would lead to identification.

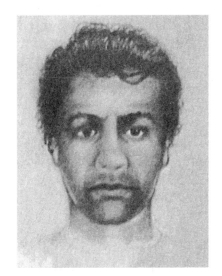

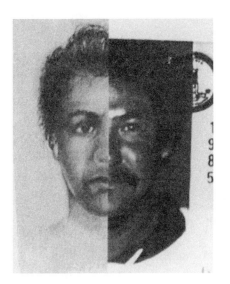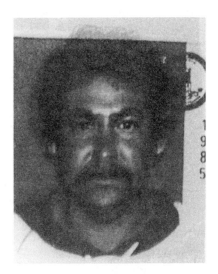

In forensic facial reproduction, unless there is supporting evidence, close doesn't count. This forensic artist's sketch from the skull of a Maryland roadside murder victim looks a lot like the photo on Blas Espinoza's driver license. "Espinoza" was the alias of an illegal immigrant who disappeared from a Maryland farm in 1985. Because no dental or medical records could be found for comparisons, however, the body is still officially unidentified.

however, it offers another benefit to the legal profession, simply by virtue of its visual drama: the display of such comparisons provides maximum impact in a courtroom setting.

My colleague Bill Maples, of the C. A. Pound Human Identification Laboratory at the University of Florida in Gainesville, provides a case in point. A Florida man, on parole and with a long criminal history, was arrested and charged with beating elderly women, obtaining their bank cards and access codes, and then removing cash from their accounts through an automatic teller machine. Apparently the man hadn't noticed a 16 mm black-and-white camera at one of the windows beside the ATM, but it noticed him. Nearly thirty photographs showed him in various poses, with sunglasses and without, as he went about his larcenous chores.

Following his arrest, the suspect's parole was revoked and he was returned to jail. Bill Maples learned that in his previous residency he had established himself as the weight-lifting champion of the state prison, so before his portrait session Maples requested that authorities provide him with some form of protection. He says they responded with the Florida version of the Incredible Hulk, who watched quietly from the sidelines, and the subsequent shoot proceeded without a hitch. Armed with a court order, Maples used a 35 mm camera to photograph the suspect, trying to duplicate the positions of the images in the bank photographs. He took about 100 pictures in a five-minute period and used the contact sheet to pick out the best match. He then employed his system of two high-resolution video security cameras to superimpose the images taken at the bank with those he had taken of the suspect. The comparison was made easier by the fact that the suspect had short hair; a variety of skin defects, including a prominent mole on the left side of his nose; and evidence of Stahl's disease, a congenital condition characterized by unusual thickening at the top of the ear.

During the pretrial conference, the attorney for the accused viewed the superimpositions. Before he fully realized what he was looking at, and perhaps sensing a trick, he asked how Maples had put the sunglasses on the photos of his client taken at the prison. Maples responded that the image was a superimposition, accomplished through the use of video cameras in his laboratory. The defense lawyer reportedly looked at the ground and slowly shook his head.

15

BUT ARE YOU SURE?

In May of 1990, in the woods of the Cascade District of Snohomish County, Washington, a millyard worker named Melvin Lloyd White killed one of his guests at a drinking party by hitting him on the head, in the time-honored tradition, with a tire iron. He then dragged the body down a grass-covered path behind his cabin off Hidden Valley Road, near Granite Falls, leaving heel marks and a trail of blood on his way to the river. One witness arrived at the launching site just in time to catch a glimpse of the corpse as it bobbed briskly downstream in the fast water. A couple of days later, some of the surviving guests talked to the police, and even though the body couldn't be found in a preliminary search of the riverbank, Mel was arrested and charged with murder.

The remains finally were recovered two months later in a logjam some distance from where the body had been dumped into the river. Some of the toes and lesser body parts had become detached in transit, but there was enough left that the identity of the victim could be confirmed from dental records; his death was certified, and an evidence package was sent off to Washington. Was there any chance that I'd be

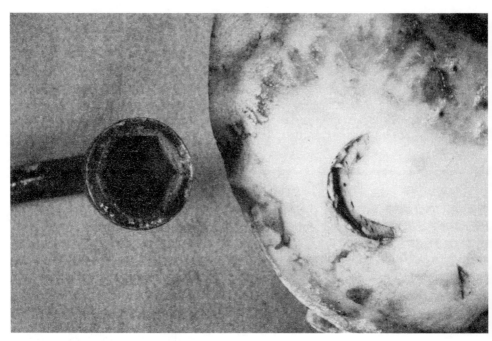

Lethal weapons leave their own signatures. Here a tire iron is shown with the skull of Melvin Lloyd White's victim.

able to match the tire iron, the police asked, with some dents and a large hole in the skull?

The principal evidence was the penetrating fracture; it went through both the outer table and inner table of the skull, knocking out a plug of bone the diameter of the lug head and driving it into the brain. It was easy enough to match the tire iron with both the shape of the plug and the diameter of the punched hole. Based on my examination, I was invited out to the West Coast to testify at Melvin White's trial.

His attorney wasn't very happy to see me. He put me through a Frye procedure, which essentially placed the science of forensic anthropology on trial, away from the jury, in an attempt to disqualify my testimony against his client. The attempt failed. Even though the killer's attorney appeared to lack a serious appreciation for my discipline, it was soon readily apparent why he had tried to stop me. When I finally did get to testify before the jury, I stood before them with the skull in one hand and the iron bar in the other and demonstrated how the lug wrench fitted exactly inside the punch hole. It was damning evidence.

Naturally the defense didn't give up in the attempt to challenge almost everything I had to say, but my testimony was fairly cut and dried, and it was allowed to stand. The lawyer even asked how the evidence had been packed for shipment to the FBI, apparently hoping to suggest that the skull got its marks from banging against the tire iron all the way across the country, rather than when his client had bashed the victim on the head. I answered that each item in the carton had been carefully insulated from every other item by Styrofoam.

Between the Frye procedure and the explanation for the jury, I was on the stand for an unusually long time, and toward the end I could feel the strain. At that point, just as I thought I was going to be allowed to step down, the defense attorney came at me from a completely unexpected angle. He pointed out that I had given all the measurements for the injuries in metrics, and he asked me to tell the jury how many millimeters are in an inch. I held up my right hand where everyone could see, and demonstrated the length in the space between the thumb and forefinger. "A centimeter, or ten millimeters, is about this long," I said.

Even as I spoke, it was crystal clear from the look on his face that my casual approximation wasn't going to be good enough, and I also realized I was so tired that I wasn't certain I could rely on my recollection of the exact number (25.4, if you run into the same attorney). Rather than risk being corrected for giving a wrong answer to a question of such obvious irrelevancy, I stated simply that I couldn't recall. He turned to the jury with a look that couldn't have been more triumphant had I admitted to the murder. With a flourish of the hand that could easily have been interpreted as the flushing of my credibility down the drain, he looked back and told me, in a tone rich with scorn, that for my future information there were 254 millimeters in an inch. Even in my exhaustion, it was obvious his number was off by a factor of at least 10.

The weekend after the trial, I was out in the country riding my tractor, clearing some land and also trying to clear my mind. I've often wished I had a baseball player's ability to "shake off the pitch" right after letting go of the ball, to put contentious issues or unresolved problems out of my mind once I leave the witness stand or the office or a dig. That's one wish that is seldom granted; as a rule, I bring them home with me. This time, as I geared down the tractor for another assault on a briar patch, the terrible thought popped into my mind that I had been wrong about the Styrofoam packaging.

Granted, Styrofoam *seemed* like the right answer, but was that the reason I had said it? My thoughts raced back to the day, months before, when I had opened the carton in my office. I kept seeing Styrofoam in my mind's eye, but now I wondered, was I seeing it because I had said that's what it was under oath and now I didn't dare see it otherwise? I had absolutely no doubt that the evidence had been carefully wrapped, and that there was no possibility whatever that the tool mark had been imprinted after, rather than during, the murder. But defendants sometimes hang or go free on trivial details such as this one, and tiny errors of memory can prove to be the nail in the horseshoe that lost the battle and the war. Even though I knew that my memory was pretty reliable, I wondered if in this case I had been betrayed by a subconscious need to produce an answer under pressure, and if the answer had been wrong. Had I confused the tire iron case with one of the many others that had subsequently flowed through my laboratory? That night, I dreamed of Styrofoam packaging.

On Monday morning, the first call I made was to the FBI. Could they look in their records to tell me how the evidence in that case had been wrapped? That's a perfectly legitimate question in this line of work, so I was confident that asking it was not likely to raise doubts about how well I was holding onto my marbles. After what seemed an eternity of waiting, the voice on the other end said, "Sure, here it is. Styrofoam."

"Thanks," I said. "That's what I thought."

A short time later, the prosecutor wrote to tell me the jury had convicted the killer. Once more, I was glad I'd made that call.

In the majority of the many and varied forensic arts, most witness work is painted on the broad canvas that stretches between reasonable doubt and absolute certainty. As a rule, the system does not require the defense lawyer to prove an airtight case for a client's innocence, and few convictions are won because the prosecution is lucky enough to have a videotape of the accused committing the alleged offense. Justice may try to be blind, but the kindred arts of prosecution and defense are often highly subjective, especially where a jury is involved, and nowhere more so than in the interpretation of evidence.

When expert witnesses are called, it is not uncommon to find equally respected, equally credible authorities testifying to exactly opposite conclusions from the same information. If the issue is mental competence, it is almost guaranteed the jury will be treated to diametrically opposing portraits by psychiatrists with equally impressive credentials. Neurologists commonly contradict each other in tort cases, and so do orthopedists. The role of the expert witness in many fields is frequently little more than the art of advocacy dressed up in a white coat. I'm glad to say that is usually not the case in forensic anthropology.

As in any other science, there are different levels of certitude in my own discipline, and as elsewhere any evidence subject to interpretation is also subject to debate. Even so, it is far less likely than in other sciences that two genuine forensic anthropologists properly qualified through the accrediting body for their field of specialization will find themselves in court arguing on opposite sides of an issue. One reason is that the standards for certification are reasonably rigorous, and the experts are all trained to those standards. Another is that the number of credentialed diplomates is still only in the double digits. Perhaps even more important, anthropology has always been an academic science, not a commercial one, and although anthropologists get paid for the work they do, I have never heard of a diplomate selling his or her skill and knowledge to mere advocacy.

I've always had the philosophy that a professional scientist, anthropologist or otherwise, should never be wrong in anything that is put into the record. That doesn't mean in forensics that every examination leads to a positive identification. It does mean that the anthropologist should be completely accurate in the degree of certainty with which scientific findings are presented. To some extent, that entails nothing more than choosing the right words, such as when to use "probably" or "maybe" instead of "without doubt," and "unlikely" or "rare" instead of "never." And vice versa.

Yet there can be differences between how one forensic anthropologist and another will testify on the witness stand. A lot of the questions we get in court ask us to establish probabilities, which is perfectly legitimate if the answers are based on observed fact evaluated against a reasonable body of experience. A relatively inexperienced expert witness may interpret that kind of question as an invitation to speculate. Besides, some anthropologists are more experienced, and therefore more confident, in particular aspects of their science than others. Forensic anthropologists are frequently asked in court—usually by the defense—to attach a numerical value to the probable accuracy of an estimate of age, race, sex, or some other factor related to the identity of the victim. What are the chances, for instance, that the bones are from a female, when I have testified the remains are male?

The answer is that the chances depend on what evidence is available for the estimate. If the remains are adult and include the pubis, it's reasonable to say the chances of accuracy approach 100 percent. If the pubis is missing, then the accuracy can range from about 70 percent to 95 percent or even higher, depending on what else there is and how clearly it models established sex criteria. There's nothing wrong with offering an opinion along with a clear statement of probability. What *would* be wrong would be to state that the skeleton of a child was a black female, aged nine, as I was once asked to do in court, without at the same time giving some sense of the likelihood of error. There can be powerful clues to all of these things even in the skeletons of children; but any science based in part on averages is subject to the anomalies that prove the rules, and to present averages as absolutes, even when you're guessing correctly, is to misrepresent your science.

On the other hand, not all misrepresentations are intentional. Professional witnesses have to be very careful not to be swayed, especially without their knowing it, by their sense of what others, such as the police or prosecutors, want to hear. It's very important for forensic anthropologists to keep in mind the independent nature of their science; the case is more commonly brought to us by the prosecutor than the defense, but in either instance we have to avoid subscribing to anyone else's agenda. Scientists should never allow their testimony to be shaped to support any scenario that has not first been proven in the laboratory, no matter how strong the personalities or how beguiling the incentive to please a client.

Even in the intense pressure often associated with a capital case, I have found that most seasoned prosecutors and defense attorneys won't attempt to influence my testimony or place me in a position where I feel expected to testify beyond my expertise. What they ask for instead is my opinion, the probabilities that are attached to it, and from that information they determine their own strategy of how to use what I am going to say.

Not all lawyers are equally circumspect, however, and there are times when I have been subjected to intense persuasion—both beforehand and on the witness stand—by advocates who were anxious to tailor my testimony to fit their suit. In those situations, the witness has to make a conscious resolve to remain true to the facts and not be caught up by the hopes or assumptions of others.

A good example of the necessity for such resolve can be found in two trials related to a double murder on Palmyra Island in the remote Pacific. I was one of the experts at both trials. I still vividly recall my sense that the defense attorney in each was determined to bend my testimony to support his own interpretation of the evidence.

These particular cases had received a lot of publicity, and feelings were pretty intense. The prosecution had developed a scenario about the murder, some of it compelling. The defense had a scenario as well. In both trials, I recall deliberately arming myself against the risk of inferring one bit more than could be proven by the evidence, regardless of pressure from either side.

The undisputed portion of the case was fairly simple. In the summer of 1974, two couples found themselves on Palmyra Island, an otherwise uninhabited atoll 1,000 miles south of Hawaii. The older couple were Mac and Muff Graham, relatively well-to-do and sailing an elegant, well-appointed yacht, the *Sea Wind*, on an adventure cruise that had begun in San Diego. The other couple, Buck Walker and his girlfriend, were on the run from Buck's drug charges; their boat was also named after the wind, but the *Iola* had been rescued from a wreck and was barely seaworthy. In the course of whatever followed, there was a major shuffling of those basic facts. Sometime later, Buck and his girlfriend appeared back in Hawaii, and they were aboard a repainted yacht that turned out to be the *Sea Wind*. Neither their original boat, the *Iola*, nor the *Sea Wind*'s real owners were anywhere to be found. Buck and the girl were arrested.

The fate of the Grahams remained unknown until after another yachting couple stopped off at remote Palmyra in November 1980 and found a human skull and other skeletal remains on the beach. Nearby were a large aluminum container, a lid, and the wire apparently used

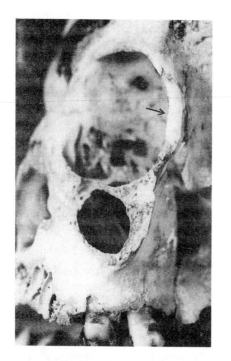

The skull from Palmyra Island. The photograph at left shows an area eroded mechanically—an effect sometimes called "coffin-wear." At bottom, the distinct borders of the burned area indicate that the remains were burned while the bones were covered with flesh.

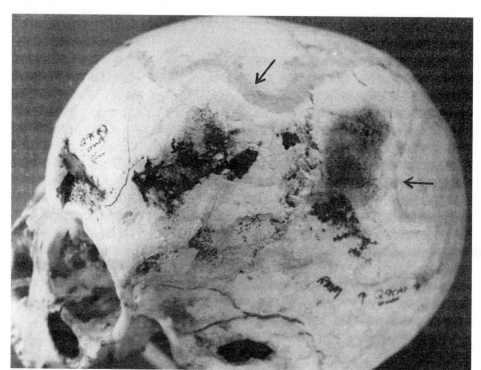

to tie it down. The remains were identified as having belonged to Muff Graham, and they found their way to my laboratory for any perspective I might provide on the circumstances of her death.

It had been six years since her disappearance, and the evidence on the bones was difficult to interpret. There were signs of intense heat having been applied to the top of the skull, and in the center of the affected area I noticed black deposits embedded in the bone. The bones of the face showed a peculiar flattened pattern of abrasion known as "coffin wear," a likely indicator of prolonged contact with a relatively flat object. Elsewhere, on one side of the skull in the thin area of the temporal bone, was a hole with outwardly beveled margins. Although it had the characteristics of an exit site for a bullet, there were no associated lead fragments on the X-rays, and there was no entrance site. One of the long bones of the lower leg showed a spiral fracture and there was evidence of rodent gnawing on some parts of the skeleton. The tibia, which had the fracture, also showed extensive erosion, as though it had been subject to the swirling of sand and water over a prolonged period of time.

Each of these observations entailed its own set of difficulties in interpretation, given all the unknown factors in the case. It was hard to reconcile the fresh, uneroded area of the black deposit on the skull with the heavily eroded tibia. Did the hole in the skull represent an unusual gunshot wound, or was it nothing more sinister than additional postmortem erosion? As the medical examiner for San Francisco, Dr. Boyd Stephens, later pointed out, gas pressure associated with contact gunshot wounds occasionally can produce external beveling even at entrance sites; however, such a wound would ordinarily be associated with radiographically dense lead particles, which were absent in this case, and the hole could have been produced by some other factor. The evidence for burning on the skull also was subject to alternative explanations. It could have been produced by a blowtorch known to have been present at the scene, but I had to admit to Walker's defense attorney that it also could have been produced by an intense beach fire if the rest of the skull had been imbedded in the sand. I gave an opinion that the coffin wear could have been produced by the hard surface of the aluminum container, but I couldn't rule out the possibility it had come from contact with some other surface.

Walker and his girlfriend were charged separately, and I was called to testify at both trials. Walker went first. At that one, my cautionary interpretations may have appeared helpful to the defense, but he was convicted anyway. For the expert witnesses, the second trial was pretty much a repeat of the first. However, the girlfriend was defended by a different attorney, who had the double advantage of having observed the first case and of being able to remind the jury that the real perpetrator of this crime was now safely in jail. Naturally, his defense built in part on Walker's conviction.

It's safe to assume that he would have been delighted if I had joined in that strategy by stating definitively that the burns in the skull had been caused by a blowtorch and that the hole had been caused by a bullet. Unfortunately, there were exactly as many unknowns the second time around as the first, and the data were still too equivocal for such exact statements. Although such events could have happened, I could not prove them from the physical evidence alone. I had already testified in the first trial that various scenarios could explain the results, and I was not about to lock in on one of them as my expert opinion at the second.

Although I did not deliver the opinions the defense apparently hoped for, other evidence suggested the defendant had not been involved in the murder. The jury returned a verdict of not guilty.

There's also a risk from the witness's own ego. No one is exempt from the human desire to be smart, to know the answers, but being the expert from the Smithsonian doesn't mean I remember everything or that I'm always right. Lawyers for both sides often play on the human temptation for an expert to say more than the facts or his/her expertise reasonably allow.

On the other hand, most scientists try to add to their expertise every chance they get. The case that opens this book, the story of the murdered Puerto Rican girl whose remains were found in a Virginia berry patch, held just that kind of opportunity—and it's also a good example of the temptation toward premature closure. Because Larry Angel had already contributed so much to the case, I had to guard against unconsciously turning any of his speculations about the cut finger, which he had offered solely to indicate future avenues of inquiry, into assumptions that might find their way into court disguised as scientific certitude. This caveat was very much in my mind that morning in the San Juan mortuary.

After reading Larry's messages on the bags, I washed all the girl's bones, inventoried them, labeled them, and made a list of those with alterations. When I finished the examination at the morgue, I then took the cut phalanx, along with several of the bones that had been chewed, to the nearby Primate Research Center, where I examined them under a dissecting microscope.

The cut phalanx was distinctly different from all the gnawed bones in having what appeared to be a relatively sheared surface. The others were extremely irregular, with depressed edges or actual tooth marks, and all the other alterations were typical of those produced by carnivores. The phalanx was broken off on a straight plane, suggesting something different from what had happened to the others, although the planar cut was not definitively the result of the clean, straight stroke of a knife.

When I called the prosecutor in Virginia to tell him I had found and examined the lost phalanx, he laughed with relief. "Waiting for your call was like anticipating word of my first baby," he said. I began to wonder if the importance being attached to this evidence had become greater than the inferences I would be able to attach to it from my examination.

I finally decided that in order to analyze the bones properly, I would need better equipment than was available in Puerto Rico, so I wound up taking them back to Washington.

Even under a higher-powered microscope at the Smithsonian, I still couldn't find the very fine cut signature of a knife. I had never seen a carnivore do that to a bone, but in examining it further and talking about it with colleagues, I developed the opinion that it was theoretically possible that the cut could have originated with a dog or a fox, if the animal had gotten the bone in his back teeth in just the right way.

I began to ask myself what other event than a knife stroke or an unusual carnivore bite could account for the same pattern. The prosecutor asked me if the shearing could have been the result of a struggle in which her finger had been slammed in the car door. Could a lawn mower or brush cutter have run over it? Could it have been something similar to a knife but cruder, such as an ax, machete, grub hoe, or some other type of large instrument?

Once again, for good or bad, because I'm not the kind of person who leaves all of his problems in the office, I kept thinking about the riddle of the phalanx all that following weekend, which included Memorial Day. On Monday we were going to have a barbecue in the backyard, and the mystery was still with me when I went down to the supermarket to buy chicken. As I picked up a package from the meat cooler, it came to me how many structural similarities there are between the cancellous bone in the end of a chicken drumstick and

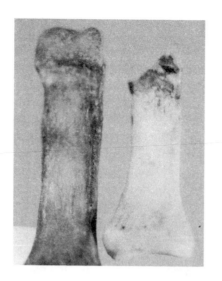

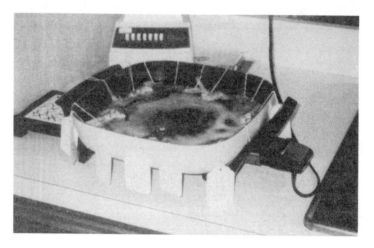

Sometimes unconventional means are necessary. At top left is the altered phalanx from the Goochland case. Attempts to re-create the fracture pattern in similar tissue led the author to experiment with chicken parts: first by cutting, then by slamming drumsticks in a car door. The bones, identified with tags, were macerated at home. At lower right is a partial drumstick exhibiting a fracture similar to that in the phalanx.

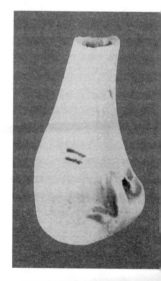

the end of a human finger. Although the cortical bone of a chicken and other birds is denser than in humans, and the internal part more hollow, the overall thickness is similar. I threw an extra pack into the cart. Much to the delight of my son Max, I announced when I got home that I was planning on using those particular chicken legs for some forensic experiments.

With the first one, I simply sliced off the end with a sharp knife from the kitchen.

The next I cut with a very dull knife.

From the cellar I retrieved a machete which I use to clear brush on my tree farm, and lopped off the end of the third.

Another I hit with the grub blade of a small mattock, normally used for digging out stumps.

With the fifth and sixth, I tested the theory of the slamming car door; on the first try, the bone was too far into the door jamb and broke in the wrong place; the next time I held the drumstick while Max did the slamming, and it hit just right.

The seventh I set in the ground and ran over it with our mower. It was a disaster: the blades picked it up and turned it to mush.

We then gathered up the five drumsticks on which the tests had been conducted successfully. I carefully used a knife to strip off most of the meat, which was subsequently barbecued and consumed by my co-investigators, and the rest I simmered away in hot water. The next day I took the clean bones to work with me and looked at their severed ends under the microscope.

As I suspected, the pattern of the knife cut was extremely different from the pattern in the phalanx. However, the form of the fracture, the amount of jaggedness, and the approximately planar surface were all closely duplicated in both the bone that had been cut by the mattock and the one that had been slammed in the car door. This appeared to rule out a sharp knife, and while it didn't tell me which particular alternative may have been involved, it pointed to the likelihood of some sort of dull-edged instrument—even, still, the posterior carnassial teeth of a canine.

Soon after I completed the experiment, I learned from the prosecutor that the defendant had pleaded guilty to the charges and it appeared the case would never reach trial. Weeks later, memories of my experiments on the chicken bones were fading when the prosecutor called back. Shortly before sentencing, the defendant had withdrawn his guilty plea and it now appeared we were going to court after all.

As before, the prosecution was intensely interested in limiting the possible explanations of the cut phalanx. I had shown that the trauma could be roughly duplicated by slamming the car door of our family Voyager on a drumstick, but the victim had been driving a 1974 Ford Pinto. Would we expect the same effect from the slamming doors of a Pinto? As frequently happens in this work, I was out on the edge of my existing knowledge, and I replied I had no idea. I'd already invested an enormous amount of time in this case, and was swamped with other work. But the prosecutor leaned on me to help once again, finding a soft spot by reminding me how long the family of the victim had been waiting to learn the truth and receive justice. I said, "Okay, can you find me a 1974 Ford Pinto close to the Smithsonian?"

Within an hour I received a call from a detective. "Doc, we've located just the car you're looking for." It was in Arlington, just across the river and minutes from my office. I have to admit I received the news with mixed emotions.

We agreed to meet at the local Safeway, where we purchased packages of wings, thighs, and drumsticks; then we drove another few blocks to where the Pinto and its owner were awaiting us. I sensed that the owner's feelings about this adventure were somewhat ambiguous as well. He was very cooperative, but he kept glancing around the driveway in a way that suggested some concern for the opinions of his neighbors. I can't say I blamed him. We were slamming and reslamming the doors and the hatchback on pieces of poultry in our continuing—and by now tedious—attempt to reproduce the angular trauma seen on the forensic artifact. We finished as quickly as possible, donated the unused parts to the car owner, hurriedly cleaned the residue from the doors and frame, and I drove home with the specimens to remove the soft tissue in the privacy of my kitchen.

The next morning at the Smithsonian, I treated the bones further to clarify the nature of the trauma. Of eighteen experiments, seventeen produced breaks with crushed and jagged edges, quite distinct from the Goochland phalanx. The one other experiment, slamming the right side of the hatchback on a chicken thigh, produced bony changes that were very close to the cut on the human sample. But the experiment had injected new caution to the limits of our interpretation, and I wasn't at all sure it had illuminated much more than our uncertainty.

Just as I was preparing for my court testimony, the prosecutor called one final time. The defendant had once again pleaded guilty. This time he had signed the necessary documents and there would be no turning back. Only he knows for sure what happened to that phalanx. But after two false takeoffs, our chicken story never got to fly in court.

By contrast to the Goochland case, where the skeletal remains were fairly complete but information on the murder was nonexistent, a fragmentary skull from Tennessee arrived at the Smithsonian some years ago with enough documentation on the killing to support a short novella.

The skull was believed by police to have belonged to a young man who was murdered while camping. He had pitched his tent on the bank of a stream, so the story went, and one evening two other campers set up next to him. While getting ready to fish the next morning, the victim noticed his money was missing, and he confronted one of the two strangers. The accused thief knocked him to the ground with a fist to the jaw, then hit him on the head with a flat rock while he was struggling to regain his feet. There was just one blow to the top rear of the skull, but it produced an enormous flow of blood and the victim immediately collapsed. Some four months later, the broken skull was recovered 75 yards downstream from the campsite by park rangers and agents of the FBI, guided in their efforts by the marvelously detailed description of the alleged murderer's associate.

The scenario was so complete on the face of it that one might assume the request for a forensic examination of the skull was little more than a formality, part of a natural, majestic progression between the thoroughly documented crime and inexorable justice. But as I continued turning the pages of the report, I was comforted to find other information to support my deeply held conviction that things are not always as they appear.

For example, I learned that the alleged killer's associate had produced this story after being arrested in another state while in possession of the missing man's car, three months after the above incident. When police checked back over his trail, they found proof that he had sold the camper's equipment a short time earlier. His story about his associate and the victim's missing money was not the first the suspect offered to explain how he happened to be in the car and, needless to say, none of his explanations, including this one, portrayed him as the slayer. Police checked with camp authorities and gas stations around the area and determined that the other man had indeed been seen driving the victim's car after the date given for the killing, and the other man's face had been badly bruised, indicative of a fist fight. But even if this latest version of the story seemed to be holding up under investigation, at least one important piece fell apart when police plugged in the lie detector. That was the piece related to the author's own involvement in the fight and killing.

Almost reluctantly I laid down the report and turned back to the only aspect of this case that was in my province to evaluate. I had fitted the fragments of bone together to form one incomplete calvarium, which included most of the base and the left side and upper frontal portion, but lacked the face and most of the right side. I had estimated the age at between eighteen and thirty-five; now I knew the presumed victim had been twenty. The morphology of the supraorbital ridges and mastoid process strongly suggested a male, which was another fit. There was no reliable basis for estimating stature, race, or weight.

In general, the evidence of trauma matched the story as well. It consisted of a compressed fracture measuring 70 mm by 40 mm and extending in an oblong shape on the back portions of the left parietal and temporal. It was just the kind of result one might expect from the impact of a large blunt object, and was in more or less the right place to support the story of the flat rock.

An unusual bonus in this case was the availability of medical radiographs of the alleged victim's head, taken seven years before, when he had been thirteen. But that potential advantage was largely canceled out by the age difference and by the incompleteness of the calvarium. The suture lines change with maturation, not so much in shape as in clarity, and any possibility of a match with the frontal sinus patterns was thwarted by the loss of the necessary facial bones.

Considered individually, none of these factors permitted me to make a positive identification of the victim, but by the same token none of them positively ruled it out. Taken together, they offered a strong circumstantial argument for the possibility that the skull was just whose they thought it was, and I underscored that conclusion in my report. It was very similar to the situation in the Karen Marsden murder: before the police located the medical X-rays from which I was able to prove conclusively that the frontal sinus patterns were identical to those of the calvarium skull, I was willing to go to court with what we had and let the jury decide the probability, for themselves, that the skull was hers.

Maybe in all of this there's a good rule of thumb for courtroom objectivity. Say everything you know that pertains, and not a bit more. The extent to which an expert witness allows himself to be drawn in at the start of a case can be exactly equal to the length of the limb he finds himself sitting on at the end.

There are limbs and there are limbs, and not every case a forensic anthropologist examines involves consequences as dire as those of murder. But professionally and scientifically, that rule of thumb is every bit as relevant.

In one such non-forensic case in 1987, I was asked to examine a skeleton thought to belong to Gabriel Duvall, who had served successively as Comptroller of the United States and Justice of the United States Supreme Court in the early nineteenth century. Duvall had been buried in 1844 in a family cemetery in Maryland, and a coffin was exhumed by his descendants, who intended to move their illustrious ancestor to a more accessible location on the family estates. But first, they wanted some assurance they had the right body.

There was already a lot of evidence that these were the remains of an individual of great prestige. He had been buried in a mahogany coffin with a green velvet lining and a thick glass window at the level of the occupant's face. The skull contained a gold tooth. The remains were exhumed from a private graveyard, which contained less than two dozen graves. But because the plot was small, it was already crowded at the time of Duvall's death and there was no room for him in the area immediately adjacent to the remains of either his first or second wife. I was therefore asked to search for other indications of his identity.

The casket had collapsed and largely rotted away long before the exhumation, and the resulting coffin wear on the skeleton took the form of a planar flattening of the nasal area of the face. The teeth were stained green, probably as the result of long-term contact with copper in the frame of the viewing port. From the condition of the teeth and jawbones, the closure of cranial vault sutures, and arthritic wear on the joints, the body could have been that of a man between fifty and seventy years or older at the time of death; historical records indicate Duvall stayed in remarkably good shape into his ninety-second year, so there was room in that estimate for a fair degree of stretch.

The record also indicated another possible clue to identity, but not one that proved helpful. Duvall had been involved in a riding accident a couple of decades before his death, and had broken his arm in two places. X-rays indicated only that either the arm had healed sufficiently for signs of the breaks to be obliterated, or those signs were destroyed by extensive postmortem damage to the same bone. However, based on all the consistencies between my other observations related to size, sex, facial morphology, ancestry, and social stature, I concluded it was likely that the remains belonged to Justice Duvall. The body was transferred to the new location and reinterred with appropriate honors by his descendants.

16

DIFFERENT STROKES

In the fall of 1892, every schoolchild in America knew exactly how a broad-browed, full-lipped, slightly pop-eyed spinster was reputed to have done away with her father on a hot August morning as he napped on a downstairs couch, and then went upstairs and did the same thing to her stepmother in their home in the coastal mill town of Fall River, Massachusetts:

> *Lizzie Borden took an ax*
> *and gave her father forty whacks.*
> *When she saw what she had done,*
> *she gave her mother forty-one.*

Although a jury decided otherwise and Lizzie was acquitted of both killings, and even though three other elements may have been in error (it could have been some other weapon than an ax; fewer whacks were reported; and the distaff victim was Lizzie's stepmother, not her mother), for many partisans that durable jingle represents the judgment of history.

A colleague of mine at George Washington University, Professor James E. Starrs, has undertaken to settle the matter once and for all. He proposes to exhume the two bodies, which will entail the clearing of a number of hurdles with both descendants and local authorities, then to match the evidence on their bones with the cutting edge of the alleged murder weapon, which is still available. In fact, the hatchet is probably the single most important historical artifact in Fall River. If he succeeds in raising the remains, I have agreed to join a team from the University of Massachusetts at Amherst to work with him, as I have several times before, on the forensic anthropology.

As a general rule, alterations in bone approximately reflect the size and shape of the instruments that made them—although a variety of alterations can derive from a single source, depending on the direction, angle, and force of the blow or insertion. Blades (including those of axes and hatchets), bullets, tire irons, and hammers may be the most frequently seen and most easily recognizable of such objects, but they are far from the only ones to leave a signature imprint when applied to bone in cases of murder. Over the years, forensic anthropology has accumulated a substantial body of evidence showing the effects of a variety of weapons on the human skeleton.

The best evidence for trauma from the time of death consists of so-called green bone response, where the bone, which is still covered with flesh, bends or twists in ways that are not possible after the organic components have deteriorated. Stabbings, for example, typically produce a slight incision where the edge or the point of the knife strikes bone, usually very slight alterations that are easily missed without careful cleaning and examination. This condition contrasts with what happens when a blade cuts a dried and perhaps brittle bone several weeks or months after death. An alteration caused by a knife inserted at or about the time of death will also have very distinct borders and lack any evidence of healing or long-term bony change.

If knife marks in green bone can point to the possible cause of death, the absence of such marks is no guarantee that a knife was not used. I examined one skeleton in a case from the Midwest where a bloody shirt was also recovered at the crime scene, and although the shirt had ten cut marks on the left side of the front and four more on the right side of the back, evidence on the bone was limited to the eighth and ninth thoracic vertebrae and the left fourth rib; of the fourteen apparent insertions, only three struck bone. And in a double murder described in Chapter 22, the only sign of the knife that was probably used to kill both victims was a tiny nick in the bone of one hand, probably the result of an attempt to parry the thrust of the blade.

In most circumstances, the green bone or bending effect from such a thrust results in the raised edge of bone curling inward along the edges of the incision. If the incision is located near the margin of a thin flat bone like a scapula or rib, a slice of bone may be bent outward instead, but it is equally characteristic of a stabbing. This is one reason a single instrument can cause a variety of incisions on different parts of the same skeleton. Another reason is that various parts of an instrument, such as the handle, butt, blade, point, hilt, or spine of a knife, each produce its own impression. A third is that the instrument, especially a blade, can change shape over the course of multiple insertions.

An example of mixed trauma resulting from different uses of the same instrument—stabbing with the point of a knife, slashing with the blade, and hammering at the victim with the handle—was a case I received a couple of years ago from Massachusetts. I found evidence on the bones of a teen-age girl that two different-shaped blades had been used in her murder, and I suggested that the marks may have come from a single blade which changed its shape during the course of the violent killing. When the murder weapon was matched against the marks on the bones, that theory proved to be correct—and it was further found that imprints of added trauma on the facial bones roughly matched the other end of the knife, which had been used as a bludgeon.

It can be difficult to distinguish between cut marks made at the time of death and those made soon after. The latter can be the result of postmortem dismemberment or, in archaeological specimens, cultural funerary practices. In prehistoric ossuaries such as those I have examined in Ecuador and Maryland, cut marks on long bones are often evidence of the defleshing and disarticulation of body parts in preparation for burial.

I also have seen those same postmortem cut marks, for the same purpose, in murder cases. A couple of years ago a package of body parts—two arms, two legs, and a partial pelvis—arrived from western Massachusetts, where they had been found at the edge of a rest area off a rural highway. The parts of the bones associated with joints showed clear characteristic marks of cutting with a smooth blade, the likely result of disarticulation with a knife. By contrast, evidence of cutting in the thicker area of the sacrum was probably indicative of a saw.

That case is unsolved.

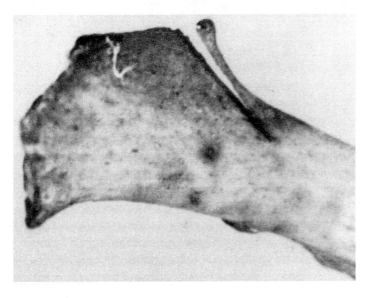

The bones above shows the bending effect that occurs when a cut is inflicted *perimortem*—at or about the time of death. Cuts in the distal ends of the two bones at right, found at an ancient site in Virginia, usually signify defleshing or disarticulation of a corpse before burial.

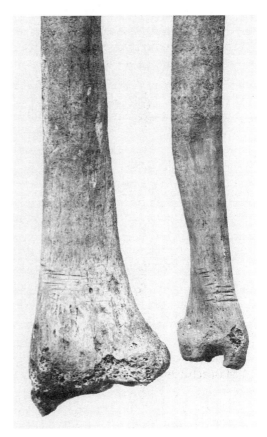

When perimortem alterations are clearly distinct from postmortem ones, because the former are on green bones and the latter are on dry, it is sometimes possible to hypothesize the chain of events by which both sets of alterations occurred. On the day before Christmas Eve in 1978, two young boys playing in a densely overgrown ravine in a midwestern cemetery found a body partially buried in a small creek. The head and the other portions of the corpse that were above the water were skeletonized, and some of the associated bones were scattered nearby along the water's edge.

There were no disturbed gravesites or other evidence that the body had ever been a part of the normal cemetery population. Police dug the remains out of the stream bed; on the parts that were underwater, the flesh was relatively intact but had turned to adipocere. Portions of the same waxy tissue adhered to some of the scattered bones which had been recovered from damp areas along the bank. From what remained of the body and from along the edge of the creek they also recovered a man's three-piece suit, shirt, tie, belt, and underclothes. On the first working day of the new year they packaged the remains in waterproof cartons and sent them on to the FBI.

Chemical analysis further confirmed that the remains had not migrated from a graveyard when no evidence of embalming materials in the soft tissues showed up. The package was sent over to the Smithsonian. I laid the bones out on an examining table. Because of the mixed environment in which they had been recovered, more tissue adhered to some than to others, but whether the bones had been in the water or in the open air, they all appeared to be in good condition. The only evidence of carnivore activity was in small tooth marks in the proximal and distal ends of the long bones of the thighs.

The brow ridges of the skull, the general large size of the bones, and the shape of the pelvis all suggested the sex was male. From the arthritic lipping on the vertebrae, the state of development of the pubic bones, and degree of wear in the joints, I estimated the age at death as about fifty. Strong projection of the bones at the front of the mouth (alveolar prognathism) suggested black ancestry, but some European characteristics were also present; lack of anterior curvature of the femorae likewise suggested black ancestry. Mathematical interpretation of data through analysis of eight cranial measurements reinforced this estimate of a racial mix. From a single bone in the leg, using the tables developed from the collections, I was able to set the person's living stature at about six feet. On the left maxilla and right ribs I detected the marks of healed fractures. There was no indication he had ever had dental work, although a number of teeth had been lost long before his death.

I estimated the time since death, based on geographical location, time of year, and stage of decomposition, at between six months and two years. Although it was not possible to determine the cause, there was no doubt that the man had been murdered. I found a triangular perforation on the left plate of the forehead; the mark was characteristic of a blow from a sharp, hard object, and the fracture penetrated to the inner table of the skull. Immediately above that perforation was a narrow incision in the bone, indicative of stabbing by a sharp, narrow-bladed instrument such as a knife. In addition, I found six other incisions in the frontal bone, all parallel with each other and relatively small, which I interpreted as signs of slashing by a blade. Similar cut marks appeared on the ribs of the right chest area and on the left side of the lower jaw. He also had fractured ribs, but it was possible they had broken postmortem, so there was no way I could associate them with his death.

This body was an excellent example of mixed trauma, which is not uncommon in murder cases. One instrument had made the triangular perforation in the forehead, and at least one other had produced the evidence of stabbing and slashing. Although the fractured ribs would not be admissible in court because they could have been broken by some natural event long after death, the combination of injuries suggested the victim had been smashed on the head, slashed, and kicked repeatedly until he was no longer able to defend himself, and then stabbed several times in the chest. I recommended to the local medical examiner that she check for hospital X-rays of any missing persons meeting the general description I had provided, and a few weeks afterward the body was positively identified by that means. Over a decade later, the crime is still unsolved.

Injuries from hard-edged triangular objects often perforate the bones of the skull, and even though that type of injury is a familiar part of the forensic anthropologist's library of imprint designs, as a rule it says little about the probable source of the wound. The triangle is one of the most basic man-made shapes, and it is usually impossible to distinguish from the imprint alone whether the mark was left by a metal bar, a tool, a box, a paperweight, the corner of a piece of furniture, or some other familiar form.

Just such a triangular-shaped fracture was imprinted on the posterior left parietal of a body I examined very recently. The break in the bone is depressed on all its edges, and fracture lines radiate from that point throughout the skull. The body was found in underbrush near a bridge outside a major eastern city, and if there were any doubt that it was murder, a large granite curbing block was found lying where it had been dropped, across the victim's chest.

This particular case provides an example of another type of trauma which is neither perimortem nor postmortem but which took place long enough before death that it had a chance to heal. In this instance the earlier trauma was to the victim's nose, evidenced by remodeling of the bone, possibly the result of an old fight. At about the time of death the nose was again broken in the same place, and the new fracture line intersected or paralleled the healed tissue from the earlier incident.

Experienced detectives are also aware that a single weapon can produce different marks depending on how it is used. Several months after an eleven-year-old girl disappeared from a family campsite in an Idaho park in 1979, a partial skeleton, a girl's clothing, and other debris were found a few miles away. All of the evidence was carefully collected, labeled, and sent to the FBI for testing; the part that crossed the street to the Smithsonian consisted of a skull and mandible, one knife in its case, and a rock. Among other things, the accompanying paperwork from the police requested a match between the impressions in the skull from both the blade and the butt plate of the knife. They also were looking for matches with the rock.

First, I set about my normal intake ritual and examined the skull for basic data. It isn't easy to estimate sex from the bones of a young girl and there was no reason for me to make a guess; I saw that every one of the teeth remaining in the skull and jaw had been filled, and it was immediately apparent that a match with the missing girl's dental records would prove her identity beyond a doubt. The teeth also told me the age at death was between eleven and thirteen, and there was evidence from the bone structure that she likely was of European ancestry.

Much of the skull was missing. The pieces which remained showed multiple fractures, including a depressed 20 mm fracture along the right rear of the skull. Most of the breaks had been produced while the child was alive or soon after death. Those on the left side were probably produced by a large, heavy object, such as the accompanying rock. The one on the lower right closely matched the shape of the butt of the knife.

A key suspect was tried but acquitted, and the case remains open.

Bullets can also produce more than one effect. Early in 1980 I received the skeleton of an apparent murder victim, found in a weeded lot in an urban section of Louisiana. Although there was some disarticulation, it was complete except for the bones of the left hand. The victim was male, predominantly white but with some black admixture, between twenty-six and thirty-two years old, and only about 5´3" tall. There was evidence in the bones of a past cyst or massive infection in the left ear. Six spent .22-caliber bullets were found along with the body. I estimated the time since death at less than three months.

There were no bulletholes in the bones. Instead, I found three fractured bones: the left seventh rib, the right side of the ninth thoracic (midback) vertebra, and the first lumbar (lower back) vertebra. The shape of the fragments told me the force probably impacted on the front surface of the bone, and the absence of any signs of healing said the breaks coincided with death. Gunshot wounds don't always make the kind of identifiable round hole in the rest of the body that they often make in the skull. Instead, when bullets hit ribs and the backbone they often cause the kind of fracture associated with other forms of blunt trauma, and in bone cases where no bullets are recovered it is entirely possible for the true cause of death to go undetected in a conventional autopsy.

Otherwise, bullets usually leave a distinctive pattern, but like almost every other object they can leave different imprints depending on circumstance. By contrast, in cases of blunt-force trauma, the patterns of impact can be so varied and so lacking in definition that there is no way to identify the tool or, when there is evidence of blunt-force injury to several sites on the same body, even to state with certainty that one object was the cause. Two male skeletons in an unsolved double murder from the Northeast provide a case in point.

The bones of the two skeletons were generally disarticulated and intermingled, but each proved to be fairly complete when the parts were reassembled in their natural relationships. The victims were male, one about twenty and the other in his early forties, and they had both been under 5´6" in height. Although there was no identification on either body, the medical examiner had speculated from skeletal clues, strands of hair, and the type and newness of their clothing that they were illegal immigrants, probably from Latin America; my own examination supported that possibility. There were no signs of any trauma elsewhere on either skeleton, but each had sustained horrific blows to the skull.

The entire right side of the cranium of the older victim was broken and missing. Fracture lines extended through the base of the skull and through the upper edge of the right eye socket. Another large fracture arched from the upper edge of the missing section across the top of the head. The most obvious trauma was related to the huge hole where his brains had been beaten in, but there were indications on the face and the opposite side of the skull that he had received numerous other blows as well. But not one of those blows left the imprint of any identifiable object in the bone.

The younger victim had died in nearly identical fashion, and very possibly from the same instrument. But this time it was different—perhaps the blow had come from a different angle, perhaps it was delivered with greater or lesser force, perhaps the victim's tissue was more pliant. Whatever the reason, the print of the instrument, clearly definable by size and shape, was recorded indelibly in the bone. If either case comes to trial, the prosecution will have access to information on the murder weapon.

In some instances the murder weapon reveals itself because it is still lodged in the bone. Usually the instrument in question is a bullet; less frequently the broken tip of a knife. In one appalling case, the murder weapon was a blunt instrument.

The female skeleton was found in a rural area by deer hunters in the late fall, and from the state of decomposition I estimated the murder had occurred the previous summer. The only evidence of trauma was across the front of the head, from the bottom of one eye orbit, across the nasal aperture, and into the maxillary teeth. She had been savagely smashed in the face with one terrible blow—probably with the branch of a tree. In the place where the nose had been and in the broken bone below the eye, a rough-surfaced, rectangular section of wood, apparently broken off by the fatal blow, was still protruding from her shattered face.

That case also has not yet come to trial.

Three years ago I had another assignment with Jim Starrs: the exhumation and forensic examination of five suspected victims of the nineteenth-century equivalent of Hannibal the Cannibal, the notorious Colorado prospector Alferd Packer. Packer had been the lone survivor of a group of six gold miners who were marooned by a blizzard in the San Juan Mountains of Colorado in 1874. Nearly ten years later, he was convicted of having murdered Israel Swan, one of the prospectors who did not survive the winter, but the decision was overturned. He was then retried for killing all five, and that time the conviction stuck.

Packer's supporters argued that he had killed in self-defense, and eaten the victims more or less as an afterthought when he ran out of more conventional food. His detractors referred to him as "the Colorado Cannibal" and said he had harvested his companions for no other purpose than to feed himself. A widespread but apocryphal story from the trial is that he was convicted only because his victims had been Democrats.

The Packer project was a high-tech operation from start to finish. The victims' burial pit in Lake City, Colorado, was located with the help of historical records and the use of a subsurface impulse radar. The scientific team Starrs assembled included experts in geophysical engineering, archaeology, anthropology, pathology, document examination, tool-mark analysis, and firearms identification.

In that case, the forensic study of the century-old crime appeared thoroughly to vindicate the conviction of the accused. The team anthropologists—including Walter Birkby of the Human Identification Laboratory at the University of Arizona—found significant evidence on the hands and arms of the victims that they had attempted to defend themselves against the attacks which ultimately hacked them to death. Although Packer was twice convicted in connection with the murders and finally sentenced to forty years in prison, he was released in less than half that time and lived out the rest of his life in relative obscurity.

17

ANGLE OF ATTACK

In 1988, a man walked into the office of a wilderness park in Florida and told one of the rangers he had found a skeleton in the woods. For those of us who like to keep track of such things, the reason the man had gone into the woods was to relieve a full bladder. He told the ranger the body was about a mile from the office, several yards off the road. The man was so offhand about his report that the ranger was suspicious it might be a hoax, and those doubts increased when the informant declined to return to the site on the excuse that he didn't want to get involved. But the ranger went down on his own, and the skeleton was just where the man said it was, visible from 15 feet away. Tampa detectives arrived a short time later and secured the crime scene.

In life the skeleton had been that of a black male between twenty-eight and thirty-four years old, about 5'6", with a medium build. He was wearing a T-shirt with a mock university seal for "Drunken State," a pair of jeans, white athletic socks with blue bands at the top, and black leather athletic shoes. An empty vinyl wallet that may or may not have been his was found nearby. He had been dead at least six months. That would seem like enough to assure a quick match with Missing Persons records, but it wasn't, and almost two years later the body wound up in Washington for a reproduction of the face.

After verifying the above estimates, I checked the remains for skeletal and dental features to guide our artist and for possible future help in identifying the man if comparison X-rays could be located from life. I found a lot: spurs on two bones of the lower legs, a small bony bump on the right hip bone, unusual bony features on the breastbone, an old healed fracture resulting in a slight asymmetry of the nose, and, what is extremely rare, a left lower eyetooth that had never erupted and was still visible in the alveolus. There were enough unique characteristics in his teeth alone to guarantee a match with the proper lead. But from a forensic viewpoint, the most informative part of the examination was related to trauma at the time of death.

In the neck, the left horn of the telltale hyoid bone was fractured, a portion of ossified thyroid cartilage was broken as well, and the right styloid process was snapped off at the base. All three breaks could have happened either at the time of death or afterward, but under these circumstances they could well have been evidence of a blow to the throat or manual strangulation. (Sir Sidney Smith was right: the killer has to get his thumbs or shoe tip way up under the chin; even in cases of ligature strangulation, the band or noose is usually too low on the neck to catch any of these well-protected bones.) Strangulation causes localized hemorrhaging, and if the body had been recovered a lot sooner after death the evidence would have been clearer. In this case, there was no associated soft tissue to examine for signs of bleeding, and no adipocere to help establish the chronology of the breaks.

Whether or not the victim died from what happened to his throat may be academic, because he was also shot in the head. There was a circular 13 mm perforation on the left occipital bone, beveled inward, with extensive radiating fracture lines. There were corresponding perforations in the right parietal and right rear temporal region, both beveled outward. A trajectory line from the entry site to either of the apparent exits showed clearly that he was shot from behind, and that the bullets exited at a higher point in the head than where they entered. There was no sign of a second entry site.

Measuring the angle of attack can sometimes lead to inferences about the events directly related to the killing. In this case, the angle was consistent with the victim lying face down, a reasonable possibility if he had just been strangled, when the shots were fired to finish him off. But until we learn who he was or who killed him, it's unlikely we'll ever know exactly what happened.

In a very similar case that came in a few months later from a country in the Caribbean, police were able to test that same type of inference by asking the murderer.

This time the body was found under a pile of debris that included a bureau drawer and a discarded refrigerator, at the side of an unused road on the western end of the island. Like the case in Florida, the skeletal remains were wearing jeans and a printed jersey (with the logo of my favorite football team), the victim was black, of short stature and slight build, and had apparently died of two gunshots to the head. A few weeks later police caught the killer, a local, who admitted to this and several other murders over the previous fourteen months.

As I understood the background of the case, most or all of the victims were Haitians who had emigrated to the Caribbean island to make their living as taxi drivers. The killer knew such immigrants were unlikely to have families with them, so there was a good chance they wouldn't be reported missing. In some instances he apparently was so sure that he stole their cars and then sold them out of the country. This all seemed to be an implausibly dangerous game on an island roughly the size of Martha's Vineyard or Santa Catalina, but his logic worked to a point; he was able to run up a total of nine victims before the police caught him. All I was asked for was confirmation of the sex of this particular victim, but along the way I was able to make some interesting inferences about how the murder had been committed.

The two gunshot wounds both entered the left side of the head, one just ahead of the left ear and the other in the lower jaw, and both exited on the right. In the United States, that would indicate the probability the driver had been shot from outside the car by a killer who thrust his gun into the open driver's-side window. But on the island where the killing occured, most cars have right-side steering and the scenario would be reversed. In the tropical climate it's reasonable to assume the window was down. In order to preserve the value of the vehicle he intended to steal, the murderer apparently leaned forward from the back seat and aimed the two shots in such a way that they would pass through their target and out the open window, leaving the car untouched.

Not every bullet fired into a victim's head goes all the way through, especially when the weapon is a smaller caliber such as a .22, .25, or even .32. In one case I examined just recently, the skeletal evidence clearly showed three clean, relatively small entrance holes and just two exit sites. A spent .22-caliber bullet was found inside the skull.

I heard recently of a case in Kansas where the anthropologist, Dr. Michael Finnegan, was presented with a skull with a single hole in it, and the policeman used the same overworked metaphor: "This guy has been drilled." He asked if there was any way to tell the caliber.

Finnegan turned the skull over thoughtfully in his hand, measured the hole, and said it looked like a .25. There aren't that many .25-caliber weapons around these days, and the detective asked if he meant a .22. Finnegan stuck with his estimate, adding he thought he could even guess the make of weapon: Black & Decker. Again, the policeman apparently thought the scientist was confused, and asked him if he meant Smith & Wesson. No, Finnegan meant Black & Decker. The hole showed none of the beveling of a bullet wound; the skull had been drilled postmortem with a metal bit.

It proved to be exactly what had happened. The skull had been recovered by the police from a woodshop located behind a beer hall in a converted railroad car. No one was certain where it had originated; perhaps it was an old war trophy or cemetery relic. For a long time it had occupied a prominent position over the bar-room cash register as a conversation piece, and the locals would try to outdo each other in making up lurid stories about what had happened to its original owner. One night, someone commented that the stories would be a lot more colorful if the skull contained a bullethole. Few suggestions have fallen on more fertile ground. A short time later, out back in the woodshop, the hole was drilled to order.

In another case an apparent exit wound turned out to be only apparent. When police found the victim, they noted a lot of trauma at the evident exit site of a bullet wound to the head. Upon lifting the body they found all the associated bone fragments in a neat pile right where they had apparently fallen. Put back together, the broken pieces completely articulated, covering up the hole.

This was a vital lead to the recovery of all the evidence. If the bullet had really passed through, those fragments would have been scattered all over the landscape. Instead, the bullet had crossed the entire skull and cracked the far wall, but at that point lacked the energy to complete its exit. For a time the skin and outside soft tissue had held the fractured bones in place, but when the skin decomposed, all the fragments fell out. X-rays showed radiodense material representing lead fragments inside the skull just behind the hole, and when the police looked a little further the bullet was also recovered from under the body.

In extreme contrast to either of those stories is a case from Hawaii in which a woman's skeleton was found face down in a shallow grave of sand and coral chips. She had been shot with a high-caliber firearm in the frontal portion of the right temple, and the entry site was sharp-edged and cleanly beveled inward, appearing from the outside as though it, too, had been punched through the bone with a drill. The exit of the bullet could only be inferred, having carried away the entire side of her face opposite the point of entry.

A case from the mountain states was even more of an enigma. There was a clear entry site in the right lower occipital, and an exit site, almost as clearly defined, near the center of the frontal, proof that the woman had been shot in the back of the head and that the bullet had come out the front. There was another major fracture near the mastoid process. If that was the second entry site of another bullet, that one might well have emerged in the area of the nose. But in this instance there was a lot of bone missing from the mastoid, and the nasal bones were missing entirely. There was no way to tell with certainty what had caused the second wounds.

Not every case involving computation of the angle of attack is necessarily a shooting. A murder victim's skeleton was dug out of the ground a few years ago in a midwestern state, and although his shirt was perforated front and back, there were no holes or fractures evident in the bones to indicate the passage of bullets. The victim was identified by dental charts, but the question remained of how he had died.

The damage to the shirt included ten long, narrow slits clustered in the upper left front area, and four additional cut marks grouped together on the right side at the back. At first glance there seemed to be a possibility the body had been run through with a long blade, but the two clusters of cuts were not opposite to each other, so it was unlikely that any of those on the rear represented exit sites. This was confirmed by a careful examination of the bones. I found knife marks on several ribs and vertebrae that corresponded to both sets of puncture marks in the fabric, with the thrusts coming from their respective sides of the body. There were still several cut marks in the fabric which could not be matched with evidence in the bones, and that disparity isn't necessarily explained away by the possibility that those other strokes of the blade were confined to soft tissue. If the shirt had been open, the fabric could have been slashed without the knife necessarily hitting the body with each thrust.

My most recent forensic case involving computation of angle of attack opened many larger questions. This was the case of Dr. Carl Weiss, the putative assassin of Louisiana's Kingfish, the legendary Huey Long. It was another historical project headed by Jim Starrs, and like the Packer and Borden cases, it holds the potential for altering the long-accepted official view of surrounding events.

According to that official version, on September 8, 1935, the twenty-nine-year-old Baton Rouge physician met Louisiana Senator (former Governor) Huey P. Long in the state capitol, where Weiss allegedly drew a .32-caliber pistol and shot Long in the abdomen at close range. In retaliation, so the story goes, Long's bodyguards fired numerous shots into the young doctor, killing him instantly. Long died thirty hours later in a nearby hospital. Despite numerous questions and widespread skepticism about that official version, neither body was autopsied, and the physical evidence was never made available to the public.

Some possibly important pieces of information that trickled out later only served to lengthen the shadow of doubt. When Long was admitted to the hospital, an attending nurse noticed a cut on his lip and asked how it had happened. Long dismissed the question with "That's where he hit me." And a few days later, one of Long's bodyguards was reputed to have been sent out of the state for a short time after allegedly making the drunken remark that he had killed his only friend.

Defenders of Weiss claim that he would not likely have hit Long in the face if he intended to shoot him, especially when the senator was surrounded by bodyguards. The alleged assassin's brother, Dr. Thomas Weiss, believes that Carl journeyed to the capitol not to kill Long but to see him about political matters. Carl may have lost his temper and struck Long with his fist. An extension of that theory is that Long's police guards overreacted, and Long was struck with one of the bullets they fired at Weiss.

The investigation launched by Starrs recovered more than the bones of the alleged assassin; it uncovered the long-suppressed police records on the case, as well as Weiss's pistol. The weapon appeared in the inventory of the estate of a prominent official in New Orleans who had bequeathed it, as personal property, to his family. A daughter of the official was located who refused to acknowledge she was still in

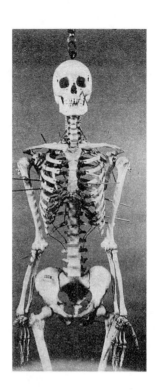
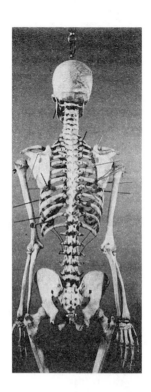

The pins in this laboratory
skeleton indicate the location of gunshot trauma in
the skeletal remains of
Carl Weiss, alleged assassin of Huey Long. At least
23 different trajectories
were identified.

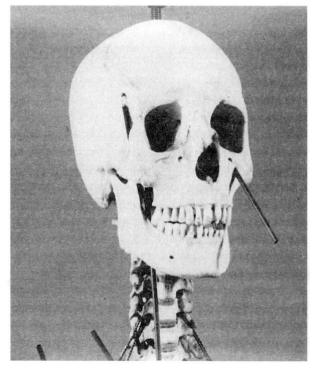

possession of the unusual legacy. Later, she turned the pistol as well as the long-lost records over to the New Orleans Sheriff after an order was issued in a civil district court. It didn't become available to Starrs or the general public even then. In a bizarre turn of events, the police announced that fifty-seven years after the two deaths they had decided to reopen the case and that under the court order the evidence could not be seen publicly.

However, Starrs was able to learn the serial number of the pistol, and by matching it with the files of the FBI for 1935, verified that it was the one that had been owned by Carl Weiss. A single spent bullet of the same caliber as Weiss's pistol, with a distinct impact site on the nose, was also included in the recovered materials.

A subsequent test firing of Weiss's pistol proved that the spent bullet had been fired from some other weapon, and could not have come from Weiss's.

As for my own studies, they began at the autopsy in Lafayette in October 1991 and continued when the remains arrived at the Smithsonian. They were limited to identifying Weiss, verifying age, sex, ancestry, and other data, mapping the evidence of gunshot trauma to the bones, and measuring the trajectories of the bullets. I found no evidence of trauma to the hand bones, although that hardly disproved the scenario in which Weiss hit Long with his fist. I did find a curious black stain on the teeth, which turned out to be mercury. Dr. Weiss was no mad hatter; the source was probably the eroding amalgam in his dental fillings.

Careful examination of the gunshot trauma identified a minimum of twenty-three distinct trajectories and a possible twenty-fourth. These suggested the occurrence of at least twenty separate gunshot wounds that affected bone (three were in the arms and could have gone on to cause further trauma noted in the chest area), although there certainly could have been any number of additional such wounds that were limited to soft tissue. Half of the measured trajectories indicated their bullets were fired into Weiss from behind his back; seven came from the front, and the other five from the sides. It seems astonishing that more people were not injured in the course of his execution. To Jim Starrs and to the surviving members of the Weiss family, that's the whole point. Starrs reported that the investigation had raised serious doubts about the accuracy of the original official account.

Surprisingly, it also raised a lot of ancient defenses. When the gun and police records were located, Starrs wrote the surviving scion of the Long family, the present senator from Louisiana, to ask for his cooperation in the case. Senator Russell Long, who has been an unwavering advocate of the official version, replied that it was best to leave the past alone. Then, after the pistol and records were discovered, a local judge issued a gag order on the forensic experts who witnessed all the scientific tests on the materials. When Starrs presented our findings to the American Academy of Forensic Sciences in New Orleans in February 1992, he was told by a police officer who attended the meeting that his disclosure of the results of the scientific testing done by the state police was a violation of that order, and that the judge was proceeding to hold him in contempt. Nothing came of the threat, and we all left New Orleans safely.

Just before that meeting, Starrs and I presented the anthropological evidence of my examinations to the Weiss family, prior to making those findings public. A few days later I received the following letter from Weiss's brother Thomas, reproduced here with his kind permission.

Dear Douglas,

My wife, Cat, and I thank you for the excellent review of your current findings on the remains of my brother, Dr. Carl A. Weiss, killed in 1935.

Your orderly and masterful description of the osseous defects and their relationship was lucid. This brought back my challenging but exciting entry into the medical world via gross anatomy, an anchor subject in those days (1936).

Be assured this recent experience in your laboratory was not emotionally traumatic. Rather, I find renewed hope emanating from those studies by very qualified forensic scientists. Though I harbored pneumonia at the time of your presentation, I was determined to hear you out.

Past frustrations have been exhausting, but I never lost hope for a fair final evaluation.

The truth I'll accept.

With deep appreciation, I am,

Gratefully,
Thomas E. Weiss, M.D.

"Fair final evaluation." That's the best description I've heard so far of what forensic anthropology is all about.

18

FAMILY SECRETS

There are few things in life sadder than the death of a child, and no amount of professional detachment ever fully insulates a medical examiner, or even an anthropologist, from the pang that comes with confronting mortality in the very young. When that death involves a forensic examination, almost always the tragedy is magnified by direct proof of trauma or the inference of suffering. The cause of death is usually deliberate, and frequently is embedded with the evidence of rage.

In May 1983, a young man told Rhode Island police that he had witnessed such a murder. He said it had happened the previous summer, and had started with his girlfriend violently thrashing her four-year-old son. When the child died a few days after the beating, the man said he wrapped the small body in a green fabric bedspread, placed it in a cardboard box, drove to a wooded area in a border town in Massachusetts, dug a pit, and for the next two days cremated the remains in a fire which he stoked continuously with wood and flammable fluids.

On the day of his statement, he led Rhode Island police and Massachusetts State Troopers from the Bristol County Crime Prevention and Control unit to the burned-out firepit. There were several empty Busch beer cans scattered around the area, including one in the pit and one in the crotch of a tree that had been partially stripped of its limbs for firewood. It was known that the witness had a hatchet in his truck. Detectives carefully collected the cans, pieces of the unburned firewood to match for cut marks, and other debris, which included fabric, cardboard, and even some relatively unburned bones from the area around the pit. They then excavated the ashes and other debris from the pit itself, including more bones, and placed it in meticulously labeled bags and boxes.

It all took some careful sorting out when my share of the shipment arrived at the Smithsonian. From among several chunks of wood charcoal and lots of ashes and organic debris, I identified the upper ends of three leg bones, six ribs, the centrum from two lumbar vertebrae, and other fragments from the skull and neck. There was no way to get at sex or ancestry. Examining the largest of the leg bones, a fragment of the femur, I was able to calculate its length prior to burning as 190 mm, and from that to estimate the victim's age at death as between three and four years. In my report I cautioned that my efforts were handicapped by the incompleteness of the fragment, and that long bone lengths vary considerably with different individuals of the same age.

As usual, my observations and estimates were all made before reading the letter of conveyance that came with the remains. When I did read it and saw that the age of the suspected victim was four, at the upper end of the range I had suggested, I added to my report that it is quite likely a child with a history of abuse would be significantly shorter than normal. The fact is, children who are loved grow faster than those who are not.

Because the remains had been burned, the amount of time since death was very difficult to verify. A year after the date given by the man responsible for the cremation, small insect larvae were still active even in the materials in my office, but it is possible they were feeding on organic material unrelated to the human remains.

The sternal end of one of the right ribs was broken, with the surface bent backward. Based on what I knew about the properties of rib bones, the nature of the break suggested the trauma might have taken place at about the time of death or shortly before. The ribs held another important clue to the events which followed death. While most of the other remains were charred or even slightly calcined, five of the ribs, though partially blackened through contact with the other material, did not appear to have been burned at all. This was puzzling, because at least two vertebrae which are anatomically close to the ribs in question had been burned black. I examined all the bone fragments under magnification and was unable to detect any sign of cut marks. Even without them, considering all the other evidence of the young man's admitted zeal in the disposal of the remains, I suggested the possibility that the body had been dismembered before being fed into the fire.

This bizarre case was to take another couple of strange turns before it was finally resolved. Although the body was found in Massachusetts, it was determined the murder had taken place in Rhode Island and the trial was to be held in Providence. Under ordinary circumstances, whether I would be called upon to testify would depend on what I had been able to extract from the evidence, and perhaps on whether there were other expert witnesses to the same findings. But just as the case was about to go to court, the prosecutor announced that in moving to new storage facilities, Massachusetts had misplaced the child's remains—and without the bones and ashes, the prosecution would have to offer some other proof that the child had died. Under those new circumstances, my testimony could now be critical in establishing that proof.

I flew to Providence, only to find I had to wait two days before being called as a witness. When my time finally came, it was at a pretrial hearing, where I testified on my findings on the case and showed the court X-rays and photographs of the bone which I had taken in my laboratory. In the absence of the remains themselves, these visual documents became the evidence. It was a lesson in the importance of carefully photographing and retaining photos and X-rays of all such evidence. Later, while I was still waiting to testify in the trial itself, the defendant pleaded to the charge of harboring and was sentenced to five years suspended and five on probation. The child's mother, who was a co-defendant in the case, pleaded guilty of manslaughter and was sentenced to twelve years imprisonment with seven suspended, followed by another seven on probation. I returned to Washington without ever having to appear before a jury.

In another Massachusetts case, human remains were found in a trunk recovered from the cellar of an abandoned house. Because of its size and apparent time since death, the skeleton was suspected by police to be that of a boy reported kidnapped some six years earlier. From careful measurement of the teeth and long bones, I estimated age at about six years. Since it isn't possible to reliably estimate sex or racial affiliation from a skeleton of that age, I didn't try. The bones were well preserved and covered with desiccated soft tissue, and I saw numerous fly pupal cases, but because the secure, dry conditions in which the body had been preserved were obviously different from those of a burial or of a body exposed to the weather, I was willing to say of the time since death only that it was more than a month and perhaps several years. I observed no signs of trauma or other cause of death, a fact which sometimes points toward strangulation or asphyxiation.

That was not a very promising response to the request of the police that we match the remains with the description of the missing boy. But fortunately, the police had also submitted some X-rays along with the body in the trunk, and I was able to report that a comparison of the radiographs of the missing boy with those of the skeleton strongly suggested they were the same individual.

In cases of this sort, "strongly suggested" is about as close to positive as one can reasonably hope for. Radiographs of skeletons and mummies always differ from those of living people because of differences in the density of the bodies. The intensity of the radiation was different as well. Moreover, in murder cases there is almost always a space of months or even years between the taking of a medical X-ray and the time of death, and if the victim is a child, the bone changes in size and shape as it grows. Even with all those negatives, I didn't find a single point on which there was an obvious mismatch, and enough traits agreed in this instance to favor the probability it was the same child. If that weren't enough, my estimate of the age at death came within four months of the age when the boy in the medical X-rays was reported missing.

On that evidence, despite the caveats, Massachusetts authorities determined that the body in the trunk was the missing child, and issued a death certificate. The case is still open.

Another trunk case involved an even younger skeleton and a death that probably had occurred half a century earlier. This one was in a trunk from a house in Baltimore. The homeowner had cautioned her children not to open it until after her death. They followed her instructions for many years, and soon after she died they went right to the forbidden trunk in the expectation of finding a will or possibly a valuable legacy. What they found instead was a mummified infant, wrapped in a multicolored house dress imprinted with designs from the 1939 World's Fair in Flushing, New York.

I suppose her warnings to her children suggest the possibility that the homeowner was the mother of the baby, but whatever the truth of this past tragedy the secret outlived the woman who held it, and she succeeded in taking it with her to the grave. I estimated the remains were those of a newborn or a child of only one or two months. There were some indications the baby had been female, and although there were no signs of trauma, it was possible she had suffered from an infection or disruption in growth at around the time of death or shortly before.

Two other women who died at about the same time as the mother in Baltimore nearly succeeded in taking their own secrets with them as well, but even so their cases ended differently. Both had bled to death as the result of botched abortions, and I was asked to examine the fetal remains in order to help determine whether the procedures had been performed illegally late in pregnancy.

On the first of these cases, I was called in after the young woman's autopsy to examine two small pieces of the fetus which were found in her uterus. I turned to the Smithsonian's fetal collection, which consists of skeletal remains through the whole range of development up to full-term delivery. After carefully comparing the scraps of bone with the collection and reviewing the extensive literature in that area of fetal forensics, I was able to determine that the abortion had taken place at about five months, which is late enough to be murder under the law. In this case, because of the alleged illegal protocol and inept technique, the abortionist was subject to the charge of having caused the death of the mother as well.

In the second case as well we recovered only two bones, but again that was enough. Measuring them against standards published in a guide entitled *Fetal Osteology*, I estimated the age of the fetus at six months. It was a different abortionist, but the same illegally late procedure led to the same lethal result for both the mother and her unborn child. In this case, the family claimed that the man who performed the operation made a practice of raising his prices once the term of pregnancy crossed the line that limits the time of legal termination. Each time the pregnant woman managed to save enough to meet his last price, she was that much more pregnant, and he would tell her the figure had risen again. When she finally was able to collect the required amount, it was obviously past the point where the doctor's venality intersected with his competence.

Other family tragedies take place under less explicable circumstances. In the winter of 1984, police found a burned vehicle on a rural road in New York and identified it as belonging to a young man who had been reported missing earlier that same day. Behind it was a pool of blood, later determined to be human, containing brain tissue and several bone fragments. Police had developed a pretty good circumstantial case that the victim had been lured to a meeting at this isolated place by his older brother, who then killed him. I was asked to examine the fragments to determine whether they were human, and for anything else I could find that might illuminate the mystery or help establish that the missing brother had been there.

When the case went to trial, the principal witnesses to the medical forensics were myself and a brain specialist, and in conference with the attorneys and the judge in pretrial it became apparent that we both had the same problem. We could say that the materials we had examined were fully compatible with human tissue: the brain had all the measurable human characteristics, and the bone had all the measurable human characteristics. But under oath, because of the extreme smallness of our samples, neither of us would be able to rule out the remote possibility that our specimens were of non-human origin.

The area where the killing was alleged to have occurred was deer country, and although the hunting season had closed two months before, the judge said that expert testimony of this sort required greater certitude than we were willing to offer, and that mere probabilities, however weighted, were little better than guesswork. In that context, a beginner might feel a certain amount of pressure to suddenly find a way to be sure. But everybody in the system recognizes—or should—that professional witnesses are not meant to be advocates. Where certitude is not scientifically possible, its lack may diminish the impact of the expert's testimony; but it has never hurt anyone's scientific reputation.

For reasons I no longer recall, assuming I understood them at the time, Solomon decided to cut the baby in half, and the brain specialist was allowed to testify although I was not. In this case, half a loaf proved to be better than none; the jury found the surviving brother guilty of murder.

When a forensic examination fails to produce evidence of guilt, defense attorneys sometimes like to interpret the absence of such evidence as proof of innocence. Most forensic science is aimed at testing evidence of guilt only: yes, that's John Doe's fingerprint, or no, the bullet could not have been fired from that gun. The fingerprint might prove John Doe committed the crime, but ruling out one scenario doesn't prove him innocent in any other.

Take the hyoid bone as an example. The fractured hyoid of an adult may be pretty good evidence of manual strangulation, but an intact hyoid in a child is no proof that manual strangulation didn't take place anyway. Sir Sidney Smith notwithstanding, modern estimates of fractured hyoids in manual strangulation cases range from 17 to 71 percent, which even on the upper end is a long way from universal. The variance in these estimates likely reflects differences in the ages of the victims, as well as variances in autopsy techniques and thoroughness; but collectively, the data suggest that hyoid fracture occurs in only a third of all strangulation cases.

The difficulty in interpreting hyoids is illustrated by a case from Louisiana in 1988. On the afternoon of August 3, a postal employee and sometime telephone and cable TV installer named Gerald Estrade appeared at the Metairie Day Camp, where he said he had left his daughter that morning. Camp officials could find no record that the ten-year-old had been there at all that day, and Estrade called the police.

Police interviewed children and adults at the day camp, and while forty-nine said they hadn't seen the girl, thirteen children thought they recalled seeing her that morning. One child even offered that he had seen the missing daughter being abducted. She was sitting on a blue Dumpster, throwing rocks, and a man with a black beard threw a brown rope around her waist and tried to pull her into a car. The story began to deteriorate when the boy said she got away and ran into the gym where she called the police. In subsequent interviews, all thirteen stories, including this one, changed. In the end, the police were satisfied that the missing girl had been seen at the day camp on that date by no one.

The National Center for Missing and Exploited Children was contacted, and one of the familiar fliers was prepared with her picture on it, asking for information on her disappearance. But even as the flier was being circulated, detectives on the case began to wonder whether the circumstances were exactly as Estrade had given them. Details of his story did not hold up under further inquiry. For example, the father said that when he had left her there were so many cars at the curb he had to park some distance from the usual drop-off place; all other parents reported no such congestion. A camp employee recalled something else that seemed odd: when Estrade had arrived in the afternoon, he went directly to the counselor to ask if his daughter was on the attendance list, rather than stopping first to look for her around the playground. Numerous other people found it strange that in the days that followed, the father never displayed anxiety, grief, or any of the other expected painful emotions that would be normal for someone whose daughter was missing.

The day after the reported disappearance, a workman found a gym bag containing the girl's lunch in a trash container at a nearby apartment complex and called the sheriff's office. In addition to the sandwich, a box of raisins, chips, and a Thermos, there was a pair of neatly folded pink shorts, a pair of black sunglasses, a red bandana—and a pair of mismatched men's work gloves. The father was confronted with the work gloves and immediately denied ever seeing them before. Police asked others who knew him, however, and the suspicion grew that the gloves were his.

By this time, police were developing a pattern on the father. Estrade was compulsively neat, the kind of person who washed his hands frequently and could never bring himself to throw anything away. He had a history of marital problems and difficulties at work, characterized by anxiety, depression, and fits of rage. Two months later, in the trunk behind the bench seat of the father's truck, police found a second pair of gloves, identical to the first except they were for the opposite hands. Estrade responded in character, claiming that he was being framed.

That December, the skeleton of a child found by hunters in nearby Mississippi was identified as the missing ten-year-old girl. In due course, the father was arrested, and the remains followed the gloves to the laboratories of the FBI. In my examination I found that the greater horns had not yet fused with the body of the hyoid—the main reason one would not expect that bone to be fractured in a child strangulation. There was no physical evidence of choking or of any other sort of trauma.

Even though the newspapers reported that my examination had proven nothing, the father later admitted to the crime and was sentenced to prison. He said he had shaken her to death, but at least two of the detectives in the case still believe he strangled her. It illustrates the fact that you can never prove a positive with negative evidence. Perhaps even more important, it demonstrates one of the great truisms of forensic law: all the science in the world doesn't have half the convicting power of a guilty conscience.

The Louisiana case also illustrates something else that can surface during a criminal investigation, and that's the extreme hypocrisy with which people sometimes attempt to shroud their guilt. Before Estrade confessed, he managed a call from jail to a local radio station to protest the way the case was being handled. In particular, he was upset with the treatment of the remains of the victim, which he complained were being held as evidence and had not been released for interment. "We have not had a decent Christian Catholic burial ... this is the most gruesome thing I have heard in my life." Later, he admitted to hiding the body in the woods, 400 feet off a rural road in Pass Christian, Mississippi. I wonder how many of the people who read about that part of the case in their newspapers could remember how they felt when they heard his call to the radio station. And I wonder how they feel now.

By contrast, even the clearest proof of murder is no guarantee a killer will ever be brought to justice. In another case involving a child of nearly the same age which I examined at about the same time, the skeleton showed evidence of gunshot wounds in the chest. Despite the youth of the victim we were able to find strong characteristics of a white racial affiliation, and to match several facial features with a photograph of a suspected victim. We used radiography to prove the presence of projectile fragments on the shattered margins of the bones, along with a technique called X-ray fluorescence to identify the elemental composition of those particles. We also found possible evidence of blunt-force trauma to the head. But none of that was enough to prove the identity of the missing child, and the police have never been able to make a strong enough case against a suspect in lieu of this positive identification. There has never even been an arrest.

The skeleton of another murdered little girl, another inconclusive forensic examination, and another guilty conscience all combined again for the same result in a case on which I testified in court in the District of Columbia in 1991. This one started off five years before, and the original examiner was Larry Angel.

The victim, a cute, pigtailed fifth grader, had disappeared in May 1986, three days before her father was to remarry. At first the police believed she had been taken by her natural mother, who had left the family six years earlier, but that theory evaporated the following October with the discovery of a badly deteriorated body in a thicket on the grounds of a junior high school just eight blocks from the missing girl's home. Larry told the press the body was definitely a black female in the age range of the missing girl, but in the absence of a lower jaw or any evidence of reconstruction in the maxillary teeth, identification from dental records seemed unlikely. He proposed a facial reproduction.

Larry turned the case over to me a few days later; although I agreed with his estimates, I wasn't quite as willing to state them conclusively. We looked at the calcification of the crowns and roots of the teeth, using dental standards, and came up with an age which we then found was very close to that of the missing girl. Ancestry is difficult to determine in skeletons this young, although I agreed there were numerous characteristics supporting Larry's findings: she exhibited an extremely wide nasal aperture, lack of definition at the base of the nose, and pronounced prognathism. Other matches made by the FBI Laboratory's hair and fiber specialists helped confirm the likelihood that the remains were those of the little girl.

I had less trouble agreeing fully with Larry's observations regarding evidence of foul play: there was no sign of any kind to indicate how she had died.

The case went into my files and remained dormant for the next two and a half years. Then, in April 1989, just a few weeks short of the third anniversary of the little girl's disappearance, the stepmother turned herself in to the D.C. police and admitted to murder.

She had killed the child, the woman said, as a way of getting revenge on the father after a fight. "I figured if I hurt her, that would get to him." In a forty-five-minute videotaped statement, she demonstrated how she held the little girl's head under the water in a bathtub for five minutes, long after the body went limp. At the time of her confession, she was not sure whether the killing had served its purpose: "If he cared, I couldn't tell." At least it didn't interfere with their other plans; three days after the murder, the couple was married.

When she came to trial two years after her confession, the woman changed her mind about the events she earlier had described so vividly. Perhaps her perspective had changed as a result of being held in the county jail and contemplating what the next twenty years of her life would be like in prison. She had been confused, she said, and most of what she said on the tape was the result of the taunts of relatives and coaching from disembodied voices from such unlikely places as the toilet, under the rug, and from the air around her while she was riding on the bus. Only one member of the jury didn't know what to believe, but that was enough to require a retrial.

At both trials, I was asked to testify on my examination of the remains five years before. On the face of it, there may appear to be a paradox in the government calling a witness to the fact that the corpse in a murder case exhibited no evidence of trauma, and that inferences as to age and race are tentative. However, I was allowed to present slides illustrating the basis for the inferences about the victim's identity, and they appear to have been pursuasive. I also was able to testify that the absence of any forensic evidence of trauma was absolutely consistent with the method of murder to which the defendant had earlier confessed. The second time around, the jury convicted.

19

FAIR PLAY AND FOUL

A big part of the challenge to forensic anthropologists is distinguishing the evidence of foul play from changes to the skeleton due to factors that precede death or follow it. The most common post-mortem factors are carnivore activity, damage from lawn mowers, plows, or other heavy equipment, fire, and accidental alterations in the remains by those who discover them, whether hunters, hikers, or the police. These factors, especially when combined with such natural changes as erosion, bleaching, coffin wear, or the development of fungus activity which mimics burning, can appear as very deceptive evidence to the untrained eye. Conversely, real evidence of crime can sometimes be lost in subtlety or confusion, and escape detection or follow-up.

At one point in the Palmyra Island case, the defense suggested that the abrasive flattening of a part of the skull, which most likely was the result of chafing from ocean wave action on the metal cannister in which it was found, was instead evidence that the death blow had been delivered by a machete. There was no more evidence that it was a machete than a lawn mower or a band saw, but someone had decided the machete might make an acceptable scenario based on the way the abrasion mimicked a planar cutting action, as in slicing or shearing. That suggestion never made it into court, perhaps because it was absurdly speculative and unprovable, but more likely because it didn't improve the defense.

That kind of question comes up all the time, and the witness's experience in observing the effects of a lot of different conditions is really the only reliable credential for distinguishing one result from another. For example, there was evidence of two totally unrelated forms of trauma in the skeleton of a twenty-nine-year-old woman that was recovered two years ago from a rural southern roadside. She had been shot in the head, and the bones also displayed extensive fracture and shearing in the midsection of the back. I was asked to offer an opinion on the cause of the latter injuries.

There was no doubt whose body it was or how she had died; the woman had been identified from dental records and anthropological comparisons, and the skull contained a well-defined bullethole just ahead of the left ear, with a jagged exit fracture on the other side of the head. In the other trauma, the cuts were not inconsistent with the results that might be made by a large mower blade, but they also could have been related to her murder. When I reassembled the fractured bones in their natural relationship and determined that the shearing had occurred while the body was still articulated, the timing of the mid-body damage moved a lot closer to the time of death.

The marks on the bones were indicative of a large blade, such as an ax, machete, or mower. Again, there are lots of possible scenarios, and this is a case where it is not inconceivable that the victim was first hit in the back by a sharp-bladed instrument, then shot executioner-style once the blow had brought her down. There was no indication in the planar cuts that the blade had been used on the limb joints or long bones, so if the trauma were postmortem rather than perimortem, it was not related to any attempt at dismemberment. Considering that the victim disappeared in late spring, just before the start of the grass-cutting season, and her body was recovered in a deeply weeded roadside area the following winter, odds would appear to favor the mower theory.

There are no records that the highway department or the landowner mowed that particular stretch of grass during the eight months her body lay near the roadside, but that doesn't rule out the possibility it was done anyway, or that a tractorborne mower passed over the body while on its way to another destination. Her killer was convicted

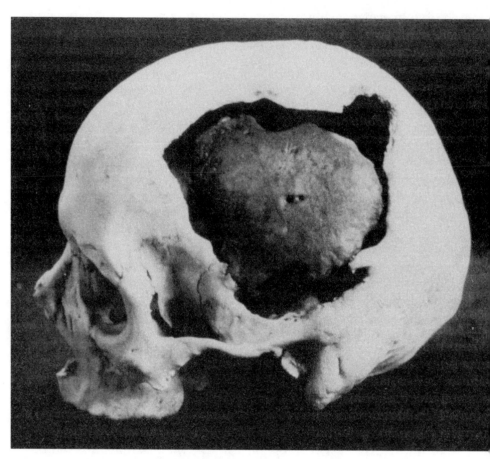

The irregularly shaped piece of bone found inside this skull fit a large hole in the cranium. Partially healed edges and regularly spaced perforations—stitching points—indicated that the cut was part of an outdated surgical procedure not related to cause of death.

a year after my analysis of the remains, but only of firing the shot through her brain. If he indeed knows what would account for the victim's sheared vertebrae, he is an unlikely source of information; he still denies having anything to do with the crime.

Not every perforation of the skull is a bullethole or the evidence of blunt-force trauma, and for that matter not every hole in the head is necessarily even the cause of death. Just a few days after police recovered the body of the shot and possibly lawn-mowered woman, the scattered bones of another skeleton were discovered in the woods beside another highway on the opposite side of the same state by a deer hunter who was searching for his dog. This body proved to be that of an old man, but like the woman in the grass, the preliminary medical examination noted a large, circular hole in the cranium.

This time the trauma could not have been related to the victim's death, because the edges of the hole showed signs of much earlier healing. Moreover, inside the cranial vault was a large, irregularly shaped piece of bone which fitted neatly into the perforation. As I rearticulated the flap of bone into the hole from which it had been cut, close examination of both margins showed regularly spaced perforations, the stitching points where the plug of bone at one time had been reattached. I called a friend of mine who is a brain surgeon at George Washington University, and when he stopped by to confirm the analysis, he told me the cut in the bone had been made by a long-outdated technique involving the drilling of five burr holes and the use of a surgical device called a Gigli saw. The pattern suggested the focus of the surgery was on a subdural or epidural hematoma.

The craniotomy was not the only evidence of trauma long predating death. The skeleton contained a number of other healed fractures, especially to the bones of the face, the collarbone, and the upper ribs. It would not be unreasonable to speculate that both the fractured bones and the surgical sawing may have been related to the same cause: an industrial accident, a fall from a high place, or, more likely, an automobile accident. Based on the victim's age, the type of procedure, and the extent of remodeling of those earlier injuries, I estimated the time of the original facial trauma to have been about fifteen years prior to death.

If you can stand four hole-in-the-head stories in a row, Doug Owsley had one in the fall of 1991 that provides a wonderful example of how a forensic anthropologist can unscramble clues to even the most improbable scenarios. It's also a good cautionary tale for anyone who thinks our troubles are over once we're dead.

The skeleton in this case was discovered by a farmer who was plowing his field, and before the bones came to the Smithsonian they had already been identified as the remains of a thirty-seven-year-old man who was last seen alive almost five years earlier. On the ground near the body was a rusted shotgun, with an empty shell casing still in the chamber. The top of the head had been shattered, and the bones were variously bleached from the sun and stained from burial, grooved and splintered from plowing, and riddled with shotgun pellets. The pellets were not in the skull but scattered throughout the lower abdomen and pelvis.

It's one thing for a suicide to shoot himself in the head. It's another when he apparently has been shot more than once.

Doug set about reassembling the head, and laid out the bones from the rest of the body more or less in their original relationship. In the skull, the mandible was badly fractured, most of the facial bones had been lost, and there was a triangular wedge missing from the top of the right parietal bone.

As for the pellets, he counted seventy-one entry sites in the skeleton and clothing, and placed wooden markers in each of those he found in the bones.

One of the first keys to the mystery was still in the shotgun. The shell casing in the chamber evidently had contained no shot at all. It was a rifled slug, commonly used for hunting deer.

The next clue came from the test results by a Smithsonian laboratory. Although X-rays revealed none of the radiopaque evidence of lead, infrared spectrometry indicated the presence of plastics containing cellulose nitrate, the common residue of gunpowder, imbedded in the spongy bone inside the braincase above the eye orbits. For Doug, this was a powerful clue to where the rifled slug had gone. He inferred from the location of the residue that the victim had placed the muzzle of the shotgun under his chin, and the projectile had exited either through the face or the triangular hole nearer the top of the head. If there had been any imbedding of lead, called "bullet wipe," it would have been on the bones which were carried off by the slug.

Next, Doug checked the alignments of the markers, and because they came from so many different directions on the reassembled bones, they proved that the skeleton was already disarticulated at the time of the second shooting. This meant the two events were separated by at least several months. Bird season doesn't reopen until the fall in the state where the body was recovered, so on that evidence alone the space between the two events would have been the better part of a year.

However, he also observed the relationship between the pellet holes and cracks in the bone from weathering. In normal conditions for that climate, weathering cracks don't appear until two or three years after skeletonization. When the pellets had entered the bones, those cracks had already formed. Probably the birdshot had been fired into the bones just a few months before their recovery.

To extract the cause of death and such exact inferences for the timing of the secondary trauma was a virtuoso performance even for a forensic anthropologist, but Doug went further. Almost as an afterthought, he identified cuts on the bones of the arms and hips as having come from the blade of the farmer's chisel plow.

The range of possible explanations for how alterations in bone occur often expands or contracts with what we know about the setting where the remains are found. It's logical to look to the blade of a plow to explain the grooves on bones recovered from a plowed field. It is also logical to consider mower blades in the analysis of sheared bones found in tall grass. In the case just cited, Doug Owsley was able to match the groove with the tool that made it. But where the blade of a particular mower, for example, is not available for comparison, inferences can be risky.

A decade ago, I was sent some bones that had been recovered from the grassy slope of a roadside railroad embankment—just the kind of place that gets mowed with heavy, tractor-towed equipment. The remains consisted of two legs and two feet, the pelvic region, and several vertebrae from the lower portion of the spine. It was midsummer, and based on the extent of larval activity, odor, and remaining soft tissue, I estimated the time since death as between three weeks and three months. There was evidence of large-blade trauma at three different points on the vertebrae. Combined with the grassy recovery site, it might seem natural to consider the possibility of postmortem trauma from heavy equipment. In this case, there were several good reasons why that would have been a mistake.

First, all the evidence of cutting was limited to one area of the spine. Second, no other portions of the body, not even splinters of other bones, were recovered at the site. Third, the nature of the cut surfaces and the angles involved did not match those expected from mower damage. And finally, when I checked the report, I found that the remains had been wrapped in an old newspaper, then a checked plastic tablecloth, then a black polyethylene bag, and over all of that a contoured bedsheet. And the package was bound with electrical cord.

That's a little too tidy for a sleeping hobo whose upper half accidentally got mulched. What we had was a twenty- to twenty-five-year-old white male, almost certainly a murder victim, whose body had been cut in at least two parts with three powerful blows of an instrument resembling a butcher's knife. But as far as I know, police never recovered the rest of the body, and the case is still open.

Context was even more important in a query I received from Alaska back in the early 1980s; in fact, it was half the case. This particular mystery consisted of nothing more than a slide transparency and an interesting story.

In the fall of that year, an old man drove up to an automobile dealer in a coastal city and said he needed to sell his pickup truck in a hurry. He told the salesman he had been hearing a lot of demon voices lately, and had decided to get out of town fast. The letter that came with the picture omitted all the theological details—for example, how the salesman wrestled with the ethical conflict between the man's need for sound spiritual counseling and his own desire to do the best thing for his dealership and his family—but the bottom line was that the truck changed hands on the spot "for a low price." The old man disappeared with cash in hand, and the personnel at the dealership divided up the personal effects he had left behind in the truck.

One of those things, the last to be divided, was a toolbox filled mostly with personal papers that didn't seem to have any particular value. But at the bottom of the toolbox was a small cardboard container, and inside the container were several photographic slides. On one of them, number 9 to be exact, the salesman discerned what appeared to be human skeletal remains.

I looked at the same slide a week later, and sure enough, that's just how it appeared to me as well. The bones were laid out on what seemed like a rug, and although each one was dry and disconnected from its neighbor, an attempt had been made to reassemble them into their normal relationship.

I couldn't tell if they were human—although probably they were, judging from the skull. I couldn't tell if the bones represented one person or if there were spare parts. It was obvious the reassembly was not exact; some of the ribs were in the wrong order, and there had been a lot of switching around of the long bones. But, beyond the fact that it's illegal to keep a dead body for private purposes, there was no evidence that the bones in the picture represented the victim of foul play. The date on the slide was from a decade earlier—now more than twenty years ago. It was impossible to tell more without being able to examine the bones themselves, so I copied the slide for its curiosity value and returned the original to the FBI. From time to time, I've wondered if the demons who drove the old man out of town included the voice of the body in the picture.

I may never find out, but that doesn't mean the truth will never be known. Sometimes it takes decades for material evidence to catch up with a story. In 1985, I was asked to examine a partial skeleton that had been found in the Tidewater section of Virginia.

The skull was found by a local fisherman in July in shallow, muddy water off the shore of an old, abandoned estate in Westmoreland County. A local medical examiner tentatively suggested it was from a woman who had been dead between ten and fifteen years, but several days later both estimates were revised when more remains were found in the rotted remains of a submerged coffin. The skeleton was wearing an ancient pair of hip boots, and under the body, in the bottom of the burial box, was a spent .45-caliber bullet. After a summer of widely varied conjecture, much of it in the press, about the body's age and origins, the bones were packaged up and sent to the Smithsonian.

I determined that it had been a black male between thirty-five and fifty-five years of age, about 5'7" in height. There was evidence of trauma to the right cheek and jawbone, and the presence of barnacles in the broken areas suggested the damage occurred a considerable time earlier—although it still could have happened after death. There was no evidence on the bones to explain the spent bullet. Meanwhile, the Westmoreland Sheriff's Department had been talking with the former Chesapeake waterman, who told them a story that had been passed down to him by his father from the time of World War I.

In 1917, according to the story, a fisherman named Bigbelly Marmaduke had found the body of a black man floating in Chesapeake Bay. Local authorities of that era were aware of the practice of some local fishermen recruiting help from among the itinerants along the Tideland waterfronts, working them for a couple of weeks or a month, then when it came to payday, killing them and dropping their bodies into the bay. The locals favored the home team in those days, and Marmaduke was told to keep quiet about his discovery and bury the body himself.

One of the men who helped in the task was the present-day waterman's father, who told his son the body was interred, boots and all, under a cherry tree some few yards from the water's edge. When the waterman was taken to the recovery site by the police, he pointed to the same tree, still alive seventy years later, and—due to the same erosion that had exposed the grave—now standing at the water's edge.

There is a saying in science that nothing can be studied without changing it. It's hard to see how that caveat applies to astronomy, but it's probably true in chemistry, where I believe it originated, and it should also be kept in mind in the analysis of forensic cases. A certain amount of the damage we observe in skeletal remains is not trauma at all, but the result of someone else's earlier analysis. By the time a case gets as far as Washington and is delivered to my office by the FBI, there is a good chance that it has already been through a local sheriff's department, perhaps has briefly detoured to the nearest university for a brief examination by a professor of something like zoology or biology, then been checked out by the city or county medical examiner or coroner and perhaps also picked at by the local dentist. That's a long trip, and any one of those intermediate stops may have involved cutting and sample taking which, unless properly noted and the data forwarded with the remains, can be indistinguishable from evidence of foul play.

I have had numerous cases in which I identified clearly defined cut marks on the bone, only to find after reporting them that the local examiner had used a scalpel or strong knife to cut away the soft tissue, leaving a whole series of little nicks which were indistinguishable from the evidence of assault. Ideally, a report on the methodology and result of destructive examinations by others would travel along with the remains to the next analyst in the line, but this rarely happens. When I find cut marks on bones, I frequently get on the phone and talk to earlier examiners to find out what they did that might explain it.

Sometimes the explanation of such marks takes more than a phone call. About ten years ago in the West, a concession cashier in a national park left her tent and disappeared without a trace. Four months later, two hikers found some skeletal remains beside a rock-climbing trail, and dental comparisons proved they belonged to the missing woman. The Park Service wanted to know when she had died, and how. The case is a good example of problems in interpretation from circumstantial evidence.

The body was found on a pile of shale and other debris at the foot of a nearly vertical rock cliff. The park was mountainous, and its main highway passed through several tunnels, one of which was located within the cliff. Directly above the remains, far up the rock face, was the exit for a large ventilation pipe that carried air to the tunnel. The scenarios offered by the criminal investigator who referred the case all related to the vent pipe. One was that the girl had walked down the pipe from the highway tunnel and jumped or fell to her death. In another she was thrown, either while she was still alive or after being murdered.

Regardless of how she had died, the basic problem was that all of the violence to her remains was explicable by events in and after the fall. There was no evidence on the bones of cut marks from a knife, no metal fragments or the telltale fracture marks associated with shooting, no ligature around the cervical vertebrae, and no imprinted signature of a recognizable blunt instrument such as a hammer, wrench, or gun butt. There were lots of other fractures, of course, and two of them— one that broke the right femur in half, and one in the right parietal of the skull—were mildly ambiguous; they could have been produced by the impact of the fall, or they could have been associated with some murderous event before the fall.

The long drop down the cliff would certainly have killed the girl if she hadn't been dead already. On the other hand, if she had been murdered first, some of those other signs might have been available to analysis for the first few days after death. But in the intervening months, two other opaque veils had been hung across our field of vision. The body had decayed and begun to disarticulate, and it had been disturbed by wild animals. The fact that the vertebral column was still intact although it showed large tooth marks suggested a dog or coyote rather than one of the park bears. Carnivore activity probably also explained the many bones that were missing.

Circumstantial evidence, by its nature, gains more weight by accrual than by science, and is more subject to judgment than to proof. In this case, the judgment of the police was based on the location of the body directly below the vent pipe, combined with the circumstances related to her disappearance, which pointed toward misadventure at the hands of a friend or acquaintance, and to some lesser extent on the possibility that the fracture to the right parietal and the snapping of the femur occurred earlier than the other skeletal damage. A decade later the investigation is still open, and it is still considered a homicide.

Another case from the same part of the world was similar in many ways to that of the missing cashier, with one notable difference: the evidence of trauma, though still not conclusive, was far more suggestive of murder.

The inventory of materials was a forensic anthropologist's Christmas carol: five animal bones, four packages of feces, three photographs of the recovery site, two packages of pine needles and soil, a pair of men's boxer shorts, and one nearly complete but badly gnawed skeleton of a white male of twenty to thirty, just under six feet tall, dead between one and twelve months. The police thought they knew the identity of the victim, but they requested an examination of the feces for evidence that it was the dogs who had been responsible for the chewing, and in particular they asked for an opinion on trauma to the skull. I decided to address the last issue first.

Three areas of the skull had been traumatized at or near the time of death. Perforations of varying sizes were located on the lower center of the front, on the left side, and on the right. There were extensive fracture lines throughout the skull except in the area furthest from the holes; most appeared to originate from the trauma site on the right side.

This evidence fit the classic pattern of death by gunshot. If that's what it was, a single bullet had entered the upper left temple and exited slightly higher on the other side of the head; the extent and pattern of the bone loss suggested that the trauma occurred while the brain and other soft tissue were still intact. Due to irregularities in the shape of the three perforations, it wasn't possible to determine the caliber of the bullet, or even to state conclusively that it had been a bullet that did the damage. That's generally the case in gunshot trauma; the projectile flattens out and reshapes after initial impact, and by the time it completes its entry or makes an exit, the distortion is so great as to make it unidentifiable.

My report doesn't show that I examined the dog feces; it's too long ago to remember. However, I'm a former student of Bill Bass, and the absence of a record may indicate that I didn't do the work, but chose instead to send them back across the street to be X-rayed.

One of my most bizarre cases involving evidence of foul play was one in which the killer had already admitted to the murder but lied about how he did it. There was a good reason for the lie.

Several summers ago, a boy of seventeen was reported missing from his home in upstate New York. It's possible the police didn't have much to go on at first, and besides, lots of kids get itchy feet at that age, especially at that time of year. Five weeks later a charred and decomposing body was found in a pile of partly burned brush in a remote section of the county, in an area of stony ravines and steep gorges. The skeleton was relatively intact except for the upper portion of the head, and that was found later, buried nearby. Comparison of the mandibular teeth with dental records proved it was the missing youth. Within twenty-four hours, police had arrested another boy of the same age, a friend of the deceased named Charles Shortridge.

The suspect quickly acknowledged that he had been responsible for the death, and he felt awful about it. The two boys had gone into the woods to drink some beer and after a time a fight had started. At first the struggle was more a boyish tussle than in anger, but it accelerated and Shortridge hit his friend several times in the face. The victim fell against some rocks, and Shortridge ran, leaving him unconscious in the woods. Then he realized his own tan shirt had gotten some blood on it, so he pulled it off and left that behind as well. Later, when his friend didn't return home and the family called the police, Shortridge realized that what started in relative innocence was turning into a nightmare. A few days afterward he set off into the woods again, hoping against hope he wouldn't find what he expected. But there in the clearing where he had left his friend was the body. It was a pretty sad story—technically a murder, but more of a tragic accident in which both boys were victims.

What Shortridge did next sounded like sheer panic. He told the police he dragged his friend from place to place within the gully, seizing on one idea about what to do with the corpse and then abandoning it a moment later for another. It was high summer, and decomposition was well under way. The flies had been at work, the stench was overwhelming, and he was half crazed with remorse and fear. The last time he moved the body, the cranial portion of the head fell off, leaving the scalp and mandible still attached to the neck. He buried the head separately, piled brush on the body, got some trash from his house to serve as kindling, and ignited the pyre. The fire went out. He covered the remains with tree branches and went home.

Under the law, there are several types, or degrees, of homicide. The definition of each type can vary from state to state, and so can the consequences. In most states, even though the differences between first-degree and second-degree murder are spelled out exactly, the distinctions are often blurred by circumstance, by frame of mind, and by subtle interpretations of intent. That October, by the time the evidence inventory of fifty separate items arrived at the FBI Laboratory, the police already had a positive ID of the victim, they had the perpetrator, and they had a confession. For the most part, the forensic examinations were to focus on Charles Shortridge's intent.

The first five items in that inventory were the skull, the jaw, one tooth from the fire, seven more teeth from the fire, and the skeletal remains. I laid them out on the examining table. The skeleton was relatively clean and very well preserved. Some soft tissues were present, and so were numerous insect larvae. As usual, after a preliminary inspection of the bones, I searched the remains for trauma or evidence of foul play.

Because the authorities had been told the boy died as the result of a fight, they expected that any skeletal evidence I found would be of either a blow from a fist or from the impact of bone against rock when the body had hit the ground. As demonstrated by the case of the skeleton under the ventilation tunnel in the national park, those distinctions aren't often possible. If I found fractures, it would indicate a degree of violence, whether from the blow or the fall. As it happened, I found none.

What I found instead were numerous small incisions in the bone. Seven in the shoulder blades. Six in the bones of the neck. Eighteen in the left ribs. The thirty-three wounds were produced by at least twenty-nine separate forceful insertions of a thin, sharp object such as a knife. One of them passed through the area housing the spinal column and by itself would have caused instant death. All of them had been dealt from behind and were clustered just left of the midline in the upper back. Notwithstanding Shortridge's story of how the fight had started, it appeared to have finished in a murderous rage.

This new perspective had a predictable effect on the way the police and prosecutors viewed their case. What was entirely unpredictable was the chain of events that followed. Sometime after the defendant was advised I had found cut marks, Charles Shortridge's father committed suicide, leaving a note in which he confessed to the killing. It had happened, the note said, in the family home, and after murdering the boy the elder Shortridge claimed to have compounded the tragedy by enlisting his innocent son, Charles, to help dispose of the body. Charles immediately verified the confession.

By now, however, the prosecution no longer believed either the dead father or the son. Charles had demonstrated a pattern of consistently amending his story to meet new turns in the trail of evidence, and although the authorities were convinced the note had been written by the father, they were equally certain its contents were a lie. At the time of his death the father knew about my report that the victim had been stabbed, but the prosecution had not yet revealed the location and number of the injuries—so his letter made no reference to the knife thrusts to the back.

When confronted with the inconsistency between his father's confession and the real nature of the killing, Charles responded in character. He adjusted his story yet again, claiming that in the course of disposing of the dead body, he had added a few thrusts of his own—hoping, he said, to make it look like the results of a motorcycle accident.

The final version didn't persuade the jury any more than it had moved the police or prosecution. Despite his father's extraordinary final gift, Charles Shortridge was convicted of first-degree manslaughter, and is serving a sentence of up to twenty-five years in prison.

20

SOME ASSEMBLY REQUIRED

At about the same time Alferd Packer got out of jail for his crime in Colorado, another, far lesser frontier celebrity named Elmer J. McCurdy was shot to death by a posse in a hayloft in Oklahoma. McCurdy's crime had been the robbery of a train of the Missouri, Kansas & Texas Railroad, and although the adventure netted him only $46 and a case of liquor, a comparison of his end and Packer's seems to suggest that the tolerance for cannibalism in the Old West was considerably higher than for the crime of stealing booze. Six and a half decades later, McCurdy's mummified remains turned up in Long Beach, California, as a prop at the Laugh in the Dark Funhouse.

The discovery that the remains were real, and not just a man-made dummy, came during the filming of an episode of the television show "The Six Million Dollar Man"; one of McCurdy's arms came off when hit by a stage light, revealing bone. The forensic anthropologist Clyde Snow was able to confirm cause of death by gunshot, but although

McCurdy had died violently, he was provably not a victim of murder. Working in collaboration with Los Angeles County medical examiners and others, Snow was able to trace the cowboy-bandit's remarkable show-biz odyssey through sideshows and roadside attractions across the West for the last half century, starting with a career in 1916 as a nickel-a-peek curiosity in the back room of an Oklahoma funeral parlor. My contribution to this case involved helping to assess age at death from microscopic examination of thin sections removed from the bone.

When McCurdy's saga was reported in the *Wall Street Journal*, it was noted that the historical detective work was aided by the presence of numerous carnival ticket stubs found in Elmer's mouth, and that two rival bed-and-breakfasts were then engaged in an ugly duel of wills over their rights to the use of his pulling power as a tourist attraction. After one final blaze of glory in which his remains dressed the set for a eulogy by CBS superstar Lesley Stahl, Elmer was certified dead at long last. His remains were returned to the state in which he died and he resides there today in a casket securely anchored by a shroud of concrete two feet thick.

In the last century the theft, usually by substitution, of noted skulls was so epidemic that the head of the Swedish mystic Emanuel Swedenborg was switched three times. A modern forensic examination proved that the cranium in his present crypt is not the one he was wearing when he died in 1772, and a parallel examination produced a strong possibility that the real Swedenborg skull is in the collection of a woman doctor in Wales. (I mean, is that mystical, or what?)

In *The Human Skull: A Cultural History* (1966), Folke Henschen shows that some of the most famous people of their times—aside from numerous saints, they include Voltaire, King Henri IV of France, the philosopher Descartes, the poet Schiller, and even the revered Papa Haydn—have not been immune from the theft of skulls or even entire bodies out of the shrines to which they were committed. Before we snicker too loudly at such ancient foibles, consider the present day. The illegal collection of modern bones, especially skulls, is not the sole province of the deranged serial killers in orange jumpsuits and iron manacles seen staring blankly at the camera on the late-night news.

After World War II, trophy skulls of the enemy dead appeared all over the country, not just on bookshelves and mantelpieces but at dumpsites, in trash receptacles at roadside rest areas, in people's gardens, and in all sorts of other places where they had been disposed of by collectors who apparently developed second thoughts about the meaning of victory. Another wave of trophy skulls arrived on these shores after Vietnam, and in at least two instances wholesale quantities of immaculately clean, carefully packed crania were recovered by police still in their shipping crates, evidence that the spoils of war had become a profitable import industry.

It doesn't stop there. Every state in the Union contains cemeteries that have been plundered for their bones by looters whose motives range from childish derring-do through morbid curiosity to Satanism and plain old-fashioned madness. As the anthropologist Kenneth Kennedy of Cornell University has pointed out, "the desire to possess a human skull, however acquired, is a perversity not confined to physical anthropologists."

By the same token, the desire to identify a skeleton by name is not limited to police, members of the Swedenborg Society, or descendants of dead poets. The Roman Catholic Church frequently needs to verify the identity of skeletal remains of candidates for sainthood, and sometimes calls on the techniques of modern forensics; an anthropologist at Berkeley named Theodore McCown provided just such a service in connection with the remains of Father Junípero Serra, the founder of California's Franciscan missions, who died in 1784. McCown also positively identified the remains of Juan Bautista de Anza, the founder of San Francisco. But he may be best remembered by the general public as the scientist who put a wet blanket on a claim that the remains of Amelia Earhart had been recovered from a South Pacific island. A Hearst newspaper reporter brought McCown a skeleton that had been dug out of a seaside grave in Micronesia, suggesting it was the missing aviator. McCown said it was more likely the body of a Micronesian male.

Bone cases seldom arrive from the FBI or other agencies without at least a few missing parts. Ideally we'd like to see the whole skeleton in order to derive the maximum amount of information, but in reality we rarely get it, and sometimes all we see are a few isolated pieces. Even so, in a surprising number of such fragmentary cases we are able to develop a picture of the dead person and of the events attending death.

One of my earliest cases involved a severed hand that had been sent to the FBI Laboratory in a bottle of saline solution. It was found in an open field in New Mexico; inquiries at area hospitals had revealed no history of hand amputations, and local laboratory tests produced no evidence of agents associated with embalming. Although the referring medical investigator was hoping for a positive ID from what was left of the fingerprints, there wasn't much to work with. He also knew enough to ask the FBI for an opinion on possible age and sex.

We started with an X-ray, which disclosed that the amputation had occurred just above the wrist. The thumb was severed through the distal end, the index finger was severed at the midshaft, and the tips of the remaining three fingers had been cut off as well. For the most part the borders of the cuts were very even and clean, although the lacerations on the thumb and index finger were slightly irregular and showed some evidence of tearing. There were also some marks from the gnawing of small rodents. Skin color suggested that the racial origin was Caucasian, and the large size of the hand suggested it was from a male.

A suggestion, however, can't be expected to stand without some form of support, and there is not a lot of information in the literature about the comparative size of finger bones. In order to provide a range of scientific probability for our inference, we went back to the Smithsonian's collections and began to measure the length of metacarpals from known skeletons, establishing size parameters for male and female. There is a large area of overlap in the middle-size range, but this hand was at the end of the spectrum where there was little doubt that it was male.

We didn't have to create a database in order to determine that the the hand was from an adult: the X-rays disclosed that the epiphyses had all been united, which meant the victim was at least twenty years old. There was no sign of healed fracture or any other earlier traumas, and the state of preservation of the tissues indicated that the time since death—of the limb if not of the owner—was no more than a week.

Shortly afterwards, working with what remained of the patterns beneath the severed tips, FBI fingerprint specialists were able to identify the owner of the hand. It had come from a twenty-two-year-old Hispanic male who had been reported missing just about a week before the severed member was found. No other remnants of the body were ever located. It was decided the hand was insufficient proof that its owner had died, and fourteen years later a death certificate has still not been issued.

Sometimes we get far more of the body but can extract far less information. Back in the summer of 1980, a man bought an old house in Sioux City, Iowa, with the intention of tearing it down and putting up another building in its place. The house had been vandalized, and neighborhood kids had broken in on several occasions to play in the empty rooms and third-floor attic; but despite the derelict condition, there were numerous items such as old books, letters, and even antique typewriters which the new owner planned to salvage for sale before calling in the wreckers. Many of the best items were in the attic, and he decided to go through it systematically, starting in the north corner. It was there that he came across a wooden crate containing a partial skeleton. All of the bones were still in their original relationship, and it appeared to represent the portion of the body between the bottom of the rib cage and the midsection of the thighs.

Local police began collecting information on the history of the house and they sought opinions from a succession of analysts, including a medical examiner, a pathologist, a radiologist, and an archaeologist. The remains were variously identified as belonging to a boy of fourteen and a man of twenty-one to sixty but most likely around forty. Because a medical article entitled "End Results in Surgery of Female Pelvis" was found in a nearby pile of papers, there was additional speculation on gender by the police, although not by the consultants.

All the bones except the right femur were still articulated when the remains got to Washington. They had been stained dark brown, and I noted that both femora had been cut with a saw about a third of the way above the knee. The police report said that attic temperatures in the house ranged from 32 degrees to 150 degrees. There was considerable grease and soft tissue still present, but no odor. I knew that under some circumstances, including such temperature extremes, similar tissue condition can be maintained for several years, so an estimate of time since death would be so broad as to be worthless. I agreed with the other examiners that the sex was male, and I set the age between thirty-five and sixty. As it turned out, those conclusions weren't worth much, either.

Further investigation by the police revealed that a couple of the prior owners of the house had been physicians, although many years before. It was finally decided by the police that the bones had been used for teaching and were not evidence of a crime. I think they were right. Medical specimens of this type can retain dessicated soft tissue long after the odor has gone away, and it would have been easy for an absent-minded physician to forget a skeleton once it went up to the attic. The remains were buried and the case was closed.

Hannah Arendt said of her studies of the Holocaust that what most impressed her about evil was its sheer banality. That isn't true only of the evils of war and genocide. Time and again, as I have read the reports that accompany the evidence of murder, I find myself marveling at the persistent relationship between even the most terrible crimes and the commonplace, everyday things that make up normal life.

A few years ago, a twenty-eight-year-old family man near Spokane invited an old friend over to his house. The two had known each other since high school, and police suspected that in the intervening years they had become confederates in the international drug trade. The family man may have been under some pressure from members of the drug ring who apparently considered the friend a security risk, so he led his old classmate down into the cellar and hit him in the head from behind with an ax. He then called a second friend over to give him a hand with the body. Maybe there's some other word; this isn't really a story about friendship.

When the second visitor arrived, he pointed out that the body at the foot of the cellar stairs was still twitching. I don't know what Miss Manners would say about that kind of comment, but it apparently didn't offend the killer; he strolled over to the body and gave it a second whack, then together the two men dragged it up the stairs and out into the backyard. They set the body down, moved the redwood table where the murderer frequently picnicked with his family, got some shovels from the toolshed, dug a grave, dropped in the bloody corpse, refilled the hole, smoothed out the dirt, and set the picnic table back where it belonged.

For the next couple of years, it was pretty much business as usual at the old homestead. The killer and his family occasionally dined al fresco, weather permitting, just as they always had, although they may well have had to level the table from time to time with an additional shovelful of dirt to compensate for settling. But two summers later the killer invited the second man back and announced his decision to disinter the victim. He intended to throw the remains into the river.

Digging the dead body out of the ground turned out to be not quite as easy as excavating the raw dirt had been two years earlier. Most backyard burials don't involve such niceties as embalming or watertight coffins, and when an unprotected corpse is placed in an unlined grave, it quickly forms a union with the earth. Flesh rots, fabric disintegrates, and under certain conditions the more durable portions such as the skull, spine, pelvis, and long bones can become imbedded in the surrounding soil. The two toilers soon despaired of getting it all, so they loaded a bedspread with those parts they could pry loose, refilled the hole, and headed for the Spokane River. They waded into the fast-moving water to the tops of their thighs, then flipped the spread between them like an Eskimo blanket, scattering its contents far out into the flood.

Two more years passed before the inevitable happened and the police heard about the murder through a convict who wanted to make a trade. The convict's source was the second friend. That's another banality about this kind of crime: if any other people know what you did, eventually they will tell.

The police were wonderfully thorough in building their case. With the exception of the suspect, they interviewed everyone who could possibly illuminate what had happened, including the co-digger. Under his direction, they sent divers out into the river and retrieved several bones, including one that looked like an arm or a leg. They even spoke to scientists who told them what to expect when they finished the exhumation from under the redwood table. Then they dug up the backyard, packaged up forty-four bones from the gravesite, two dirt samples from under the skeleton, three bones from the river, twenty-nine bags of unknown debris, seventeen bags of clothing bits, and "seventeen teeth attached and loose," and sent everything off to Washington.

I didn't know at the time that local pathologists had already tentatively identified two of the river bones as a human metacarpal and tibia, and had expressed an opinion that the third was petrified, so I felt no pangs of collegial guilt in reporting with certainty that they had come instead from a bird, a cow (*Bos Taurus*), and some unidentified large animal.

As to the body from the backyard grave, the remnants consisted of a right clavicle, eleven vertebrae, eight ribs, seven hand bones, and fragments of the hyoid and skull. All I could say of them was that they had belonged to a white male between thirty and forty who had been dead between six months and ten years—which was consistent with the time of the alleged crime. That was close enough; I was invited out to testify. The state got a conviction, but this is one case where I'm sure my role wasn't the deciding factor.

Another case evolved from a police investigation of complaints about trespassing and vandalism in an abandoned building. In a corner of one room they found a small cardboard box which contained a circular wooden canister. Inside that was a severed human hand, resting on a bed of cotton wadding.

The accompanying letter to my office requested help in determining origin and, if possible, an opinion on age, sex, whether a preservative was used, how the limb was severed, blood type, whether the bones were intact, and fingerprint ID—all things one might reasonably expect to learn from such an artifact, depending on circumstances.

The chemical test for preservatives, the serology, and the fingerprinting would all be done across the street, although I knew it was unlikely the latter two would produce any positive results. Dried blood is difficult or impossible to type, and three out of four Americans have never been fingerprinted. For my part, I reported that the small size indicated the likelihood of female sex, the epiphyseal closure was adult, and there was no indication of ancestry or cause of death.

The hand was mummified, indicating a time since death of certainly more than a year and probably several decades or more. Anthropologists deal with these types of remains all the time, and I have seen many such examples of natural soft-tissue mummification from the arid areas of the western hemisphere, particularly in the American Southwest, Chile, and Peru, which date back centuries or even millennia. Most medical examiners don't get to study many ancient remains, just as most anthropologists don't get to examine recent ones, so this was one case where the dual perspective was especially useful.

I felt this was an archaeological relic because of the irregular margin of the desiccated flesh at the wrist, which gave no evidence of cut marks. Apparently the hand had not been severed from the body by a knife, but was removed after mummification had already occurred. There was also a red stain, certainly not blood but very likely fingernail polish, on the severed end of the hand and on the white fiber within the container. Since the stain was on the internal structure of the hand, it would have been applied after the hand was removed from the rest of the body, and probably soon after it was placed in the container. The artifact had less the characteristics of a modern crime than of a recent sinister prank.

Another severed left hand, recovered by police from an associate of the Pagans motorcycle gang in Delaware, was not an archaeological relic, but it appeared to have served pretty much the same function as the one in New England. This one was in a Lucite block, which preserved it relatively intact, and it was found in a tattoo parlor owned by the biker. The hand had been sawn or cut off rather than torn or broken from the wrist, and the little finger and the end of the second finger were missing. Those bones too showed signs they had been cleanly cut, but only the phalanx in the second finger showed any sign of healing, which told me the little finger had been removed at or after death, while the other segment was at least several months earlier. It was not possible to tell from the size whether it had belonged to a man or woman (just as a guess, I'd say female), but from radiographs of the epiphyses I estimated age at between twenty-five and fifty. That's a fair amount of information, under the circumstances, but not enough, by itself, to suggest cause of death or to make an identification.

It was possible, of course, that either of these hands was part of something else. I have seen lots of human remains used to scare people, either in ritual or as decorative art, and sometimes even to hurt them. There are many examples in archaeological literature of human bones being modified to serve as bowls, medallions, or trinkets. I once examined a knife handle made of a human femur, which hung from the center of the meeting room in another renegade bikers' clubhouse in the Midwest; in fact, artifacts of death and violence can be an important part of biker chic. Lots of fake shrunken heads, made from monkey heads with hair attached from either humans or horses, have been coming up from South America for the last century, not to mention the real human skulls that are excavated from plundered graves for use by such groups as the Santorini cult in the Caribbean. Some of those cults call for the raising of special altars on which to place ceremonial objects, which frequently include human bones.

These things rise and fall with the tides. In the time of Byron and the Romantics, it became fashionably scandalous for the cognoscenti to toast each other's health from ornately decorated drinking steins made of human skulls, sometimes even from the heads of their friends or intellectual celebrities of the day.

Scientists in general tend to be puzzle solvers, and there are times when it seems that the best metaphor for forensic anthropology would be the jigsaw puzzle. For one thing, most jigsaw puzzles that have been around a while are missing a piece or two, and by the same token it's not uncommon for parts from one puzzle to show up in the box for another. In our business, the errant piece is almost always an animal bone. Perhaps most frequently the long bones are from deer and other ruminants, and the smaller ones are from rodents, birds, lesser farm stock, and domestic pets. Except in mass disasters or the disturbance of a mortuary site, human bones almost never migrate from one skeleton to another. But there are times, because of the nature and timing of the materials that are brought to us, when the forensic examiner finds himself playing a mental game of mix-and-match.

For the barnacled skull from the Chesapeake, the connection with the body found a week later in the same general area was obvious. By contrast, in the case of the headless, handless man whose remains were found off the interstate at Virginia Beach in summer 1991, there was nothing to match; the missing parts had been removed by deliberate cutting with a knife. And a mummified corpse from further south a couple of years before, also displaying the incisions of perimortem decapitation, was equally incomplete. In both of those latter cases, and dozens like them, it's very unlikely the puzzles will ever be fully assembled.

On second thought, there are times when all the missing pieces have come together at last. The severed head found in a plastic bag in a field in Indiana turns out to be an exact match with the headless torso recovered from a bog in Florida. The mummified remains of a human female forearm and hand retrieved from a cellar crawl space in Poultney, Vermont, precisely fit the distal ends of an incomplete radius and ulna from a woman's body found the year before in an abandoned washing machine in Texas. The skeletal remains of another arm, this time a man's recovered in 1986 between the chimney and wall during the demolition of a house in Pennsylvania belong on an incomplete body recovered at the crash site of a drug plane in Mississippi.

All of these wonderful resolutions occur at approximately the same time of day, following my return home after many hours at the office. More exactly, for people who might want to use the same technique in solving puzzles of their own, they come to me within a few minutes of laying my own fully articulated body in my bed, turning off the light, carefully arranging my still-connected head on a soft pillow, and closing my eyes.

21

SERIAL KILLINGS

B y almost any standard, Ted Bundy was a product of what we like to think of as the good life. He was handsome, intelligent, engaging, well educated, came from an apparently decent family, and had even been trained as a lawyer. A couple of years ago, he agreed to a final interview with an evangelical minister in the hope that together they would be able to identify what had gone so terribly wrong in his life. In character to the end, the most notorious U.S. serial murderer of his day came to that interview equipped with an answer: the reason for his tragic downfall, he told the minister, was pornography.

It sounded a lot like the prizefighter explaining the loss of his championship with the famous old line, "Booze done it." Maybe pornography was part of Bundy's particular trigger, but the idea that being exposed to dirty pictures is a direct route to serial murder defies logic. If that were the case, droves of adolescent boys in America would be doomed to kill, and there wouldn't be enough victims to go around. As smart as he was, I don't think Ted Bundy had the foggiest idea why he did what he did, and asking a sociopath to psychoanalyze himself, even in the hope of rescuing his soul, makes as much sense as expecting him to explain the cause of cancer or to take out his own appendix.

What makes serial murderers fascinating, beyond the fact that they're dangerous, is that they seem to be so much like the rest of us except in the one particular which makes them different. How different? It has been estimated by the FBI's National Center for Analysis of Violent Crime that there are as many as fifty serial killers at work in America today. That number may seem high, especially in context with another estimate by a leading criminologist that serial murders in this country average about twelve in a year. But even if the FBI's estimate is accurate, it means the serial killer is a rare bird indeed, a statistical anomaly that shows up only once in every 5 million members of the overall population.

Statistics also explain why the other estimate—of serial victims—is comparatively low. Because that estimate is from a different source, it uses a different minimum criterion for its definition of the offense; a killer has to murder something like eight people, not just in a rampage but spread out over a period of time, before it conforms to the definition. It may also be that the estimated number of victims is low because a lot of serial killings go unrecognized as being parts of a larger pattern.

I expect both estimates would be subject to sharp upward revision if the entry requirements were less rigorous. My own definition of serial murder is more democratic: three or more related killings, each separated by at least a week. In part, the logic behind that definition is that it allows me to include a couple of my most fascinating assignments along with some that are better known or have been in the headlines more recently.

One case that perfectly demonstrates the wisdom of such flexibility came to the FBI from the Orient in 1982. Although it was not certain whether it involved three or four victims (that was the FBI's challenge: to determine which number pertained), there was no doubt at Royal Hong Kong Police Headquarters that they were dealing with the work of a serial murderer. This case illustrates another feature of such killings that continually impresses me: that they can escape detection despite prolonged, repeated, and sometimes incredible risk on the part of the perpetrator. But what appears to normal people to be breathtaking derring-do may not be that at all; more probably the murderers are so sunk into their obsession, so detached from the concept of guilt or consequence, they become anesthetized to the possibility they will be caught. For example, they take pictures of their killings, as happens frequently in such cases, not in an impulse to flirt with danger or flaunt their crimes to others, but rather because murder is such an ephemeral event, they hope to preserve the moment and make it endlessly retrievable for future reverie. In this instance, that was how the perpetrator was caught. He went back to the photo store for enlargements.

The story began with a woman hailing a taxi in Hong Kong. She had been drinking, and before reaching her destination she became ill in the cab. The driver objected vigorously to the soiling of his vehicle, and events quickly escalated into a major scene. The details of what followed are uncertain, but when it was all over the woman was dead. Reluctant to report the death and not knowing what to do with the corpse, the driver decided to take it back to his apartment and think things through. It was there, he later confessed, away from the stress of traffic and in the peace and privacy of his bedroom, while he contemplated the dead body before him and weighed the unhappy situation he was in, that he first became aware of a powerful urge to forgiveness, even of overwhelming affection, toward the young woman who only a short time before, while living, had been the object of his terrible wrath. In addition to taking still photographs, he made video recordings, with sound, of everything that happened next.

He was arrested months later, the second time he collected a particular batch of processed film. Since all of his earlier photographs had been developed automatically and no one had bothered to look at them, his irresistible impulse had had plenty of time to blossom into a serious bad habit. When the police later searched his apartment, they found several bottles of formalin under his bed, and in them were the sexual organs and parts of several women, dissected with varying degrees of surgical finesse. When confronted by the cache, the taxi driver attempted to negotiate with the prosecutor: a confession of four murders in trade for the videos and stills. That's what I mean by detached.

Because of the pictorial record, the police obviously had no reason to bargain, and I doubt they would have entertained such an offer in any event. They came to the FBI because the photographs and video recordings clearly showed the sexual violation and dissection of four victims, but the remains of only three were more or less positively identified from the bottles under the bed. It was hoped that if one of the two sets of pubic bones found in those bottles could not have come from one of those three, then there would be another confirmation of the fourth victim.

The shape of all three pairs of pubic bones which I examined in my office showed strong evidence that they were female. I estimated their ages at death as about thirty-three, twenty, and thirty-three, respectively (all of which were found later to have slightly overshot the real ages of twenty-nine, seventeen, and thirty-one, though within the ranges I had given for each). Two of the pairs of bones showed the small pitting on the dorsal surface which usually indicates a woman has given birth to at least one child; police later verified that in each of those two cases the victims had two children. I was also able to confirm that each pair corresponded to a single individual. Fortunately, the skull of the fourth victim was recovered elsewhere about a month after the consulting forensic pathologist from Hong Kong came to see me, and she was positively identified by dental data and photographic superimposition, so my evidence and testimony were not required at the trial.

The defensive strategy of the current reigning king of the pit, Jeffrey Dahmer, took a different tack. By the time Milwaukee police finally caught up with him in the summer of 1991 (not including the time they caught up just long enough to return a naked, bleeding fourteen-year-old boy who almost got away from him), Dahmer had murdered and dismembered at least fifteen victims. The severed head of one of them was in his refrigerator, the heart of another was in the freezer, and his bedsheets were encrusted with their blood.

Apparently recognizing that there are few plausible excuses for that kind of untidiness, Dahmer admitted to everything and gambled on a defense of insanity. It was hard to imagine anyone would believe him sane, so the question really was whether the jury felt crazy also meant not guilty. Before they decided it did not, and Dahmer was sentenced to more than a dozen consecutive life sentences without parole, authorities did everything in their power to identify his victims, prove his guilt, and guarantee he would never be free to kill again.

The extent of that effort is illustrated in the case of Dahmer's first alleged victim, killed in 1978, whose remains were examined by Doug Owsley just down the hall from my office. The bone fragments had been recovered from a semi-rural disposal site of approximately two acres in Bath, Ohio. The area where the fragments were scattered had been gridded off under the highly professional direction of the county medical examiner, William Cox, and the remains were systematically excavated by his staff and the police a painstaking trowelful at a time. The resulting evidence included hundreds of bone fragments, both human and non-human.

Doug's first task was to inventory the bones and sort them by kind and size. He and his assistant, Bob Mann, were aided in the inventory by a Smithsonian zoöarchaeologist, who helped separate and identify those bones belonging to cows, sheep, pigs, chickens, dogs, rabbits, cats, possum, and woodchucks. In one of the larger animal bones—a dog femur—someone had driven a nail.

Dahmer told police he had dismembered the victim beneath the house where he committed the murder, then taken the parts outside in plastic bags and stored them behind a shed. Weeks later he returned and crushed the bones with a heavy implement, then went out into the woods and scattered the fragments like seeds, casting them into the underbrush.

Owsley and Mann set about surveying the human portion of the recovered bones for any indication of postmortem modification. Most of those alterations were cut marks or fractures associated with the breaking up of the bones. There was not a single intact bone, and the size of the fragments ranged from one centimeter in length to just over two inches. "We kept a careful list, plotting everything we had against a diagram of the skeleton," Doug said, "but by the time we were finished we found that only about twenty percent of the body had been recovered."

Even with that limitation, they were able to determine that the bones had belonged to a young adult; the stage of union of the epiphyses produced an age estimate of between seventeen and twenty years, consistent with the actual age of the suspected victim at death. From their size, they were likely from a male.

The primary objective of this effort was to establish identity, and to that end Doug conducted a variety of different examinations. One of them involved several fragments of the broken teeth, which he hoped could be compared with dental X-rays of the victim. Another entailed comparisons with a medical X-ray of the cervical spine, neck, and part of the face. Both the dental and medical radiographs had been taken some years before the time of death, so if the comparisons were to mean anything, the subsequent size of the bones and teeth had to be extrapolated from the images in the film. Moreover, the quality of the X-rays was reduced by the fact that they were so old.

In the remains of the fragmentary teeth, Doug found two molars which he was able to identify by their original locations in the lower jaw. By comparing the dental X-rays with radiographs taken of those two reconstructed molars, he found a high degree of correspondence in the curvature, size, and spacing of the roots. "They were characteristic enough that I was able to identify several features common to the antemortem and postmortem records," he said. "But in order for these results to become significant, we tried a couple of techniques that had never been done before."

One of those techniques was a radiographic subtraction procedure, borrowed from the X-ray technology associated with mapping the arteries of the heart. The antemortem and postmortem images of the reconstructed molars were superimposed, and the match was nearly exact.

The next step involved the new application of a technique called morphometrics, and Doug was aided in that effort by a statistician, Ralph Chapman, who had honed his art in the measurement of dinosaurs. The reason this technique seemed so likely to apply to the forensic case was that dinosaur bones are frequently recovered in fragments, and their shapes and sizes have to be extrapolated from comparisons with carefully measured reference collections, just as anthropologists work with data from reference collections of the bones from humans.

On a computer, Owsley and Chapman traced the outline of the teeth in both the antemortem X-rays from the dentist and the postmortem X-ray of the reassembled teeth, digitized those two shapes, and then compared them on the screen through the use of statistical programs which Chapman had developed to quantify the degree of correspondence. The correlation was very high. They then ran similar comparisons with fifteen of the same molars taken from other white males in the Smithsonian's collection. This test proved that the original high correlation was statistically significant. That is to say, there was a strong probability the teeth recovered from the site and those in the dental X-ray had come from the same boy.

"In addition to what we learned about this particular case," Doug said, "we also gained important new insight into the variability from one individual to another in molar-root morphology. From focusing on a very small area of a tooth, the mesial root, we learned that based on a random sample of individuals, only about one person in ten shares a similar appearance. At present we cannot use such similarities, no matter how many there may be in one skull, for a positive identification. But we can build a very strong inference of identity with such comparisons, and conversely we can use them to positively rule out mismatches."

Doug's next morphometric statistical comparison was based on the most nearly complete element in the partial skeleton, a neck vertebra. That vertebra was in the medical radiograph, and he used the same digital technology as in his comparisons of the molar roots. Here again he had to correct a problem of legibility in the X-ray.

X-rays are very dense, and older films tend to become faded and cloudy. So Doug had a contact print made from the original, which resulted in much greater clarity and definition—including very clear structural features in the vertebra which were previously hidden. As in the comparisons of the teeth, the correspondence was high. They then digitized specific landmarks on the vertebra and again went to the Smithsonian's collections for validation. In this case they compared the same shapes, distances, and angles on cervical vertebrae from twenty skeletons of males in the same age group as the victim. On these morphological statistical comparisons alone, not even considering the similarities of structural landmarks, Owsley and Chapman feel they have ruled out the possibility of a match with 95 percent of the white male population.

"We're making our main case for positive identification on the features of the cervical spine," Doug said, "but thanks to these new techniques, we have been able to support that inference in a lot of ways that were previously unavailable in this field. We feel very confident in the result."

What they have added to this case, they have also added to their science. Those same techniques, with refinements, will be available on other forensic examinations in the future.

The longest-running active serial murder investigation in the United States is the Green River Murders in King County, Washington, now ten years old and with forty-one known victims. I have examined some of the evidence in that series, but because the case is still open I am not able to speak on it from my own experience. You're not missing much; my role was very minor.

The series began with the discovery of a total of five bodies in just thirty-one days in the summer of 1982. All were in the Green River or on its banks near Kent, Washington, all were women, and all had a history of involvement with prostitution. In the intervening years the pattern stretched to a total of twenty-six sites in the same general area, some containing up to five bodies. The geographical scope increased slightly to include nearby Pierce County, and Tualatin in neighboring Oregon. The pattern of sex, age, and victim history has remained the same. The time since death in these recoveries has ranged from two days to six years, with the majority of the corpses having gone to skeletons. The fact that a couple of the bodies were found fully or partially buried raises the possibility that more are still out there, and police believe the killer is still active. A multijurisdictional Green River Task Force has identified over 8,500 items of evidence.

The Green River investigation was hampered to some degree, especially in its earlier stages, by the wildness of the terrain, by a lack of understanding of locating techniques, by poor appreciation of the significance of skeletal remains among those who first found them, and by improper training in recovery techniques on the part of some of the autonomous local authorities. In a few instances the bones were simply gathered up in boxes or paper bags and dropped off at the police station with virtually no documentation. That's a fairly congenial environment for a murderer to work in; now that conditions are less relaxed, the killer's productivity has declined—or else he or she is doing a better job of hiding the evidence.

One aspect of this series I have followed with some interest is the use of various facial reproduction techniques for the identification of unknown remains. Nine of the skeletons could not be identified by dental charts or similar methods at the time of recovery, and some two dozen facial reproductions have been made on those nine skulls by nine different forensic artists, working with a variety of media, in the hope of generating leads. Three of these victims were identified following coverage by news media. The reproductions have included both sketches and sculpture, and have varied widely in the extent of agreement between one artist's version and another's, and in the degree of apparent resemblance once the remains have been identified. Of the nine original unknowns, only four remain unnamed.

Another notorious series in which I have had far greater involvement is the so-called Roadside Murders of 1988 through 1990 in New Bedford, Massachusetts. So far, eleven women whose sex, age, and career patterns match those of the Green River victims have disappeared from the streets of this historical former whaling capital in southeastern Massachusetts. The skeletal remains of nine of them have been recovered and identified, mostly from roadside locations to the north, south, and west of the city.

I'd worked with the Bristol County Crime Prevention and Control

(CPAC) unit on several previous cases, and they asked me in on this one in the hope that my particular expertise might supply a useful new perspective.

I first became acquainted with CPAC through work on three related murders that took place in and around New Bedford's sister city of Fall River ten years earlier. This series and the Roadside Murders had in common that all the victims were young women, and all had some apparent involvement with drugs and/or prostitution. While the first series involved up to seven different participants, many believe that the Roadside Murders were likely to have been the work of one individual.

As usual, I worked closely with the medical examiners and detectives in the case and conducted the basic anthropological examinations, most of which were aimed at identifying or verifying the identity of all of the recovered young victims, searching for evidence of trauma, and trying to establish times since death. The project was complicated by the advanced state of decomposition of most of the victims. But eventually all the recovered remains were identified, and some other anthropological observations made in the course of the examinations may also prove relevant to the investigation. Although the series appears to have ended, the crimes remain unsolved.

22

ONES THAT ALMOST
GOT AWAY

couple of years ago, the skeletons of a man and a woman were found in a wooded roadside area in a midwestern state. They were both identified through Missing Persons reports and by comparisons with dental records, but medical examiners had been unable to find any evidence pointing to the cause of death, so they sent the remains to me to Washington. I laid each of them out in turn and examined them from head to foot, and on the surface I had to agree there was no obvious sign of trauma. There were several alterations in the man's skeleton, particularly some long, narrow cut marks down the length of one rib, but microscopic examination revealed a trough-like appearance characteristic of postmortem abrasion rather than the V-shaped signature of a blade. There were similar marks on some of the girl's bones, also apparently postmortem, as well as evidence of cutting away of soft tissue at the time of autopsy. Then I looked at the girl's left hand.

On the lateral surface of the second proximal phalanx, between the index finger and the thumb, was unmistakable evidence of the single stroke of a blade. The cut was at an angle, the proximal margin was sheared, and the distal aspect was curled outward, suggesting a downward motion of the knife. There had been no remodeling and the cut had been made while the bone was fleshed, indicating it had occurred at or about the time of death. It was a classic defense wound, and although the knife had made no other impression on the bones of either body, I was convinced it was the means by which both victims had been murdered. An investigation is proceeding on the basis of that conclusion.

More recently, the skeletons of another couple were found in a similar setting in the Southwest. Again, the only evidence of trauma on the body of the woman was a tiny planar incision, this time on the fourth cervical vertebra, and on the man a nearly invisible nick on the joint of the lower jaw. But as small as they were, to the trained eye those two discoveries spoke as eloquently of murder by stabbing as a signed confession or a photograph of the crime.

I'm sure that before the value of the techniques of forensic anthropology gained wide acceptance, more people got away with murder. Those who nearly got away include a onetime insurance salesman in Yakima, Washington, who beat his wife to death with a hammer in 1975, set the incident up as an accident, and escaped arrest for almost a decade.

On the face of it, he was the kind of killer one would expect to get caught a lot earlier. He would put away half a quart of scotch and a six-pack of beer in a typical day. He advertised his intentions in advance to at least one of his numerous girlfriends. His former in-laws were so certain he had murdered his wife that they went to the expense of an exhumation, private autopsies, and an appeal to the district attorney to reopen the case based on evidence that contradicted the official cause of death. His second wife divorced him and told the police he had boasted to her of the crime; she even recited in detail how he had done it. For all that, it finally took a special petition to the governor by the dead woman's sister to bring the man to trial.

According to his second wife's testimony in court, the killer's whole approach to the crime, and his explanation for why he was so lucky for so long, was that the cops were stupid. Anybody can get away with murder, so he said, if they just commit the crime in a way that can be plausibly explained as an accident. He hit his wife three times on the head with a claw hammer because sideways it made the same kind of impact mark as a horseshoe, placed her body in a horse stall of the barn behind their house, then drove down to the local bakery where he paid for a bag of assorted donuts by check. He told the police that when he returned home and didn't find his wife in the house, something prodded him to look in the barn. Imagine his horror when he found she had been kicked! He thought she was still alive when he called for the ambulance—a nice touch. Later, one of his children said he cried for a week. I can believe he did.

The killer was wrong about the police being stupid. They did what they were supposed to do, but sometimes that's not enough protection against a good lie and a killer's good luck. Deputies from the sheriff's office recorded a detailed report of what they were told and what they found, investigated the murder scene, took pictures, and removed the body.

The medical examiner wasn't stupid either, but the killer's biggest break was the fact that the state didn't require forensic training for physicians who certify accidental death. The coroner did what he could, considering that lack of training or experience. He found a gaping laceration in the right temporal parietal area, exposing a depressed skull fracture, and a similar injury with a broader fracture on the opposite side of the head. He removed the scalp and then the top of the skull, measured and described the two depressed fractures, and reported in detail on the linear fractures connecting them. He compared those injuries to the story he had heard, then with a detective sergeant he returned to examine the horse stall. Two feet above the floor, directly adjacent to a wall still stained with the brush marks of the victim's bloody hair, they found a timber with a projection on the end which corresponded to the injury in her right temple. The coroner wrote in his report: "The bloodstains indicated that the deceased's head had been moving in a direction away from the timber which would be logical as a result of her falling forward after being kicked against the timber." Under Manner of Death he entered: "Being kicked by a horse."

A few months later, the killer married one of his girlfriends, to whom he had told his crime. It's hard to imagine that a union based on such a bond would ever end, but when it did, several years later, there was an unpleasant disagreement over who got the furniture. As a general rule, it is imprudent to argue too vehemently with an adversary you know has an ace up her sleeve. She settled the furniture issue by going to the police with the story of the murder.

There was a big difference between the first medical examination and the studies of the remains that preceded the formal trial. The second time around, the evidence was reviewed by experts who knew what they were looking at: three forensic pathologists, two forensic anthropologists, and detectives trained in reading the evidence of murder.

My report said there were two principal points of focus on the skull, and that they produced separate, unconnected fracture lines, which contradicted the observations of the original examiner and pointed to the possibility of a different type of event than the one he had described. I also said the object producing the puncture mark at the smaller site was sharper than the other, and that it produced an ovoid hole measuring 14 × 21 mm with a sharp upper margin and crushed, flattened lower margin. The pattern suggested the trauma was inflicted at this site from above rather than from below or from the side.

The killer had allowed the murder weapon to turn in his hand before delivering that particular blow; an ovoid hole of that type and size does not come from an object resembling a horseshoe, but is the signature imprint of a hammerhead. The other forensic anthropologist even computed the exact angle of the hammer's attack and the force of the blow. A pathologist demonstrated that it was physically impossible for the body to have contorted in such a way that the puncture wound could have been caused by the knob on the beam. And finally, another specialist demonstrated that the swipes of bloody hair on the wall were not the consequence of a kick, but instead were painted there by hair that had time to become fully saturated and had brushed against the wall not once but twice, as the dying or dead woman's body was being carefully lowered by the killer into its position on the floor of the stall.

In his summation, the prosecutor addressed the essence of the difference between the first examination and the second. He said that the first medical examiner "did what I'm sure many physicians, not forensic specialists, would have done under similar circumstances. He took what appeared on the surface to be a reasonable explanation, a horse kick killed her, and did his autopsy and subsequent examination of the scene with that in mind. He made one of the fatal mistakes: to assume that [he knew] what happened and then try to fit the facts into those assumptions.... [F]orensic pathologists ... are trained not to make that mistake."

I hope he's right.

Part of a detective's job is to include any relevant information, even when it is speculative, that might be of use to the examiner in searching for evidence. Like the examiner, the detective is expected to remain reasonably neutral and not to anticipate the result of such a search. Even when the policeman is careful to express no such anticipation, however, there is a risk that the examiner will find more clues in the letter accompanying the examination request than in evidence from the remains. A letter accompanying the skeletal remains of a young girl from Swansea, Massachusetts, offers a case in point.

The identity of the victim had already been established, the letter said, as a young woman who had disappeared two years before. "She was age 16 at the time. She had run away from home three times already, and had returned. She was a known drug (marijuana) user and had been in trouble with the law." The letter went on to describe two specific physical characteristics—a chipped mandibular front tooth, and an old injury above the left eye from a rock thrown up by a lawn mower blade when she was only two—by which the identity might be confirmed. In addition to the positive ID, the letter asked for "possible cause of death," adding at the end: "Several weeks before her disappearance, her mother stated that she had been threatened with bodily harm by her boyfriend."

On the face of it, the detective didn't appear to express a bias toward either possible cause of death: a drug overdose or violence at the hands of her boyfriend. I later learned, however, that police in Massachusetts were leaning heavily toward the probability that she had died of an OD. The detective who sent the remains to the FBI was apparently a better guesser than most of his peers; he addressed his letter to the Microscopic Analysis Laboratory. After a body has been skeletonized, a microscope doesn't reveal much information about drug use, but it often can reveal insights to violence. In this case, it hit the jackpot.

My examination began with sex, age, race, and time since death, all of which were consistent with the information on the supposed victim. I confirmed a chipped front tooth, and despite the tremendous growth and remodeling that a face undergoes between the ages of two and sixteen, the old fracture from the lawn mower incident, long since healed, was still visible on the frontal bone above the left eye orbit. Without reasonably current medical X-rays or dental records for comparison, neither was positive proof of identity, but added to other evidence recovered at the site they reinforced a strong circumstantial case that these were the remains of the missing girl. Then I began examining the bones for signs of trauma.

The first one was in virtually the first place I looked, on the left twelfth rib, a 2 mm incision produced by a knife or a knifelike instrument. There was another one, this time 12 mm in length, on the next rib. Because it had been two years since the girl's disappearance and presumably since the time of her death, her skeleton had largely disarticulated. But as I examined bone after bone, I kept encountering more and more evidence of brutal stabbing.

She had been stabbed just below the right knee and three times more above and below the left knee. She had been stabbed once in each buttock from behind, and in the groin from the front. There were seven separate stab marks scattered around the back, four more in the nape of the neck, and one in the left side of the neck. There was a total of ten more such wounds in the head: one behind the left ear, three more in the left occipital bone, two on the top of the head, and four in the face—including one through the left eye. Some of the incisions in the skull were so violent they had bent back the bone. Ordinarily wounds that result from such obvious frenzy are grouped in a particular area, but in this case they appeared to travel the full length of the body. I still remember the surprise of the police when I called to tell them their case of suspected drug overdose was in fact a violent murder.

A few weeks after my examination of the remains, an important new piece of evidence was recovered near the murder site as a consequence of my report. A man who lived in the area came forward after reading in the newspaper that the death had been by stabbing. He said he had found an object which he now realized was a likely murder weapon only a short distance from where the skeleton had been subsequently discovered. It was a folding trench knife with brass knuckles on the handle and the word "Assassin" written on the eight-inch blade. By matching the curve of the blade exactly with some of the incisions in the bone, I was able first to prove that the knife could have been the murder weapon, and then to demonstrate that the blade likely had become bent in the fury of the attack.

Matching the murder weapon to the signatures it had left on the skeleton was only part of the necessary equation, however, and the case remained unsolved for another two years. Finally, one of the neighborhood boys went to the police. He said the killer was a friend from high school, and that he had shared the details of what had happened the day of the murder. One of those details was that the folding blade of the knife had snapped shut against the killer's thumb during the attack, and that night he had gone to a walk-in medical center for stitches. Police verified that the suspect had indeed received treatment on the night of the date the girl disappeared. They finally had enough

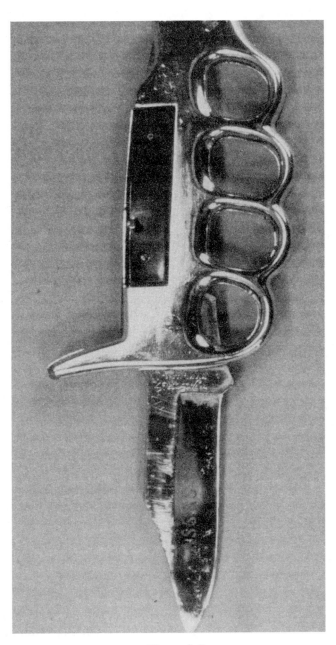

"Assassin"

evidence to arrest the boyfriend—who had been suspected by the victim's mother from the beginning.

When I flew up to Massachusetts to testify at the trial, I couldn't help but think how unlikely it was that this murder should have gone so long without being solved. Totally unplanned, it had been carried out by a heavily drugged young man in a rage. The body was left out in the open where anyone could have tripped over it in a walk through the woods. The murder weapon was recovered within just a few yards of the corpse, and the perpetrator had been identified as a prime suspect even while the case was nothing more than that of a missing person.

Those thoughts were reinforced when I arrived at the courthouse. During the trial I learned that the killer had confided his crime to at least six other boys in the weeks following the murder, yet it was five years before a single one of them came forward.

Strangest of all was what the killer recalled of events when he had gone down to the walk-in medical center for the stitches in his sliced hand. "One of the nurses said, 'It looks like you killed somebody from all the blood.'"

An extremely able assistant district attorney named Ray Veary asked the defendant what he had replied.

"I don't think I said anything. I don't think I remember saying anything."

"Did you say anything to yourself," Veary pressed, "—inside?"

The boy nodded. "Yeah," he answered softly. "I felt guilty."

23

UNWARRANTED

CONCLUSIONS

In addition to judging from surface appearances and being influenced by someone else's expectations, the third greatest danger in forensic anthropology—and perhaps in any other forensic science—is premature disclosure of unproven results. To some extent, almost every case contains some elements of all three perils.

In the late 1970s I received a cardboard box from one of the northwestern states; inside were several plastic packages containing most of a human skeleton. The bones were well preserved from aging, wear, or weather, but most of them had been cut, broken, or damaged by fire. The only remaining soft tissue was on the left foot, which I saw from the package label had been found still inside its boot.

I noted that the sex was female, the age somewhere between seventeen and twenty-one, and the probable racial affiliation Mongoloid. The absence of most soft tissue and the condition of the bones suggested that time since death was at least several months, and probably several years. Other evidence was available which I'll discuss in a moment, but consider the potential pitfalls in what I had already observed.

First, in the area where the remains were found, the population included a number of American Indians. If the referring authorities had sent no other information about the body, or if they thought it might be a specific Indian woman who had disappeared a year earlier, it would be easy enough for the forensic examiner to inherit the assumption that Mongoloid meant Indian, and to mark his or her report on racial affiliation accordingly.

Second, if the forensic examiner weren't familiar with the varied effects of burning, it would be easy enough to assume the fire had occurred at the time of death.

Third, it was apparent from the planar cuts on the bones that they had been made with extremely powerful strokes of a blade. It wouldn't take Sherlock Holmes to combine that observation with the elements above and deduce that the missing Indian woman had been murdered, her body hacked to pieces by a maniac, and the remains burned in the hope of destroying the evidence.

All of the assumptions in that lurid scenario would have been wrong.

More information was available on a closer look. The skeleton was relatively clean, and there was abundant evidence of the action of insects and larvae, the detritus of which still adhered to the remains along with some soil particles and other debris. The larval-stage cases on the skull told me the victim had been dead long enough for the insect to complete part of its life cycle; it had laid eggs, the eggs had hatched, the larvae had pupated, and the adult flies had emerged and flown.

The signs of fire contained clues of another kind. Most of the bones had been burned; some were black and some were white. As discussed more fully in Chapter 11, observation of the changes in bones from different degrees and conditions of firing can sometimes help determine whether a person died in a fire, whether fire was used relatively soon after death to help cover up a crime, or whether the fire took place long after death and was irrelevant to the question of foul play.

From an examination of the cut marks in the skull, mandible, sacrum, hip bones, shoulder blades, and ribs, I concluded that the blade marks were also probably postmortem.

Then I turned to the documentation accompanying the remains. The skeleton was thought by the police to belong to a female who had disappeared seven years earlier at the age of eighteen. The missing woman had not been an Indian, but an Eskimo. A brush fire had swept the area two years before the discovery, and if the body had been there that long, it would have been in it; the bones had been found in the grass by the roadside.

In computing stature based on measurements of the bones, I discovered that the skeleton was a couple of inches shorter than the height given for the missing woman. The height difference could be explained in one of three ways: it wasn't the same woman; it was the same woman but the measurements in the letter were inaccurate estimates; or it was the same woman and her stature happened to be at one end of the reasonable range of variability.

I also concluded that the skeleton contained no apparent indications of cause of death. The blade marks as well as the rougher breaks could easily have resulted from the body's being run over by a power mower. As for the fire, the location and appearance of the burning indicated it had taken place after most of the soft tissue had disappeared and after many of the bones had become disarticulated, which would have been long after death. All my other observations on sex, race, age, and time since death were compatible with the data on the missing woman. I noted three dental fillings in the molar teeth which would provide positive ID if the dental records could be found. The probability of Indian versus Eskimo could have been more exactly determined had not most of the facial bones been broken or missing.

No matter how compelling the false clues may appear at first glance, a prime rule of science is that first glances are never enough.

A couple of years ago I examined a murder victim from a mid-Atlantic state—a rare instance in which I knew from the newspaper that the killer had already confessed and had described the means of death. Accordingly, I was particularly watchful for signs of manual strangulation. But to my surprise, in addition to evidence of trauma to the bones at the back of the head from severe pressure, on the neck I found the unmistakable marks of a knife. One incision, 4.4 mm in length, was located on the first thoracic vertebra, fairly high up on the back. A short distance away, near the end of the right first rib, was a second cut. Next to that were two more.

All were clustered in an area on the right side of the victim's neck; they were very fine, less than 1 mm in width, and had been produced with a sharp, narrow blade. I called the medical examiner and asked if there were any possibility they represented scalpel damage from the autopsy. The answer was no. Accordingly, I carefully noted the details of the cuts in my report and returned the evidence, with my comments.

Several months later, an FBI agent who had worked on the same case happened to come by my office on another matter, and in the course of our conversation, he asked me if I recalled the strangled girl. I said I did.

"I thought there were also cut marks in the area of the neck," he said.

"There were," I acknowledged. More than that, I recalled that this same agent had been in my office when I was writing my report, and knowing he too was involved in the case, I had even shown him the evidence on the bones.

The agent shook his head in puzzlement. "It's funny nothing was said about them last week at the trial."

At first I wasn't sure I understood him. "I didn't go to the trial. The medical examiner got back the bones, so I assume he testified from his own observations."

"I did go," the agent said, "and the medical examiner testified all right, but only to the evidence of manual strangulation. Nothing was said about stabbing."

I couldn't think of what to say, so I just nodded my head and came out with something like "Hmmm."

When the agent left, I immediately picked up the telephone and called the pathologist in question. I told him what I had just heard, and asked if it were true. I half expected a moment's silence on the other end of the line, but what I heard instead was a surprised laugh. "You got me," he said.

The medical examiner told me that after getting my original call about the cut marks, he went to the freezer and his records and carefully studied the soft tissue which he had removed from the murder victim's body before sending the bones to the Smithsonian. Even under a powerful magnifying glass, the skin that had covered the area in question was free of any sign that a blade had penetrated from the exterior of the body. He made another examination when the bones returned from Washington, and there was no way the marks could have come from any other instrument than his own scalpel, as I had suggested.

Probably the most dangerous class of unwarranted conclusion is the kind that ruins a whole lot of good science by adding just the slightest pinch of wishful thinking, usually in an attempt to turn a possibility into a sure thing. At worst the result can be disastrous or heartbreaking, and at the least embarrassing. A good recent example is a case that started with the discovery of the decomposing remains of a young girl in a blue picnic cooler beside the Henry Hudson Parkway near Dyckman Street in Manhattan.

The body belonged to a child between three and five years old, but she was small for her age, and as the case grew in celebrity, local newspapers began referring to her as "Baby Hope." She was malnourished, and there was evidence of sexual abuse. One of the reasons for the attention was that she couldn't be identified, and the crime seemed all the more horrific for the fact that a small child's cruel life had been without a rescue, and her violent death without detection or redress. Then, in what could have been a nearly miraculous combination of good luck and great detective work, the police made a potentially astonishing connection.

They noticed that the little girl in the cooler answered the same general description as another child whose face was seen in five pornographic Polaroid photographs which had been found a month before in a paper bag, also recovered from the side of the highway, in a neighboring state. The skull of the child from the cooler and the photos from the shopping bag were sent to the FBI to determine the possibility that they represented the same individual.

In a child of that age, the bones of the skull are still a long way from final union; after death, they easily disarticulate. The flesh had been removed from the skull, and partly as a result the several loose bones in the package I received in my office had totally lost their natural relationship. My first task in making such a comparison was to rebuild the skull as closely as possible to my estimate of its original shape. We then oriented the skull in the same position as the face in the Polaroids and digitized both the skull and the photographs, using our computer video equipment, so that they could be compared by the technique of superimposition.

Given all the variables, I indicated in my report that we found many points of similarity and no points of dissimilarity in the comparison. I cautioned, however, that this should not be regarded as an identification. Very little research had been conducted on such variability in children's faces, and we had little knowledge of the probabilities involved.

By the time the report and the skull completed the return trip to the North, the initial speculation had congealed into a virtual sure thing. In the chain of events between the writing of my report and a press conference, my cautionary remarks had been lost. Newspapers announced that Dr. Douglas Ubelaker and the FBI had determined the girl in the photographs was "almost certainly the same" as the one in the cooler.

A short time later, the little girl in the pornographic photographs was identified. She did indeed live in the state where the pictures had been found. The man in the Polaroids was identified as well and charged with a sex crime. He escaped being charged with murder; his victim is still alive. I didn't hear whether another press conference was called, but the girl in the pictures obviously was not the girl in the cooler. The good news in that story is that one little girl was rescued from terrible abuse. But Baby Hope, the child from the cooler, is still without any other name.

It's easy enough to see why forensic evidence is sometimes used as a springboard to inappropriate speculation, even by those who should know better. Science and the law are two of humankind's principal expressions of the age-old hope for symmetry and order, while murder involves chaos, evil, and our deepest dreads. But paradoxically, even after two decades of scientific research in hundreds of investigations as a forensic anthropologist, the case that still stands out as the best—or worst—example of such a leap from fact to fancy did not involve forensics at all. It was related to an archaeological discovery at Hull Bay in the U.S. Virgin Islands, which I examined with Larry Angel back in 1975.

Two skeletons had been found, and they were thought to date from the late prehistoric or early historic period. Morphologically, our estimate of their ancestry was that they were black. The archaeologist there argued that pottery found attached to a wrist of one of the skeletons was an Indian artifact, which would have dated the bodies even earlier. Larry and I challenged this with the argument that blacks were not thought to have arrived in that part of the world from Africa until long after the last Indians had left. Our explanation of the pottery was that, assuming the archaeologist was right and it was of Indian origin, it must have been an early example of acculturation: the early blacks had found pottery left behind by the vanished Indians, and they liked it so much they either made their own or adopted the artifacts as heirlooms. We believed the pot had been buried with this particular black as a valued antique, and we published an article on it.

It happened that Larry was in a carpool at the time with a man who worked in public relations at the Smithsonian, and he told him about the paper. The story captured the publicist's interest, and he asked Larry why it couldn't have been the other way around, that there were blacks in the Caribbean prior to the known historical records—prior to Columbus—who were in contact with the Indians? Larry and I had already addressed that possibility in the paper, and the answer was the good scientific one: there was no other evidence for it. With the tremendous amount of archaeology that has been done throughout that part of the world, if there had been an earlier black presence there, it would have surfaced long ago. Besides, we specifically pointed out that two carbon datings of the skeletal remains indicated they were relatively modern burials and certainly did not date back to 1200, which was the period in which pottery of that design was made by Caribbean Indians. When the PR man pressed, Larry said anything was possible, but that scientifically such a scenario didn't represent the best explanation of the pottery in the grave.

Best explanation or not, the PR man decided to do a news release. Ostensibly the release was about our article, but its main result was to provide a showcase for the publicist's own theory; it went out under the headline: SMITHSONIAN SCIENTIFIC MYSTERY: WERE BLACKS IN THE WEST INDIES BEFORE COLUMBUS? By the time Larry and I saw the release, it was too late. The Associated Press shortened the headline to BLACKS BEFORE COLUMBUS? and, swept on by the rushing tide of interest in long-neglected black history, the story ran around the world.

We knew we were in trouble before we heard the first response, but within a few days the article triggered an avalanche of letters and phone calls from teachers and schoolchildren in every part of the country. For many of them, it was obvious that the little clay artifact on the wrist of a skeleton had grown into positive scientific proof that the western hemisphere had been discovered by pre-Columbian Africans. The same wave rocked our boat a bit when it rippled through academia, but Larry and I held hard to the gunwales and rode it out.

A year ago, when I stopped at St. Thomas to assist archaeologists with the Tutu excavation (see Chapter 1), I inquired about the latest thinking on the Hull Bay discovery. New evidence indicated it was typical of pottery made by the early Caribbean blacks. The 1740 journal of a St. Thomas plantation owner described slaves making this "Jyde pattern, without legs ... used by whites and blacks for cooking, baking, and warming the food." It turned out that the pot was copied from the earlier Indian models, but the date of its manufacture was contemporary with the black man who had taken it with him to his grave.

I doubt if there's a moral to any of this, but I have to admit that the experience forced me to do some serious thinking. For one thing, I began to wonder who handled the PR for Columbus. It seems really strange, perhaps even sinister, that the name of the genius responsible for five centuries of great press has been lost to history.

24

BRIEF LIVES

A tradition of forensic anthropologists—as of coroners and policemen—is that they keep a certain distance from their cases, or try to, in order to preserve their objectivity in court. Beyond the ethical demands of each of those professions, however, that same aloofness is a defensive barrier against learning more than they need to know, especially the kind of knowledge that breaks hearts and burdens souls.

But there's a risk in being too careful. For any of those professions, the result of deliberately suppressing human values in a case is that the real meaning of a life can disappear under piles of data: the circumstances of discovery, the measurements of long bones, the condition of the symphyses, the probable cause of death. For anthropologists, this tendency is balanced—or at least it should be—by an awareness that they represent the victim's last chance to be heard, to reveal a major insight into how a person lived and perhaps into how he or she died. If the balance works, the detachment never quite allows the professional examiner to forget that the remains belong to a fellow human being who deserves that final hearing. Sometimes their last words speak not just for the life of the victim but for society, and we ignore them at our peril.

Although I am limiting this chapter to just two case histories, they speak for legions, and the voices have a message for us all. The chapter could be a lot longer; medical examiners all over the country see more and more of these kinds of cases every day.

The first is the body of an elderly black female which I examined just last spring. Hers was the only occupied apartment in a derelict building, and she had lived there alone. When police arrived to investigate reports from neighbors that she had not been seen in weeks or months, they found both the front and rear doors of the apartment ajar, and a mountain of mail had accumulated under the slot in the front hallway, almost all of it directed to "Occupant." From the dates on some of the envelopes, the last time anyone had picked it up was January, in the dead of winter.

It was obvious the moment the police crossed the threshold why no one else in the neighborhood had bothered to check personally on the woman's condition. The stench in the apartment was overwhelming. Lined up neatly against the wall in a room in the rear was a row of metal cans containing human waste. Rat feces were all over the floor, mixed in with a few scattered items of apparel, and months of dirt, trash, and fallen plaster. There was very little in the way of furniture. The apartment had no running water, no electricity, no heat. The woman's body was lying on its back on the floor of the living room.

A green-and-red floral-patterned window drape, with the hooks still in it, was swaddled about her for warmth. Under the drapery was a loosely woven ropelike shawl. She had on a white coat, and beneath that, a blue suit jacket. Under the jacket was a tan sweater, and the layer below that was a set of heavy underwear. She was still wearing one nylon stocking. The right foot had been gnawed from the leg and dragged to a far corner of the room by rats, and the chewed bones of her hands were scattered as far as the entrance hallway. The medical examiner arrived, gathered together all the parts that could be found and, because it was a bone case, put in a call to the Smithsonian.

When I arrived, they told me they had put the body in the "Stinker Room," a special area designed for the storage of fetid cases. At first we intended to do our examination in the main autopsy room, but because of the odor we wheeled the table further down the hall to the loading ramp at the rear entrance, where there was still relative

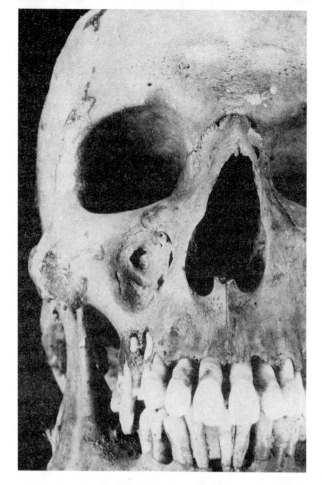

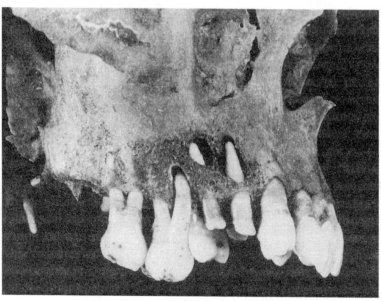

Remains of the man under the bridge.

privacy but plenty of fresh air. Even with the spring breeze, everyone in the building soon knew which case we were working on and they maintained a respectful distance.

The apartment where the woman died had been infested with rats, which had probably attacked the corpse en masse as soon as she was dead; but for all their destructiveness on her bones, they had come nowhere near to devouring all the soft tissue. It was a warm spring day and the body was swarming with some of the largest maggots I have ever seen. Maggots have a character of their own. They vary widely in size and ferocity. They can bunch their bodies up and jump distances far beyond their own length, in some cases as much as several inches. In the course of my examination, one of the largest of the teeming mass separated from the rest, jumped off the body, cleared the side of the table, and landed audibly on my shoe. I kicked it across the driveway and kept working.

Although the cause could not be determined with certainty, the evidence pointed to the probability that the woman had frozen to death in the middle of winter. The police had collected some information from the neighbors, and they said that the resident of that address was in her seventies, which agreed with my observations of her joints and skull, and the only problem she ever complained about was old age. In her final months she had probably suffered from some mild form of senile dementia. As I continued with my examination, it seemed likely she had also suffered from malnutrition and neglect.

Perhaps the case has stayed in my mind in part because of the particularly gruesome circumstances: the odor, the maggots, and the conditions under which we did the autopsy. But when I think back on it, those aren't the things I remember first or strongest. Most of all, I recall being nearly overwhelmed by the horror and loneliness of a death that was simply a mirror to the horror and loneliness of her life. It occurred to me that the only thing that really made her death any different was that at last, here on the medical examiner's loading platform, she was finally getting the one thing she had lacked in life—understanding and attention. I keep thinking, even now, what that says about our country.

Here was a lost, lonely, unstable woman, freezing to death in the midst of this great city in the richest, most powerful nation in the history of the world. Wrapped in her print drapes, unnoticed, unreached by the resources around her. This work we were doing on her remains was her last opportunity to be recognized, to express her plight, to have her identity documented and to leave some record of her life.

Except for what was recorded here, she would drift off into oblivion.

The other case is from five years earlier, but it has stuck with me just as firmly. The remains, skeletonized and partly destroyed by fire, had belonged to a homeless man who lived the last of his life like a fairytale troll in the crawlspace under a bridge. That's where they found his skeleton.

His death had remained undiscovered for some length of time, until there was a fire in a complex of electrical cables that ran through the area that became his crypt. As the police pulled out the burning materials, they also pulled down his desiccated body. My analysis of the remains was more than a forensic examination to determine if he had died as the result of a crime; as in any anthropological case, it provided a chance to look at part of the life history of another human being through the bones he left behind. It was a life few of us see except at a safe distance.

He was a very robust male, and there was evidence on his skeleton, particularly in the facial region, of physical violence during his life. It was possible to see some of his earlier history in his teeth. He had had good dental care when he was younger, evidence that he had a family capable of providing that kind of attention in his childhood. But there were several untreated cavities that had developed a few years prior to his death, and these had festered into abscesses around the roots and gum sores that would have been causing real pain by the time he died. This is a dental portrait common among indigent homeless people, and it matched the evidence of his lifestyle in the skeleton.

The homeless have discovered that some bridges with enclosed substructures offer even better protection than just the shelter of their spans. These include crawlspaces, like the one in which this particular body was recovered, which are used as tiny apartments. All the prospective tenant has to do is find a way to pop off the access plate, which usually isn't too difficult, and slither up into a snug refuge. Lots of people in America live under bridges, with oblivious traffic passing just a few inches above their heads. Like the woman in the abandoned apartment, the man in this case retreated to this last haven, probably grateful to God for any shelter at all, and froze to death.

Nothing is going to happen to the people who wrap themselves in drapes for warmth or who live under bridges until enough of us are willing to admit they are there. If you don't remember anything else from this whole book, I hope these two stories have the same effect on you that they've had on me, and that you can't get them out of your mind.

25

ANOTHER HELPING HAND

In late May 1991, I took my family down to Tennessee for a visit with my old friend Bill Bass. The excuse for the trip was the annual Mountain, Swamp and Beach Forensic Gathering, a very informal get-together of anthropologists and related specialists from the eastern states which was held that year in Knoxville.

The MSBFG had been formed a few years earlier in response to a similar organization in the western states, the Mountain, Desert and Coast Meeting. Both groups attract a lot of students, and this particular gathering in Knoxville naturally included a good number from the University of Tennessee, where Bill headed up the Department of Anthropology and runs his forensic research facility. The assemblies are a social highlight of the year. Multi-institutional and multi-generational, the affairs have been described by one colleague as a gathering of the clans, and they have that same sense of festive ritual and extended family. In part, this owes to the fact that the field is still so small, it's hard to attend any meeting of forensic anthropologists, social or professional, without running into both teachers and students from one's own past. The particular virtue of the MSBFG was that it provided the opportunity to get together and trade stories with old friends, colleagues, former protégés, and associates in law enforcement, and to meet new people who for one reason or another had an interest in our specialized corner of scientific research.

The gathering was going to open Friday night with the first American viewing of a television documentary produced by the BBC on the relationships between scientists, mostly forensic anthropologists, and the police. In England, the police don't relate with academia nearly as freely or productively as in the United States. The program examined Bill's work at the University of Tennessee as an outstanding American model for fruitful collaboration between science and the law. As it turned out, some of us were going to miss the showing.

Hugh Berryman, another of Bill's former students—not from Kansas but from Knoxville, where Bill has taught since 1971—was coming up from Memphis, where he is director of the regional forensic center. Like the Ubelakers, the Berryman family would be staying with the Basses. So would the family of Doug Owsley, another Bass alumnus who was now a colleague of mine at the Smithsonian.

The Owsleys and Ubelakers arrived on Thursday in order to spend some family time together with the Basses. On Friday morning, we were in the middle of a vote on whether to take in the nearby water slide when Bill got a telephone call from the Tennessee Bureau of Investigation (TBI). An agent in Fayetteville said they had torn up the concrete cellar floor of a rural home, and he would need help with identification and removal of the body that had been buried beneath it.

Up to that point, my son Max, aged eleven, had been one of the leading advocates for the water slide, but I could see from his expression that this latest development, far from being a disappointment, represented an even more exciting prospect. He looked at me expectantly, not sure whether he should ask outright if he could come along. Bill and Doug Owsley saw the look, too, and grinned. Under the circumstances, I decided there was no reason this particular clan expedition shouldn't be open to a younger member.

On the way down to Fayetteville, Bill told us the police had been tipped to the burial site by the alleged killer, who claimed to have been hired by the wife of the victim. Max hung on every word. Nothing is more compelling to a great teacher than an eager student, and Bill couldn't resist passing on some of the lessons he had learned from the forensic side of his career. "There's a big lesson here for people who are planning to kill their mates. First, if you're going to do it at all, do it yourself. It's never a good idea to get someone else to do your dirty work. Second, if you hire it out, don't ask two people to do it because that doubles the risk one of them will talk."

Max nodded thoughtfully.

"People who accept contracts for murder are usually not very savory," Bill went on solemnly, "and down the road a piece, there's a pretty good chance they're going to get arrested for something else. If they find themselves in a bind, they often try to make a deal with the police: in exchange for a reduced sentence on their present problem, they'll give them the story on the earlier murder. In this case, it took seven years."

Fayetteville was a four-hour drive southwest of Knoxville, near the Alabama border. When we finally arrived at the TBI office in the local jail, both the sheriff and the agent who had called were in the middle of an interview, so Bill, Doug, Max, and I were led out to the site by a couple of investigators who had come up from the Limestone County, Alabama, Sheriff's Office. The house was about 12 miles from town. We could tell we were there from the swarm of TBI and local police cruisers in the driveway and along the roadside. The road to the house had been sealed off with crime scene tape, but a uniformed officer signaled us to pass when he recognized Bill.

The house was relatively new and well built, but its overall condition provided a fine example of accelerated rural decay. It needed paint and the roof was in bad shape. There were several derelict cars among the overgrown weeds on what had once been a lawn. Max was especially fascinated by a giant boar's skull sitting on the hood of one of the wrecked automobiles. Beside the cellar door was an immense pile of concrete chunks that the police had broken up with sledgehammers and removed in their search for the buried body.

An investigator wearing a bright blue TBI slicker came over to the car when he recognized Bill. He told him the body was wrapped in black plastic sheeting and was still where they had found it, in a shallow grave in the northeast corner of the basement.

We followed him into the house. The cellar was low and dimly lighted, but our noses told us we were in the presence of death as soon as we stepped down across the threshold into the excavation area. In the far corner, where the police had removed the final pieces of cement, we could see bits of a plastic sheet sticking up through the dirt. The remains appeared to be lying in a shallow depression about one foot lower than the rest of the soil, and if there were any doubts about what was in the sheet, they were dispelled by the white, soapy hands that protruded from the wet earth.

Max held the flashlight while Owsley and I worked with shovels, trowels, and buckets, carefully skimming away the surrounding soil and sludge to reveal more of the grave's contents. As we worked, Bill discussed the case with the investigators. They obviously assumed we were Bill's students, brought along to help the master and learn a little technique in the process. Both Owsley and I had left Bill's academic nest many years before (over twenty years before, in my case), and though the setting was grim we were moved by the *déjà vu* nature of the project. I smiled at Doug. "This seems like old times, doesn't it?"

Before long, we had removed all the soil from above and around the body, without touching or moving it. It now could be seen and studied in the exact position in which it had been placed.

Max continued to hold the flashlight while the grave was photographed. Then Bill, Doug, and I folded back the plastic shroud. Inside, the body was lying on its back, nude except for a clear plastic bag that had been placed over the head. The skin and flesh had turned to adipocere by the moisture in the soil, and the corpse had taken on the look of a sculpture in soft white paste.

There was a red beard, as well as reddish body hair. The arms were bent at the elbows and the right hand lay across the chest in classic funerary repose, while the left hand rested on the lower abdomen. The fingers of both hands were bent, perhaps as a record of the flexing that had occurred at the moment of death. Because the grave was shallower at one end, the feet were higher than the head.

"This used to be a dirt cellar," the TBI investigator told us. "They buried him here in 1984, then poured a foot of cement over the entire basement. In this corner, right over the body, they had a big freezer." The detective shook his head thoughtfully. "He sure doesn't look like he's been here seven years."

Throughout this whole procedure, I had been keeping an eye on Max. Although he was still a child, he was only a few years younger than I had been when Bill Bass took me on my own first dig. I knew this was different, but even so, I could see some of the same early wonder in his eyes. He was experiencing something most people never see, and the impulse toward knowledge was palpably greater than the natural repugnance toward death. More pictures were taken. As before, Max held the flashlight steadily on the subject and didn't look away.

With the deputy's help, Bill, Doug, and I picked up the four corners of the plastic sheet, lifted the body from the grave, and carried it out of the cellar. Subsequently, a medical examination found two bullets in the victim's chest. Police arrested his widow and another woman and charged them with complicity in the murder.

Most of the trip back to Knoxville was driven in the dark. I was sorry we had missed the opening of the Mountain, Swamp and Beach Forensic Gathering, not for myself so much as for Bill. He had been one of the principal organizers, he was the star of the BBC production which we were all missing, and the meeting was taking place in his hometown. But if Bill had any of the same thoughts, he never showed the slightest sign. Instead, he talked eagerly with Max, cheerful, full of information and wonderful insights, just as I remembered him from twenty years before when I had first been a student in his class in Kansas.

For the first few miles, he answered Max's endless stream of questions about the case, about other police work Bill had done as state forensic anthropologist, and about the science that undergirded all of it. But gradually he turned the conversation back to other subjects, such as school and sports and summer vacation. Max had been a scientist long enough for one day, and with loving care Bill was bringing him back to age eleven.

About halfway to Knoxville, Bill suddenly hit the brakes and pulled the car into the parking lot of a roadside store. "Come on," he said, jumping out and holding the door for Max. "We can't let you come to Tennessee without buying some fireworks."

Needless to say, Max took no persuading; he shot out of the car before I realized what was going on, and by the time I got into the store after them, they had already settled on a rocket half the size of a Cruise missile. It was a trophy beyond imagining for any kid from the staid Commonwealth of Virginia, and I could see Bill was getting almost as much out of the occasion as Max.

For the rest of the trip, I kept thinking about that immense rocket in the trunk of the car and the problems it was certain to create, especially for the father in our family, when Max showed it off to his mother. If Max had any thoughts about her probable response, they were no doubt colored by the illusion that my presence guaranteed safe passage. But I knew better. At least we were both certain that when we got back to Knoxville, we were going to see some spectacular fireworks.

But I also knew from the expression on my son's face that this gift was the perfect capstone on the biggest day of his life. By allowing Max to be included in this assignment, Bill Bass had given him a chance to be an adult. And then, with the same generous instinct for natural magic, he had defined the adventure with a gift that gave him back his childhood.

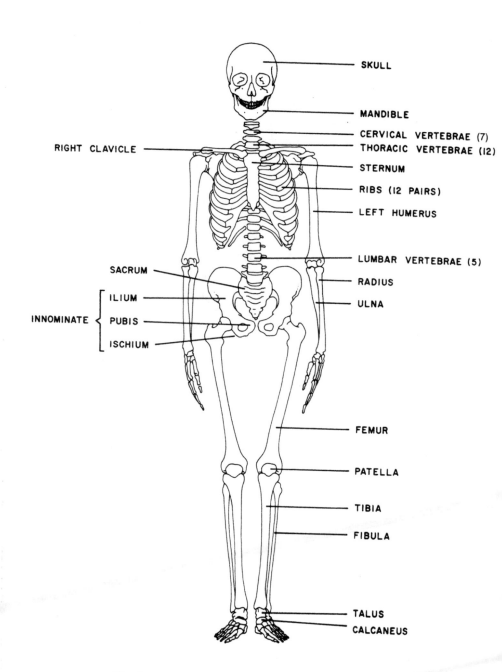

SKULL

MANDIBLE

CERVICAL VERTEBRAE (7)

THORACIC VERTEBRAE (12)

RIGHT CLAVICLE

STERNUM

RIBS (12 PAIRS)

LEFT HUMERUS

LUMBAR VERTEBRAE (5)

RADIUS

SACRUM

ULNA

ILIUM

INNOMINATE

PUBIS

ISCHIUM

FEMUR

PATELLA

TIBIA

FIBULA

TALUS

CALCANEUS

The human skeleton with principal bones identified.

GLOSSARY

Articulation. The point where two adjacent bones are in contact; the normal anatomical arrangement of adjacent bones.

Calcification. The process of formation of bones and teeth.

Cancellous bone. The spongy or porous internal structure, particularly characteristic at the ends of long bones.

Cartilage. A tough, elastic tissue.

Circumferential lamellar bone. Original bone deposited by the periosteum in the cortex of long bones.

Collagen. Submicroscopic protein fibers found in skin, bone, and ligaments.

Cortex. The outer portion of a bone.

Cremation. The act of burning a body or the remnants of a burned individual.

Cranial suture. The junction between two bones of the skull.

Demography. The study of vital statistics within populations.

Diaphysis. The shaft of a long bone.

Dimorphism. The occurrence of two forms in members of the same species; most commonly applied in Homo sapiens to differences between the sexes.

Distal. Farthest from the center of the mid-line of the body; in limbs, farthest from the point of attachment to the trunk.

Dorsal. Back.

Eburnation. A polished surface produced when destruction of the intervening cartilage allows the bones in a joint to rub together.

Epiphysis. A bony cap at the end of a long bone.

Eruption of teeth. The emergence of teeth through the gum.

Femora. Plural of femur.

Haversian canal. A small canal in the bone cortex; one of the features used in estimating age at death.

Inhumation. Synonym for burial or interment.

Long bones. Collective term for the bones of the arms and legs; specifically, the humerus, radius, ulna, femur, tibia, and fibula.

Malocclusion. Condition in which the upper and lower teeth do not meet.

Medullary cavity. The canal through the center of a long bone.

Metaphysis. The area between the diaphysis and epiphysis, where bone growth occurs.

Morphology. The form and structure of an object.

Non-Haversian canal. A canal formed within the cortex of long bones during the deposition of circumferential lamellar bone.

Ossuary. A communal grave containing the secondary remains of individuals initially stored elsewhere.

Osteoblasts. The specialized cells that produce bone.

Osteoclasts. The specialized cells that destroy bone.

Osteology. The study of bones.

Osteophytes. Abnormal bony extensions that develop on the surface of bones.

Partial articulation. A condition in which two or more (but not all) bones of a skeleton remain in articulation, indicating that decomposition was incomplete at the time of burial.

Parietal thinning. Change in the skull with age, in which the inner and outer layers move closer together producing scooped-out depressions on the exterior of the parietals.

Pathology. The study of disease.

Pelvis. The portion of the skeleton composed of the sacrum and the left and right innominates.

Periodontal disease. An abnormal condition of the tissue adjacent to the teeth.

Periosteum. The membrane of connective tissue that covers all surfaces of bones except the areas of articulation.

Post-cranial skeleton. All bones except the skull.

Primary burial. An articulated skeleton, buried in the flesh.

Proximal. Closest to the center of the mid-line of the body; in limbs, closest to the point of attachment to the trunk.

Pubic symphysis. The junction of the right and left pubic bones at the mid-line.

Resorption. The process of destruction of bone by osteoclasts.

Scaffold. A wooden platform used by some Indian groups to hold their dead.

Secondary burial. An interment of disarticulated bones.

Stratigraphy. The superposition of layers of strata of differing geological or cultural origin.

Symphyseal face. The articular surface of the pubis.

Symphyseal rim. An elevated margin that forms around the edge of the symphyseal face of the pubis.

Symphysis. The area where the left and right pubes articulate.

Trabeculae. An internal network of bone fibers.

Trauma. An injury inflicted by force by some physical agent.

Trephination. A surgical procedure involving cutting a hole in the cranial vault.

Radiogram. An image produced on photographic film by the passage of X-rays. Synonyms: Roentgenogram, radiograph.

Ventral. Front.

Ventral rampart. A ridge of bone that forms on the ventral surface of the symphyseal face of the pubis.

Diplomates of the American Board of Forensic Anthropology, 1992

William M. Bass, III, Ph.D.
Professor and Head
Anthropology Department
University of Tennessee
Knoxville, TN 37996

Walter H. Birkby, Ph.D.
Human Identification Laboratory
Arizona State Museum
Univeristy of Arizona
Tucson, AZ 85721

Hugh E. Berryman, Ph.D.
University of Tennessee, Memphis
Regional Forensic Center
1060 Madison Avenue
Memphis, TN 38104

Sheilagh T. Brooks, Ph.D.
University of Nevada
Maryland Parkway
Las Vegas, NV 89154

Jane E. Buikstra, Ph.D.
Department of Anthropology
University of Chicago
1126 E. 59th Street
Chicago, IL 60637

Michael Charney, Ph.D.
Forensic Science Laboratory
Colorado State University
Fort Collins, CO 80523

Michael Finnegan, Ph.D.
Osteology Laboratory
204 Waters Hall
Kansas State University
Manhattan, KS 66506

Diane L. France, Ph.D.
Laboratory for Human Identification
Department of Anthropology
Colorado State University
Fort Collins, CO 80523

Eugene Giles, Ph.D.
Department of Anthropology
University of Illinois
Urbana, IL 61801

George W. Gill, Ph.D.
Department of Anthropology
University of Wyoming
Laramie, WY 82071

David M. Glassman, Ph.D.
Department of Sociology and Anthropology
Southwest Texas State University
San Marcos, TX 78666

Rodger Heglar, Ph.D.
7450 Olivetas Avenue # A-B
La Jolla, CA 92037

Madeline Hinkes, Ph.D.
U.S. Army Central ID Lab
Fort Kamehameha Building 45
Hickman AFB, HI 96853

J. Michael Hoffman, M.D., Ph.D.
Department of Anthropology
Colorado College
Colorado Springs, CO 80903

H. Yasar Iscan, Ph.D.
Department of Anthropology
Florida Atlantic University
Boca Raton, FL 33431-0991

Kenneth A.R. Kennedy, Ph.D.
Ecology and Systematics
E-231 Corson Hall
Cornell University
Ithaca, NY 14853

Ellis R. Kerley, Ph.D.
98-1421 Onikiniki Way
Aiea, HI 96701

Linda L. Klepinger, Ph.D.
Department of Anthropology
University of Illinois
109 Davenport Hall
607 S. Mathews
Urbana, IL 61801

John K. Lundy, Ph.D.
Consulting Forensic Anthropologist
Oregon State Medical Examiner
301 NE Knott Street
Portland, OR 97212

William Maples, Ph.D.
C.A. Pound Human Identification Laboratory
Florida Museum of Natural History
University of Florida
Gainesville, FL 32611

Turbon A. Murad, Ph.D.
Department of Anthropology
California State University-Chico
Chico, CA 95929-0400

Michael Pietrusewsky, Ph.D.
Department of Anthropology
University of Hawaii
2424 Maile Way
Honolulu, HI 96822

Anthony J. Perzigian, Ph.D.
Department of Anthropology
University of Cincinnati
Cincinnati, OH 45221

Ted A. Rathbun, Ph.D.
Department of Anthropology
University of South Carolina
Columbia, SC 29208

Kathleen Reichs, Ph.D.
Department of Sociology-Anthropology
University of North Carolina-Charlotte
Charlotte, NC 28223

Laboratoire de Medecine Legale
1701 rue Parthenais
Montreal, Quebec H2L 4K6
Canada

J. Stanley Rhine, Ph.D.
Maxwell Museum of Anthropology
University of New Mexico
Albuquerque, NM 87131

William C. Rodriguez, III, Ph.D.
Office of the Armed Forces Medical Examiner
Armed Forces Institute of Pathology
Washington, D.C. 20306-6000

Stephen I. Rosen, J.D., Ph.D.
P.O. Box 3589
Rancho Santa Fe, CA 92067

Norman J. Sauer, Ph.D.
Department of Anthropology
Baker Hall
Michigan State University
East Lansing, MI 48824

Frank P. Saul, Ph.D.
Associate Dean CME
Medical College of Ohio
P.O. Box 10008
Toledo, OH 43699-0008

Mark Skinner, Ph.D.
Department of Archaelogy
Simon Fraser University
Burnaby, British Columbia
Canada V5A 1S6

Clyde Snow, Ph.D.
2230 Blue Creek Parkway
Norman, OK 73071

Richard G. Snyder, Ph.D.
BioDynamics International
3720 North Silver Drive
Tucson, AZ 85749

Marcella H. Sorg, Ph.D.
Sorg Associates
P.O. Box 70
91 Mill Street
Orono, ME 04473-0070

Judy Myers Suchey, Ph.D.
Department of Anthropology
California State University
Fullerton, CA 92634

Robert I. Sundick, Ph.D.
Anthropology Department
Western Michigan University
Kalamazoo, MI 49008

James V. Taylor
Metro Forensic Anthropology Team
Lehman College, CUNY
Bedford Park Boulevard West
Bronx, NY 10468

Douglas H. Ubelaker, Ph.D.
Department of Anthropology
National Museum of Natural History
Smithsonian Institution
Washingon, D.C. 20560

P. Willey, Ph.D.
Department of Anthropology
California State University-Chico
Chico, CA 95929-0400

INDEX

Root systems, 107–8
photograph, 106
Rowley, Judge William, 127
Royal Hong Kong Police Headquarters, 263
Rural sites, and corpses, 119–20
Ruxton, Isabella, 179

Sadler, Lew, 173
Sainthood verification, 254
Santa Elena sample, 43
Santorini cult, 260
Satanism, 128, 254
Schiller, Friedrich von, 253
Schwarzenegger, Arnold, 170
Science, pure, 20
Science Digest, 24
Scientific analysis, 63
Scientific experimentation, 47
Scotland's facial reproduction cases, 179
Sculpturing technique, 172–73
Sea Wind yacht, 197
Serengeti Plain, Tanzania, 34
Serial murderers, 118–19, 253, 262–70
victims of, 263
Serology Unit (FBI), 67
Serra, Father Junipero, 254
Settlements, permanent, 43–44
Sex determination, 4, 45, 67, 86–88, 212
and bone shrinkage by fire, 141
Shapiro, H. L., 21
Shoe print identification, 64, 73
Shortridge, Charles, 249–51
"Shovel shape," 93
The Silence of the Lambs (film), 26
"The Six Million Dollar Man" (television show), 252
Skeleton, human
diagram, 296
effects of weapons on, 209
Sketching technique, 172–73
Skull(s)
and adult aging landmarks, 97
of black woman with matching photograph, 57–58
photographs, 183
bullet's failure to exit, 221–22
child's, found in paper bag, 153–54
"coffin wear" from Palmyra Island, *photographs,* 198
conceptual drawings and victim identification, 167, 169, 170, 172–73
photographs, 168, 171
front, side, basal views of, *figures,* 90
with hole from Black & Decker drill, 221
of illegal immigrants with massive damage, 215–16
made into drinking steins, 260
missing body parts found for, 261
and race determination, 91, 93

size and gender indication, 87
Styrofoam packaging testimony, 192–94
sun-bleaching of, 4, 135–37
theft of, 253
as trophies, 253–54
unidentified, found in Knapp, Wisc., wrapped in plastic bags, 138
photograph, 139
of unidentified victims, 132–33, 138
of woman found in English canal, 151
See also Calvarium skulls; Hydrocephalic calf skulls
Smith, Capt. John, 40, 42
Smith, Sir Sidney, 151, 219, 233
Smithson, James, exhumation, 36–37, 40
Smithsonian Institute, Department of Anthropology, 8, 48, 148, 200
author as chair of, 130
and Dr. Angel, 18
evidence from FBI, 64
Goochland case, 3–7, 9
and Hrdlička, 20
and knowledge for its own sake, 28
reference collection of human remains, 20, 53, 55–60, 255
cervical vertebrae, 268
photographs, 54
skulls, 185
Terry Collection, 57
Smithsonian magazine, 24
Snow, Charles E., 21, 25
Snow, Clyde, 252–53
Soft tissue removal, 161
Soil sample analysis, 64, 69
time since death calculation, 165
South America, 28, 56, 260
Special Projects Section (FBI), 181–82
Spectrographic print matching, 65
Spelunking, 149
Sperber, Dr. Norman, 133
St. Thomas, 10
Stabbings, 209–10, 213, 276
Stahl, Lesley, 253
Starrs, James E., 209, 216
and Huey Long's assassination, 223, 225–26
Stature determination, 4, 6, 86, 88–89, 212
Stephens, Dr. Boyd, 199
Stewart, T. Dale, 21–22, 25, 28, 34–35
career and background, 48–49
on facial reproductions, 170
Maryland ossuary excavation, 40–42
morphological dating of ancient remains, 49
photograph, 19
Smithson's forensic examination, 35–37
studies on adipocere, 150–51
Strangulation, 118, 152, 219, 281–82
and fractured hyoid, 233